presents

Paul Krassner's

Psychedelic Trips for the Mind

Stories by and about Timothy Leary, Ram Dass, Ken Kesey, Wavy Gravy, Groucho Marx, Jerry Garcia, Mountain Girl, Andrei Codrescu, Todd McCormick, Squeaky Fromme, Abbie Hoffman, Michael Hollingshead, Eldridge Cleaver, Steven Hager, Susie Bright, Dave Marsh, Michael Simmons, Steve Parish, Augustus Owsley, Steve Bloom, Dawna Kaufmann, Stanley Krippner, Jerry Hopkins, Roy Tuckman, and many others...

Produced by Steven Hager & Jim Ski
Editor: Paul Krassner
Copy Editor: Gabe Kirchheimer
Art Director: Frank Max
Managing Editors: Zena Tsarfin & Keith Chong
Production: Rob Braswell

First Edition May 2001

ISBN#: 1-893010-07-4

Printed in China through Palace Press International

To Todd McCormick and all other political prisoners of the war on some people who use drugs.

* * *

Also by the author:

How a Satirical Editor Became a Yippie Conspirator in Ten Easy Years

Tales of Tongue Fu

Best of The Realist

Confessions of a Raving, Unconfined Nut: Misadventures in the Counter-Culture

The Winner of the Slow Bicycle Race: The Satirical Writings of Paul Krassner

Impolite Interviews

Pot Stories For the Soul

Sex, Drugs and the Twinkie Murders: 40 Years of Countercultural Journalism

"I lay down and sank into a not unpleasant intoxicated-like condition, characterized by an extremely stimulated imagination. In a dreamlike state, with eyes closed, I perceived an uninterrupted stream of fantastic pictures, extraordinary shapes with intense, kaleidoscopic play of colors."

Albert Hofmann,
LSD: My Problem Child

"Dock wound up and threw a hot one over the corner of the plate—a swinging strike! It was no ordinary pitch: The ball burst from Dock's hand and left a blazing, comet-like tail that remained visible long after the ball was caught. Dock felt wobbly on the mound and his stomach was churning with acid cramps. His concentration, however, was superb. As long as he kept to his fastball, the comets kept burning across the plate. All he had to do was steer the ball down the multicolored path. Dock had a crazed look in his eyes and his lack of control was evident to the batters, many of whom were feeling increasingly vulnerable in the batter's box.
Dock easily retired three batters in a row..."

Eric Brothers in *High Times*, describing a no-hit game which Dock Ellis pitched for the Pirates after ingesting three hits of LSD

"The left side of my upper body was flat and muscular, just like the chest of a boy. I reached up with my boy's large, clumsy hand to touch my right breast and felt my penis stirring. It was a hermaphroditic phantasm that held me entranced as I discovered my divided body."

—Esther Willliams,
The Million Dollar Mermaid

CONTENTS

Introduction

Who could have predicted that I would end up collecting stories for a book like this? Not me. While I was growing up, I seemed to absorb mainstream values by cultural osmosis, so when it came to drugs, I was really puritanical. I didn't even use any *legal* drugs. I never took aspirin or sleeping pills or tranquilizers. I never smoked cigarettes, and I never drank coffee or alcohol. I had no socially acceptable vices.

The first time I heard of LSD was in a 1961 *New York Times* review of Alan Watts' book, *This Is It*: "If a simple drug can place within the reach of millions an experience that throughout the centuries has been considered the final fruit of religious discipline, then what authorities acting on what principle are going to be able to prevent usage of this drug?"

In 1962, John Wilcock wrote a column for my satirical magazine, *The Realist*, titled, "What People Are Talking About that *Vogue* Won't Admit To." Under "Names to Drop," he included: "Tim Leary—a young Harvard professor who's been experimenting with non-addicting, consciousness-changing drugs, because the sensible and unsecretive way he's been handling his research might mean the first major breakthrough in the official wall of prejudice and therefore the possible availability in the future of such drugs for anyone who wants them."

In 1963, in the only crossword puzzle I ever published in *The Realist*, the correct answer to "Causes artificial schizophrenia" was LSD. In 1964, I ran a front-cover story by Robert Anton Wilson titled, "Timothy Leary and His Psychological H-Bomb." It began:

"The future may decide that the two greatest thinkers of the 20th century were Albert Einstein, who showed how to create atomic fission in the physical world, and Timothy Leary, who showed how to create atomic fission in the psychological world. The latter discovery may be more important than the former; there are some reasons for thinking that it was made *necessary* by the former.

"Nuclear fission of the material universe has created an impasse which is not merely political but ideological, epistemological, metaphysical. As Einstein himself said, atomic energy has changed everything but our habits of thought, and until our habits of thought also change we are going to drift continually closer to annihilation. Timothy Leary may have shown how our habits of thought can be changed.

"After the outburst of unfavorable publicity about Dr. Leary in the mass magazines in November and December 1963, most readers presumably know who Timothy Leary is and what he has been doing. He is the man who, together with Dr. Richard Alpert [now Ram Dass], conducted several experiments at Harvard on 'psychedelic' (mind-altering) chemicals; as a result of these experiments, Dr. Leary pronounced some very shocking and 'radical' ideas at various scientific meetings, and attempted to implement these ideas by setting up an organization through which these mind-changing chemicals could be legally made available to whoever wanted them.

"When the authorities found out what Dr. Leary was attempting, the laws were quickly changed to make the distribution of these chemicals a government monopoly, and Dr. Leary and Dr. Alpert were removed from their positions at Harvard...."

After the article was published, Leary invited me to visit the Castalia Foundation at the Hitchcock estate in Millbrook, New York. The name Castalia came from *The Bead Game* by Hermann Hesse, and indeed, the game metaphor permeated conversations with Leary, Alpert and Ralph Metzner, the Three Musketeers of Millbrook. Leary talked about the way people always try to lure you onto *their* game-boards. He discussed the biochemical process called imprinting with the same passion that he claimed he didn't believe anything he was saying, but somehow I managed to believe him when he told me I had an honest mind. I admitted to him that my ego couldn't help but respond to his observation.

"Listen," he reassured me, "anybody who tells you he's transcended his ego..."

In 1964, Leary and Alpert did a lecture series on the West Coast. At the University of California at Berkeley, there was an official announcement that only the distribution of "informative" literature—as opposed to "persuasive" literature—would be permitted on campus, giving rise to the Free Speech Movement, with thousands of students protesting the ban in the face of police billy clubs.

Leary argued that such demonstrations played right onto the game-boards of the administration and the police alike, and that students could shake up the establishment much more if they would just stay in their rooms and change their nervous systems. But it really wasn't a case of either-or. You could protest *and* explore your 13-billion-celled mind simultaneously. During the mass imprisonment of Free Speech Movement demonstrators, a Bible which had been soaked in an acid solution easily made its way into the cells. The students eagerly ate those pages, getting high on Deuteronomy, tripping out on Exodus.

I confessed in the December 1964 issue of *The Realist* that "I'm still too chicken to try LSD should the occasion ever arise." But I became intrigued by the playful and subtle patterns of awareness that Leary and Alpert manifested. If their brains had been so damaged, how come their perceptions were so sharp?

I began to research the LSD phenomenon, and in April 1965 I returned to Millbrook for my first acid experience. I had never been high on anything before. Leary was supposed to be my guide, but he had gone off to India. Alpert was supposed to take his place, but he was too involved in getting ready to open at the

Village Vanguard as a sort of psychedelic comedian-philosopher. So my guide was Michael Hollingshead, who had originally changed Leary's life by introducing him to acid.

Our start was delayed for a few hours, and I made the mistake of raiding the refrigerator while waiting. Finally we went to an upstairs room and ingested a tasteless, colorless, odorless liquid—pure Sandoz LSD. Then my trip began with a solid hour of what Hollingshead described as "cosmic laughter."

The more I laughed, the more I tried to think of depressing things—like atrocities in Vietnam—and the more uproarious my laughter became. The climactic message I got was: IT'S VERY FUNNY! I felt an obligation to share this tremendous insight in *The Realist* with one giant headline and nothing else on the front cover. But, no, I couldn't do *that*. I debated the matter with myself, finally concluding that even though I tried to live by this universal truth, I shouldn't jeopardize the magazine by *flaunting* it like that.

"Well, the least you can do," my lunar self said, "is inform your readers that no matter how serious anything in *The Realist* may appear, you will always be there between the lines saying IT'S VERY FUNNY!" I laughed so hard I had to throw up. The nearest outlet was a window. I stuck my head out and had a paranoid flash that this was actually a guillotine and that Holllingshead was about to be my executioner. But I knew in my heart that I could trust him, so I concentrated instead on the beautiful colors of my vomit as it started moving around on the outside ledge like an ancient religious mosaic coming to life. Napalm was burning someone to death that very moment, but I was alive, and what I was really laughing at was the oneness of tragedy and absurdity.

On the stereo, the Beatles were singing the soundtrack from *A Hard Day's Night*, and I began weeping because my wife, Jeanne, and I had seen that film together. We were temporarily separated, but now I began to have *reverse* paranoia—she was doing nice things for me behind my back—and I had an internal hallucination that she had not only helped *plan* for that particular record to be played but, moreover, in doing so, she must have collaborated with a guy she considered an asshole in order to please me. What a fantastic thing to do! She had always complained about my association with assholes, yet now she had obviously worked *with* the one who had arranged for this acid trip.

Filled with gratitude, I felt compelled to call her, but I held back because I also convinced myself that she had *planned* for me to call her up *against my will*. So I figured I would call her but I would also assure her that I was calling of my own free will. I argued with myself about this for a while, as the dial on the downstairs pay phone became the inanimate object of my megalomania and changed into Dali's limp clock in *The Persistence of Memory*. I sat there, immobilized, unable to call until I could rationalize that as long as I *knew* that she had programmed this telephone call, and as long as I went through the process of deciding to call, it would be acceptable to my warped sense of independence.

The coin slot was all squiggly and vibrating, though. How was I ever going to get a dime into *that*? But then I took out a dime, and *it* was all squiggly and vibrating. My dime fit into that coin slot *perfectly*. I called collect. The operator asked my name.

"Ringo Starr," I blurted out.

"Do you really want me to say that?"

"Of course, operator. It's a private joke between us, and it's the only way she'll accept a collect call."

That wasn't true at all, but when the operator told Jeanne that there was a collect call from Ringo Starr, she *did* accept it immediately. I explained why I was calling.

"Paul, you're thanking me for something I didn't do."

And I had been so sure that we had *communed* psychically....

Later, I visited with Alpert for a while. He was soaking his body in a bathtub, preparing his psyche for the Village Vanguard gig. He had taken 300 acid trips, but there I was, a first-timer, standing in the open doorway, reversing roles and comforting *him* in his anxiety about entering show business.

"It's only an audience" I reassured him. "What can they do to you? If they don't laugh, it doesn't make any difference. What do you have to lose?"

"My ego?"

I became involved with the psychedelic community, and observed how individuals could use the drug either as a catalyst for radical change or as a tool to intensify the status quo. So I not only met a teacher of Marxian Economics who preached blasphemy at a Socialist Scholars Conference—"I am speaking of a real social process... bound up with the most scientific and technological discoveries of our epoch; it is the process of internal revolution, of consciousness expansion through the psychedelic bio-chemicals, most notably LSD"—but I also encountered a stockbroker who was grateful that acid had given him "the courage to sell short."

When I first told my mother about taking LSD, she was quite concerned.

"It could lead to marijuana," she warned.

And, in turn, marijuana ultimately led to HIGH TIMES publishing my book, *Pot Stories For the Soul*.

And now, here's the sequel, *Psychedelic Trips For the Mind*.

Enjoy your ass off.

—*Paul Krassner, February, 2001*

Chapter I

Countercultural History

Beatnik Glory
Andrei Codrescu

I remember distinctly the time, Spring 1969, going by train from New York to New Haven with Ted Berrigan who was a Guest Writer at Yale that semester. I was supposed to give a poetry reading.

On the train Ted said, "Let's split this tab of acid, you should be okay by the time you read."

It was only noon and the reading was at 8 p.m., so I thought, why not? At Yale there was a revolution going on in honor of Black Panther Day or something. Guys with spray paint cans made art like *Off the Pig* on the campus walls. We farted around checking out the revolution. Nothing, not even a twinge of high.

At 8 p.m. we went to the chapel for the reading and did the six-part brother handshake with three of Ted's students who were the whole audience. I sat down while Ted went up to introduce me and *whammo!*—the whole chapel started wiggling and Emerson's ghost stood right behind Ted making faces.

Ted introduced me for about an hour-and-a-half, and I was totally fascinated by his speech which was mostly about... Jack Kerouac. When I got up there with my big black spring binder full of poems, I couldn't remember what I was supposed to do.

I cracked open the thing and stared at my typewritten words, and then I noticed that certain words stood about a mili-inch above all the rest—they floated right off the page! I was seized by a fit of giggles and read these a few dozen times.

At the end of this performance I heard a sound like tearing silk and realized that the audience was clapping. They thought I was some hotshot poet from New York.

After that we took the whole audience to our guest rooms—set up, I thought, for German professors—and Ted talked all night about... Jack Kerouac. At some point during the night I looked to see if any of the students were girls because I had suddenly been afflicted by a powerful erotic wave, but all the students were long gone.

At which precise moment Ted asked, "Did you ever sleep with a man?"

"I have, Ted," I said, "but I don't want to."

And then he resumed talking about Kerouac. Next day he swore he never said anything of the sort, which is possible.

I guess this is more a story about Ted Berrigan than about acid, but then my funniest stoned moments always happened with someone else, particularly if there was some mishearing involved.

Around that same time I remember the Tupamaros guerrilla who started shooting a rifle into the floor upstairs—which was my ceiling—and when I rushed upstairs—just as the acid kicked in—she opened the door in all her six-foot-two naked glory with the rifle in her hand, and said, "Can you help me look for crabs?"

She had this luxurious black pubic hair, and I, with my preternatural vision, was able to pick out six of these "jewels from Venus" as she called them. We had a good laugh over that one.

How I Spent the Summer of Love
Paul Krassner

All right, get those stereotypes ready, it's the 30th anniversary of the Summer of Love. Ancient history to some, a scapegoat for current problems to others, and, for those who were there (Austin Powers wasn't), flashbacks to living an alternative to the blandness and repression of the Eisenhower-Nixon era, further fueled by the assassination of President Kennedy, leaving a void that the Beatles would begin to fill. Sergeant Pepper to the rescue.

The phenomenon was also a response to Cold-War hysteria, as personified by Pat Boone, who declared at a rally in Madison Square Garden, "I would rather see my four daughters shot before my eyes than have them grow up in a Communist United States. I would rather see those kids blown into Heaven than taught into Hell by the Communists." And that was *before* his heavy-metal period.

Stew Albert and Judy Gumbo Albert, co-editors of *The Sixties Papers*, discovered in the course of their research on the '50s that— except for the rise of the Beat Generation and Norman Mailer's essay, "The White Negro" (which would now be called "The Caucasian African-American")—there was hardly a hint that so many individuals would become agents of change.

It was as though mainstream awareness had expected *The Lucky Strike Hit Parade* to be on television forever, with Snooky Lansom crooning a different version of "It's a Marshmallow World" every week. Who could have predicted that those marshmallows would soon become laced with acid?

But the blossoming counterculture was about far more than sex, drugs and rock 'n' roll. It was, at the core, a spiritual revolution, with religions of repression being replaced by communities of liberation. And psychotropic drugs were their sacrament.

Actually, the Summer of Love began on the afternoon of October 6, 1966, the day that LSD became illegal. In San Francisco, precisely at 2 p.m., thousands of young Americans gathered for the specific purpose of simultaneously swallowing tabs of acid in front of the police. This was a cross-fertilization of mass protest and tribal celebration.

The event had been publicized by a latter-day Declaration of Independence:

"When in the flow of human events it becomes necessary for the people to cease to recognize the obsolete social patterns which had isolated man from his consciousness and to create with the youthful energies of the world revolutionary communities to which the two-billion-year-old life process entitles them, a decent respect to the opinions of mankind should declare the causes which impel them to this creation.

"We hold these experiences to be self-evident, that all is equal, that the creation endows us with inalienable rights, that among these are: the freedom of the body, the pursuit of joy, and the expansion of consciousness, and that to secure these rights, we the citizens of the Earth declare our love and compassion for all conflicting hate-carrying men and women of the world."

San Francisco became a pilgrimage to Mecca in reverse—a generation of hippie pioneers traveling *west*ward, without killing a single Indian along the way.

Originally, the CIA had envisioned using LSD as a means of control, but instead, millions of young people ingested the hallucinogen and became explorers of their own inner space. Acid served as a vehicle to help them deprogram themselves from a civilization of inhumane priorities.

A mass awakening was in process. The nuclear family was exploding into extended families. Sensuality developed into exquisite forms of personal art. The way you lived your daily life echoed the heartbeat of your politics. There was an epidemic of idealism, and altruism became the highest form of selfishness.

By 1967, there had been an evolutionary jump in consciousness. Herman Kahn, director of the Hudson Institute, a conservative think tank, was the personification of Mr. Jones in Bob Dylan's "Ballad of the Thin Man"—something was happening and Herman Kahn didn't know what it was. He asked me to give him a tour of the Lower East Side.

"The hippie dropout syndrome," he complained "is delaying the guaranteed annual wage."

Then he bought a copy of *LSD and Problem Solving*.

* * *

In the summer of 1967, if a stranger in the street offered you a pill, you might have taken it simply because you liked the look of his halo.

Today, even legal drugs are secured in tamper-proof packaging.

In the '60s, it was believed that the CIA was involved in smuggling heroin from Southeast Asia. In the '90s, it was believed that the CIA was involved in smuggling cocaine from Central America.

In the Summer of Love, marijuana was $10 an ounce. Now it's $500 an ounce. Teenagers who used to hide their pot-smoking from their parents have become parents who hide their pot-smoking from their teenagers.

In an article in United Airlines' inflight magazine, *Hemispheres*, family counselor Michael Meyerhoff advises parents to be honest with their children, but first they "must be honest with themselves. Were they truly experimenting with marijuana, or were they simply determined to get stoned? Was their promiscuity really due to an overpowering spirit of liberation that accompanied a unique cultural revolution, or was it merely the time-honored result of raging hormones combined with reduced supervision?"

Meanwhile, the quality of co-option has not been strained. "Today is the first day of the rest of your life" was used in a TV commercial for Total breakfast cereal. Tampax promoted its menstrual tampon as "Something over 30 you can trust." Classic rock songs continue to be used to sell all kinds of products. And somebody tried to trademark the Summer of Love.

In red spray paint, on a brick wall just off Haight Street, standing out among the graffiti like John Hancock's signature on the original Declaration of Independence, this cynical message summed it up: "Love Is Revenue."

* * *

True to its amorality, the Mafia had financed the printing of a popular poster with the faces of Lyndon Johnson and Hubert Humphrey superimposed on the bodies of Peter Fonda and Dennis Hopper riding their motorcycles in *Easy Rider*. During the Summer of Love, the Mafia was getting into the business of distributing LSD. A friend asked me to test a capsule, so I decided to take it at Expo '70, in Montreal.

I had been invited to speak at the Youth Pavilion and also to give my impressions, on Canadian TV, of the United States Pavilion, a gigantic geodesic dome engineered by Buckminster Fuller. Before entering the pavilion, which was guarded by marines who had gone to protocol school, I ingested the acid. I began the interview—"This dome is really beautiful, with all these flowing colors; you don't see them but I do"—and ended up burning a photostat of my draft card.

"Now, the reason I'm doing this," I explained, "is because we get hung up on symbols. People will be more upset about this than about the fact that *children* are being burned alive by napalm...."

The marine lieutenant called his captain. When the interview was finished, the captain told me it was against the law to burn my draft card. Then I took my draft card from my pocket and showed it to him.

"But he *burned* it," the lieutenant insisted. "I *saw* him, sir. He *burned* it."

"I burned a *photostat* of my draft card. So I lied on television. That's not a crime. People do it all the time."

"But," the captain pointed out, "it's also against the law to make a *copy* of your draft card."

"Well, I destroyed the evidence."

Although I knew that political demonstrations were barred at Expo, I had managed to smuggle one in. The interview was labeled as an "incident," and there was a heated argument between the US Information Agency and CBC, but the incident was already on tape, so now it had become a free-speech issue. It would be shown on TV that night and become front-page news in Montreal papers the next day.

Just as I was leaving the pavilion, a band struck up a fanfare, and I committed the error of projecting my own feelings. Suddenly I was convinced that acid had been sprayed *into the air*, that *everybody* was tripping, that peace and love were breaking out *all over* the globe at that very moment. After all, hadn't Paul McCartney stated that if the world leaders all took LSD, it would end warfare?

Walking along the midway, I started smiling at people and waving to them, and they were smiling and waving back. But then a sense of reality popped to the surface, the force of my own feedback made me turn around, and I saw that those same people were now *pointing* at me with ridicule. What an asshole!

Still blushing, I found a phone booth and called my friend.

"Well," I said, "you can tell the Mafia that I don't approve of their methods *or* their goals, but their acid is pretty powerful."

As the war in Vietnam escalated, flower children began to grow thorns. They participated in creative peace demonstrations, from launching a yellow submarine in the Hudson River to exorcising the Pentagon. While they were tripping on acid.

The CIA's scenario had backfired.

Originally published in the San Francisco Examiner.

The First International Psychedelic Exposition
Merril Mushroom

Our van-load of laughing, colorful beaded hippies was an unlikely sight to be seen driving through the gates of the Forest Hills Country Club, but, then, we were arriving for a rather extraordinary happening—an event billed as "The First International Psychedelic Exposition."

We were going to set up a sort of historical village of hippiedom on the country club premises. There we'd provide an experience for all (and sell souvenirs to) the primarily white, rich, straight American people who were curious about this newest breed of weirdos emerging out of the 1960s.

My two cohorts and I had a store in New York City's East Village. It was called Paranoia, and we sold only handmade craft items which we took on consignment from local artisans. We also served free food and provided free clothing and a place for grounding and networking to neighborhood hippies and street kids.

One afternoon, this dude I'd seen before at IFIF [International Federation for Internal Freedom] meetings and at the Paradox [macrobiotic restaurant] came strolling into the store, checked out the items on the shelves, then moved in on the three of us where we sat behind the counter.

"I'll get right to the point," he said.

JJ held up his hand. "Wait a minute, my friend. Who are you?"

"Name's Dennis," the dude says. "My partners and I are doing a psychedelic exposition—sort of like a World's Fair of the hippie culture. Most of the other shops here in the East Village are gonna have exhibits, plus some folks from uptown and the West Side, and we were hoping you guys from Paranoia would join us."

"Only one of us is a guy," Maria interjected.

"We're thinking like a five-day event," Dennis continued without batting an eyelash. "We have this place, see, and you all will have, like, so much space in it to set up a replica of your shop. You can do some kind of experience if you want, and you can sell merchandise. *Clean* merchandise," he emphasized. "The idea is to make the place look like a hippie village. We draw tourists from Long Island—the hip rich folks who come to the East Village to go slumming and have an adventure—and we give them a little atmosphere, sell our products, and have some fun."

"Sounds sort of like a gigantic Be-In with an audience," said JJ. "Where were you planning to have this party?"

Dennis smiled smugly. "The Forest Hills Country Club."

"Yikes!" Maria yelped.

"Come on," I said, "this has to be a put-on. That snooty place wouldn't allow the likes of us anywhere near them."

"Trust me, it's for real. They want us to do this. They're curious about us. Hippie is becoming fashionable."

I shook my head. "It's an awfully long commute from here."

"Hey, then listen to the best part: They want us to create a total environment, so we'll be allowed to live on the grounds and use the facilities during the whole expo. We can either camp out or sleep in our shop spaces. We'll have a cooking tent, so we can do our own health food if we want. We can use all the facilities—swimming pool, showers, sauna, gym. Man, it'll be the Ritz!"

It *was* the Ritz. Paranoia was assigned a long room with an L-shaped alcove and a door at each end. We set up a little light show at the L and the customers would enter there, then continue through the room where merchandise was displayed, and exit by the cash register at the other door. Enormous crowds of straight people showed up, and every day several of our buddies came out from New York City, dressed in their hippie drag, to help us.

I had never seen so many hippies in one place outside Central Park. We were all over the grounds and buildings, setting up tents and campsites outdoors and inside, utilizing the communal kitchen, and playing together everywhere. Perhaps what amazed me most during that week was how careful we were to keep the place clean, how nothing was trashed or damaged, how all of us were committed to leaving the grounds as we'd found them or even better.

The one matter above any other that we all had on our minds, the unspoken agreement we shared, was that there would be no dealing in substances on those premises. Even conversation about drugs was discouraged, at least with the straight people who were often disposed to ask us drug-related questions.

We were all quite clear about the risks to everyone; we understood that there would be agents and law-enforcement officers mingling among us to obtain information, that thrill-seeking tourists would try to lure us into supplying. So the drug portion of our hippie culture was not on display during the days when sightseers swarmed the grounds.

But at night, when the country club was closed to the public, we discreetly used what we had brought, hidden in the privacy of our own spaces, with people we knew and trusted.

* * *

This was my afternoon off from working our shop, my free time to enjoy the expo at large. I had ingested my substance and was eager for this trip. I wandered around the grounds, looked at merchandise in several booths, got a strobe light treatment from Max, and went to the vendors' tent where our kitchen was set up. I ate some guacamole and beans and had some conversation about social transformation, wholeness and respect with the hippies who were hanging out there.

I looked at my wristwatch. After the dial stopped dancing and the hands stopped clapping, I determined that it was almost closing time. Soon all the straight folks would be hustled off the premises and the night would belong to us. I wandered away from the vendors' tent and sat down near a circle of hippies who were drumming and playing flutes, while several lingering straights stood nearby watching.

I recalled when I was a child in the '40s in Florida, and my folks took me to an "Indian Village" where some Seminoles made a living by being who they were for tourist onlookers. I thought about that, then about what was happening for me here, in this construct of community where we, too, were on display. I considered how we each were so different, yet all so much the same. Never before had I experienced such unity, such intimacy with strangers, as I was experiencing at this happening. Through all our differences, we shared a deep-seated desire for peace, love and a gentler, healthier world.

The music was still playing, but the tourists were gone. The night was soft, the sky a conglomerate of stars, and I decided a sauna and swim would be quite nice.

Later, in the locker room, I met Jason, also tripping, and, wordlessly, we stepped out onto the deck and sat down together. I watched his face shift as he turned in the darkness—planes of forehead, cheek and jaw lit by changing pastel glow from where someone had hung flashing colored lights around the swimming pool to reflect in the water. I felt as though I could look at Jason forever, drinking in the vision of him, he was so beautiful. For a while we were silent together, each with our own thoughts.

At last Jason sighed deeply. "I'm packing it up after the expo."

"Oh?"

"One thing over all else I've learned from being here this week," he continued, "is that I want to live like this all the time, in community with people I love, people who've had experiences similar to my own, people I can share a dream with. I don't want to be afraid so much. The city is too crowded for me anymore. There's too much coming in through these open doors of perception, too much violence, hate and paranoia around."

I nodded, remembering my own trips in the city when I'd realized that so many of the feelings I experienced were really not my own but came from other people crowded together with myself in the tightly-packed spaces through which we moved and lived. People were too closely crammed against each other, even to the point of intruding across psychic boundaries. I had decided not to do any more heavy psychedelics in the city after that, after plugging into all the stresses experienced by other people in my tenement and realizing how sensitive I was to being affected by that closeness of others' vibrational fields.

Yet I still delighted in the city, absorbed the myriad experiences it still held for me with pleasure, even through the realities of violence and paranoia. Someday, I knew, this would pall, and I would join the outwardly mobile hippie stream in search of that Great Commune in the Sky, but that day was not yet, and it would not be tomorrow.

"I sure do wish you well." I leaned over and kissed Jason on the cheek, then stood up and went outside to join the rest of the party.

Excerpted from an unpublished manuscript, The Acid Years

The Great Duck Storm
Lee Quarnstrom

It was inevitable that Dale Kesey would screw up his cousin Ken's fake suicide.

Dale is a simple man in the best sense of the word—not a

simpleton at all, just a rustic fellow with no affectations, with a belief in Christianity and an unerring ability to take the wrong turn during a high-speed chase.

Like the day and night of The Great Duck Storm: We'd taken the Merry Pranksters' psychedelic bus, Furthur, with Neal Cassady at the wheel, north from La Honda, across the Golden Gate Bridge and onto Marin County's Coast Highway. We were headed to Mendocino County for no particular reason other than to cool our heels.

I remember Ken Babbs repeatedly cautioning Cassady to stop drifting the old International Harvester school bus around the hairpin curves as the road zig-zagged up the coast. But Neal, possibly the greatest wheelman of all time, found tight curves irresistible when he was on the road.

We found ourselves at Lake Mendocino. We unloaded our sound system from the bus, plugged the amplifiers into a socket in the restroom, turned up the noise to a level that would today make me call the cops, and swallowed some Owsley acid.

Only recently had it been mutually decided among "heads," as we pioneers in the interregnum between the Beats and hippies thought of ourselves, that LSD-25 would be referred to by the nickname "acid." There had been strong support among many, including Kesey himself, for "alice," as in *Alice in Wonderland*. There were no debates; it just turned out that we all called it acid.

As the weirdness engulfed us, Kesey vanished into the woods and Babbs began to quack like a duck. He quacked for an hour or so before I realized, in fact, that he was not quacking *like* a duck, he was quacking because he *was* a duck!

Gretchen Fetchin understood immediately and had covered Babbs' high-visibility red Day-Glo pith helmet as well as his not-quite-naked body with some sort of goo, then slit open a down pillow and covered him with duck feathers.

When a park ranger approached me and said we had to turn down the music, I was too stoned to respond. The ranger demanded, "Who's in charge here?" Well, no one was in charge, of course, but I pointed toward Babbs. We all pointed toward Babbs. The ranger strode up to the guy in the pith helmet and the feathers and instructed him to unplug the sound system from the men's john.

"Right now! Do you understand?"

Babbs looked the ranger right in the eye and quacked—in the affirmative. The uniformed park guard rushed back to his Jeep and radioed for help. When reinforcements arrived, Babbs nodded and gesticulated like anyone involved in a conversation would, except that he kept quacking. After all, he *was* a duck.

The platoon of rangers informed us we were 86ed from Lake Mendocino Park. One unplugged the sound system and together they forced us aboard the bus and gave us five minutes to get outta Dodge. Faye Kesey suddenly went berserk, only one of two times I saw her do so—the other being the time she smacked Ken over the head with a frying pan after he'd drunk the last of the milk she was saving for the kids; this was during an extremely tight fiscal recession at the La Honda house in the winter of '64-'65. She began to scream at the rangers.

"You can't make us leave! You can't make us leave! My husband's not here! My husband's lost!"

The gendarmes were not sympathetic. With Cassady at the wheel and Faye leaning out a window yelling desperately for her husband, we slowly motored up the road to the park exit. The rangers were behind us in their Jeeps.

The sun was setting as we left the lake, and it was almost dark when we hit the highway. Just as we left the park, Kesey popped out of the underbrush at the side of the road and hopped aboard. Babbs put "Hit the Road, Jack," our Ray Charles traveling music, on the tape deck and we headed toward the east.

Still high as a kite and swallowing another dose to make sure I stayed that way, I climbed atop the bus as we headed further. Zonker came up top with George Walker. We stared at the stars. I asked the most absurd of all possible questions.

"Zonker, what would we do if we saw another psychedelic-painted bus going in the other direction?"

We giggled; the thought that anyone else, ever, would paint an old bus with Day-Glo enamel was out of the question.

As we pondered similar deep questions about the nature of the universe, the down comforter we'd wrapped around ourselves tore and feathers began to fly. The bus' wake filled with feathers, engulfing a car following close behind. The driver of that other vehicle had to turn on his windshield wipers to see where he was going.

"Hmm," mused Zonker. "The Great Duck Storm."

Now, LSD keeps you awake, but when you decide to go to sleep, you really go to sleep. I went below, as did George and Zonker. Eventually all of us decided it was time to catch 40 winks, even Cassady, "Speed Limit," whose fondness for amphetamines kept him awake most of the time. Neal left the driver's seat and Dale Kesey took the wheel.

The bus wasn't moving when I awoke the next morning. I was still a bit high, certainly groggy—somewhat, let us say, confused. Looking out the window, I saw that the bus was parked in a pine forest, not something one sees near the Mendocino County coastline. We were on a dirt road. I could hear birds chirping.

I stumbled to the front of the bus. A couple of Pranksters were already up, standing outside, stretching, looking up the red-dirt road at a mountain towering above. Gradually, groggy colleagues stumbled out of the bus and looked around. We were all pretty fucked up. Finally, Dale came out of the bus, wiping the sleep from his eyes.

"Hey, great morning, isn't it?" he asked cheerily.

"Where are we?" some of us demanded.

"Jeez, I don't know," Dale replied.

"Then why are we stopped here?"

"Well," Dale said, shrugging his shoulders, "we ran out of gas."

The Hermit volunteered to start a fire so we could get breakfast going. Most of us realized there was no food to cook, but we all figured it was better to let the Hermit work on the fire-starting techniques he said he'd learned—along with basket-weaving tricks, while living in the mountains with the Indians—than to let him start shooting speed and running around like a madman.

Sure enough, Hermit piled a few sticks on the ground, rubbed a couple of them together and soon had what he claimed was a fire going. It had no flames, it had no smoke—"So Indians could elude pursuers," Hermit claimed—but it did produce heat. However, since the mercury was quickly rising on this mountainside, heat was the last thing we needed.

Mountain Girl wandered back down the road a couple of hundred yards, then returned with her hair wet. She'd found a water tank with a pipe and spigot, like steam engines used to require along railroad lines. We all hurried down to soak the acid bunnies out of our brains.

Where the hell were we?

Dale Kesey, naturally, had no idea. He said he'd just driven and driven and driven and suddenly stopped when the fuel ran out. As I rapidly stepped away from the water pipe, having just seen a rattlesnake coiled a yard from my feet, an old man smoking a pipe walked up the dirt road. He stopped and gazed at the brightly painted bus as though he saw them every day. It occurred to me later that he probably did.

We wondered where we were.

He informed us that we were many miles up a single-lane dirt road that led to a copper mine nine miles up the road. The water tank was the only source of water for the miners, and they sent a tanker truck down every week or two to replenish their supply. Nope, there were no phones or much of anything else, for that matter, up at the mine. We were in the Trinity Alps, inland many miles from the coast.

No, there was never any traffic on the road except for the water tanker, a fuel tanker that brought gasoline up to fuel the mine's generators every two or three months, and a truck that brought provender up to the miners every few weeks.

Jesus! Now this was starting to look serious.

How far down to the highway? Seventeen miles. How far to the nearest Chevron station? (We were broke; all we had was George's Chevron credit card.) Oh, you go down to the highway and turn right and go about 30 miles.

This did not look good. We all turned and stared at Dale. He shrugged. Kesey, though, was calm, told us not to worry, to take advantage of the situation, to make the best of a tough deal. Skeptically, we tried.

A few minutes later, as we were sitting in a clear spot watching the buzzards circling overhead, we heard the honk of a horn. We got up and walked back to the bus. Stuck behind it on the narrow thoroughfare was a gasoline tanker en route to the copper mine. It was a Chevron truck. Did the driver take credit cards?

"Of course," he said with a smile. So he pumped the bus full of gas, ran George's plastic through his machine, waited until we turned around, then continued his way up to the mine.

We headed home to La Honda.

* * *

One day, watching television at Chloe Scott's home near Perry Lane in Menlo Park, just a stone's throw from the Stanford University golf course—where Kesey had once found himself and Faye in a dream, gnawing dog-meat from the bones of countless dachshunds like his mean little bitch, Schnapps—we heard the TV actors talking about Dale.

We were stoned on Czechoslovakian acid—what the hell *were* they doing with LSD in a repressive Soviet-bloc dictatorship in the mid-1960s?—and we were watching, appropriately enough, the World War II flyboys series, *Twelve O'Clock High*. One of the characters turned to another, as their B-29 was taking flak from the Nazi gunners down below, and shouted, "Chute up and bail out!"
Kesey looked at the screen in amazement. He turned and spoke: "That guy just said, 'Shoot up and Dale out.'"

After that, Dale Kesey's misadventures, including the botched staging of Ken's suicide, were written off as another case of "shooting up and Daling out."

* * *

Kesey got busted again, in San Francisco with Mountain Girl. This time he hit the trail. He split to Mexico. It wasn't long before we packed up the Acid Test and followed.

In those intervening weeks, though, federal agents stopped by the Hip Pocket bookstore, knocked on our farmhouse door, stopped us in the street and even queried our friends.

"Where is Ken Kesey?" they all wanted to know.

"Why," we all said in amazement, "we heard he committed suicide."

Here's the suicide deal (I think Tom Wolfe had a transcript of Kesey's note in *The Electric Kool-Aid Acid Test*, but I could be wrong;

LSD does funny things to the memory): Kesey wrote a diary-like note chronicling a drive up the California coast from Santa Cruz, rambling on about his depression at being arrested twice on drug charges, etc. Then he stated he had decided to end it all.

Dale was supposed to drive one of the Pranksters' beat-up old trucks along the route his cousin had described in the fake suicide note. He was to drive to some remote sea-cliff up in Northern California and leave the truck at the edge of a precipice overlooking the Pacific. He was also supposed to leave a pair of Kesey's shoes on the front seat of the truck, next to the suicide note.

Dale got the assignment because he looked a lot like Ken Kesey: the same rugged hillbilly features, the same Bozo-the-Clown curly blond hair, the same size and shape. And he followed the plan perfectly, with one exception.

As he neared the jumping-off spot, the old truck sputtered to a halt, never to run again. Knowing he was supposed to leave the vehicle at the cliff's edge, Dale asked some local fellow to help him push the dead vehicle the final few yards.

For some reason, the FBI found this last bit of business sort of suspicious. They wondered why a suicidal Ken Kesey hadn't just walked those final few steps from the abandoned truck to the precipice where he had indicated he was jumping to his death. When they asked us, of course we said we couldn't answer that particular question.

You know," we'd tell them, "Kesey was quite strange."

But they were dogged, grilling us regularly. Of course, they could have asked almost any long-haired person in Santa Cruz, including our surfer buddies. We all knew that Kesey was in Mazatlan—where most of us would be soon, as quickly as we could get through a few Acid Test weekends down the coast in Los Angeles.

Excerpted from a memoir-in-progress, When I Was a Dynamiter.

The Merry Pranksters Meet the Hog Farm
Ken Kesey

On a sweet, clear spring day, in response to an ominous suggestion by Hugh Romney (who calls himself "Wavy Gravy" at present, who used to be known as "Dimensional Creemo," who in reality is "Al Dente"), the Merry Pranksters rendezvous with the Hog Farm somewhere on what the Hog Farm General assures us is a super secret and snugly secure mountain far back in the high desert country of Joshua Tree National Forest—just the spot for these two revolutionary bands to get together for some uninterrupted high-level plotting. Very high-level. The always-famished Hog Farmers are into the Prankster Acid stash like it was a bowl of Spanish peanuts at a cocktail party, reassuring us as they munch down hundreds of thousands of micrograms: "Go ahead, get ripped and cut loose all you want up here—there ain't nobody for a hundred miles to bother us!"

You might imagine our surprise then when we come floating out of the sage and sandstone back to where the Hog Farm's scruffy vehicles are parked about our painted bus—come sailing out of the sage, still rushing and preparing to peak—and see four patrol cars come skidding to a stop surrounding us with lights whirling and radios squawking and helicopters coming. Babbs had just strapped on his guitar and pulled on two huge green rubber hands in preparation for a little modern "Desert Song" when he found himself eye to sunglassed eye with obviously another ex-Marine just as tall and mean and threatening as Babbs was loaded, having to try to stall the guy from searching the bus while we figured out how to hide the dope that was scattered from the taillights to the dashboard. The women were frantically gathering what they could find into Shannon's Little Kiddie Kase, and Hagen and I were trying to get the sound system and camera going so we could at least leave some record behind when we disappeared up the river with so many priors amongst us that we wouldn't hit the street again until about time for Haley's Comet. I remember stammering to Hagen through the snarl of tape and film squirming between us: "Don't Panic Don't Panic Don't Panic!" and Hagen answering, with foam at the corners of his mouth: "I'm Not I'm Not I'm Not!"

An awful shadow was gliding down on us to roost for years to come. Oh, fear, fear... I finally got the tape threaded and the machine going and a microphone out the bus window but I could see it was too late; the goggle cop was breaking through Babbs' green-handed delaying tactics and, black-leather palm resting on his gun-butt, was leading his helmeted band toward us. Usually Babbs can stymie a cop with little tricks like showing his license and making sure the guy notices his serviceman's card so the guy gasps: "A captain in the Marines? *You?* Where were you stationed?" And because most cops are ex-service-somethings but of nowhere near the rank of captain, they end up calling him "sir" out of habit. But not this big eyeless bastard; he knew something was up and all of us trembling in the bus knew that it was the jig, when suddenly, rising it seemed from the very dust, there was Weavy Groovo in front of the oncoming disaster, with his eyes shining confidence and his lips already working over the microphone. I turned up the outside speakers so the mountains around rung with his rap:

"Now there's you guys and us guys. And we're all just guys. We all get up in the morning and there the day lays ahead of us and we all try to get through it. Sometimes it ain't easy. Sometimes the women want stuff we ain't got. Sometimes we see the kids heading for a life we already been through and it makes us lonely and sad. Just guys. And if you guys got something we don't and can see we could use it, you give us some. And if us guys know something you guys don't that it looks like you guys would like to know, then won't we tell you about it? Because it's like the mirror says: 'It's all done with people.' And when magic happens it's no more than just one guy helping another guy. No mystery. No sleight of hand. Just guys being guys..."

And on and on in this profound vein, stopping the search party cold in their black leather boots with a barrage of goodwill so sincerely sweet and simpleminded that they were stuck fast by the honeythick audacity of it. Even old Big-and-Mean had to remove his glasses to try to clean it away, but it was coming too thick and fast, filling not only his ears and eyes but getting also into his mouth and causing the corners of the thin mouth to lift in spite of his size, and he grinned.

This cooled everybody. Hagen finally got the magazine loaded and the camera working. Shannon took the loaded Kiddie Kase and strolled off the bus and into the rocks, a five-year-old's and completely unnoticed carrier. Out through the window I gave Babbs the old thumb-and-finger-in-a-circle sign that things were all clear—the bus was clean—and he began joyfully whanging lush green chords from his guitar with his rubber hands. Other Pranksters and Hog Farmers chimed in with flute and harp. Mountain Girl went so far as to invite the visitors in for tea. All declined except the honcho; he and MG sipped herb tea and discussed pleasantries while the rest of us played music in the desert wind. The taloned black shadow of terror rose and flapped off seeking new prey, cheated of what had been a sure kill.

It wasn't that we just avoided a bust, or that we'd fooled the cops; Hugh's monologue had carried it past that. The cops knew we were loaded and knew, as well as we did, that a thorough search will always turn up something illegal if that's what you're into. In fact, everybody knew everything and had accepted this as the basis for a truce. Maybe tomorrow boots would be kicking bare feet apart for a prickheaded harassment shakedown and vows of vengeance would be muttered in various beards, but today, for a while, on that high mountain, guys would relax with other guys and enjoy that magic moment of moratorium that is Peace.

And, a little further south, at the rendezvous between the Manson Family and the Process, that shadow would find a more comfortable roost. Everybody would be happy.

Now a tale to demonstrate the deeper side of this man's higher life:

I remember riding toward Santa Cruz in the back of Stewart Brand's pickup the raw morning after the Acid Test Graduation. And let me here confess something for the record: During that mad night, after all the hoopla about how I was going to tell the kids what was *beyond* acid, just as I was beginning to feel the half-dozen uppers I had taken to starch my front for the ordeal ahead... I saw coming across the floor toward me Doris Delay, glowing like a verse from an illuminated Bible with her blond hair trailing and her eyes like matched stars pulling her across to me through the ecstatic dancers, the apprehensive friends, the impatient cops and reporters... to stop, shining before me, and place a large white capsule between my lips like a celestial postman delivering a Registered Priority. I swallowed it like Moses getting a good deal on a hot ticket from heaven.

"Terry the Tramp told me to give it to you," Doris Delay informed me. A quick look past her golden hair and across that room of dancers and friends and cops to Tramp in his big wool sweater with his Hell's Angels jacket over it—impervious behind the bushy black hair and beard and shiny black glasses; completely inscrutable but for that grin at me!—gives me my first hint that the ticket was hot all right but wasn't going to take me quite as heavenward as I had hoped.

O an awful high-voltage humiliating public freakout! O those miserable fucking leapers that wouldn't let a crazy man keep his mouth shut. And O a psychedelic bummer, O, O, O. If you've never had one, folks, you just have no idea. Best to leave me, folks, at this midnight point in the nightmare's beginning, plunging out of sight into some discrete and subterranean agony and pick me up again drifting back into sight at dawn, battered and hell-burned, being finally maneuvered into a pickup with tenderly aghast family and friends, and watch me a while as I am driven south through the season's new sun:

Nobody speaks. None of us people, anyway. But the tires hiss and the cement whistles and the wind cries past like a newsboy calling the gossip far and wide about the scandalous spectacle witnessed last night at the so-called Acid Test Graduation Ceremonies.

I snatch the torn rubble of my mind for reasons, excuses, last-minute explanations to exonerate me—"I have been serving secretly in the Obidon Corps, friends, and it was my mission last night to act as if I..."—anything to blot out that newsboy shrill!

I finally launched out loud into a theory, something about how crossing poles need a *consciousness* at the point of intersection to serve as a kind of traffic cop at the cosmic crossroads, you understand—you understand, a sort of *human bench nark* you understand—and felt again that gathering skirl of lunacy, but I was wisely interrupted by George Walker reading kindly out loud to me the big red freeway sign flashing past: "Go back. You are going the wrong way!"

I kept quiet, holding what I learned later in jail was called my mad. We stopped a while at Stewart's place on Skyline... and remember lying in the grass and telling Babbs and Hassler: "I'm raw. Handle me really easy" and "I wish Hugh Romney had been there."

"We'll get him up next week," Babbs said. "We'll go somewhere and have a nice close trip. Just us."

"We'll get Hugh and go somewhere without police, press or para-noia," Hassler said.

"I'm raw," I said.

A week later Hugh showed up from his hill above L.A. and we packed all the instruments in the bus and drove up to LuVal's church in San Francisco. After we set up all the sound equipment and checked it, LuVal passed around a little silver box full of Owsley's newly pressed White Lightnings. With a good deal of trepidation and prompting, I joined the others and took two.

We threw the Ching and Hugh read it. It was 24, Fu *RETURN* (The Turning Point), with no changes. He started reading in a flippant, stagey voice—the L.A. voice of the time—then shifted sudden and smooth into a tone I'd never heard before, soft and so earnest and deliberate that by the time he had finished the few pages, Cassady was already stripped to the waist and hopping into the high and the walls were beginning to move. It went on for a while like that, just an ordinary high—us playing our instruments, Cassady bucking and rap-ping to the beat with Ann Murphy tugging at his arm, the Hermit zip-ping around giggling, MG flithering at the sound equipment... and I was beginning to think I was going to slide on through, that the freakout last week was just a freak freakout caused by some oddball Hell's Angel concoction, when I noticed Hugh sitting by the fireplace, crying.

We kept playing, but everybody was watching Hugh. He would sob heartbreakingly for a moment, then cease and stare at someone, his mouth agape and his eyes wide as though the person had caught his attention with an action so terrible that all one could do was to gawk in horror, gawk and then break into tears of embarrassment and dis-tress at the hopeless tragedy of the human condition.

I grew embarrassed for him. At one point I think I said: "Looks like it's Hugh's turn this week." Those that went to comfort him evoked the same reaction of horrified disbelieving shock followed by terrible weeping. Finally he collapsed to the rug, sobbing.

A guy stepped out of the shadows of the church and stroked Hugh a moment on the shoulder. This seemed to calm him. He grew still, remaining on the floor. The guy—a thin old-timey-looking longhair who I never saw before or after this event, a real old longhair who'd been wearing beads and fringe thousands of years before the word hippie—stood over Hugh holding a big russet-colored feather. The room still wheeled with drums and guitars and the Hermit's hissing and Cassady's rattling around, but now the wheeling had a hub.

Hugh rose to his hands and knees. His nose was big as an apple and his eyes puffed nearly shut, but the crying had stopped. With great effort he began to speak: "May... all beings... be peaceful." Straining in some kind of knotted prayer: "May all... beings be... happy...."

"Be peaceful... be happy," the longhair echoed, stirring the air with his feather.

"May all... beings be... peaceful!" He was on his knees, eyes and fists clenched and trembling with terrific effort. "May all beings... be happy!" Becoming louder, more urgent. George picked it up on the drums, a thick halting beat, like a horse coming out of a bag. "May all beings... be *peaceful*!" He was standing now, demanding. "Peaceful beings," whispered the longhair spreading butter on the air with his feather. "May all beings be... *happy*!" (The drums and guitars rising along with his now-stern voice.) "May all beings be *peaceful*!" (Rising, rising...) "May all beings be *HAPPY*!"

Bong. His eyes flew open. All was still. Hugh's face relaxed and for a few moments he seemed to have passed out of his paroxysm, then he collapsed again to the floor and, beginning again with the same tortured whisper—"May... all beings be... peaceful"—fought once more to rise as the drums and guitars joined softly toward another crescendo.

Each climax became louder and more drastic. Each time, in the silence following the last big "May all beings be *HAPPY*!" I would think: That's gotta be enough. Surely he's gotta be cooled out this time. Yet always would the moment of peace shatter and drop him wretchedly back to the floor. I felt impatient. I wanted to start another song, though the accompaniment we were playing was unusually musical for Prankster music, and I wanted to take a piss. But after the climax and the pause, we started right back over—from the agony on the floor.

"May... all beings be... peaceful..."

I had got my guitar notes down to a few bass strings. I could do it with my eyes closed.

"May... all... beings be... happy...."

Maybe I ought to try to add a little lead on the higher strings.

"May all... spirits... be peaceful."

Of course that'll probably mean I'll miss a few of the bass beats.

"May all spirits... be happy."

But even if I miss a beat I can lay way back and act like I meant to miss a bass beat.

"May all beings... be *peaceful*...."

Give a kinda syncopation. It could use it.

"May all beings be *happy*!"

Then a chord just for class.

"May all beings be *PEACEFUL*...."

And step on that reverb button—where is it?

"May all beings be *HAPPY*!!!"

He was looking right at me. He looked eight feet tall and fierce as a god. As I squirmed under his gaze I realized that except for Cassady and the Hermit, *everybody else was looking at me also*! That, one by one, he had gone through all the others, asking, *begging* them to make an effort, and that, as each had made the effort they had been taken into the growing circle of *peaceful beings* and *happy spirits* and that they were waiting for me to make my effort, because disquietude is painful, that they were affected by the knot of impatience in my middle and were all waiting for me to let it go. I grinned. Hugh and the others smiled back. I drew a breath and let the tenseness out of me the way one brushes a wasp out the window. For a few seconds Peace went amongst us, then Cassady and the Hermit started up and Hugh went to the floor again.

This time we were working on Cassady, all of us knew it, relishing it, concealing our knowing smiles as we watched Hugh build it, build it then *ZAP!* he had Cassady.

As realization swept over Neal we saw a rare sight. Lowering his eyes, he blushed. Then there was none left but the Hermit.

Hugh tried three crescendos on this little yipping weasel, but either Herm was unable to effect that willful calming or he was too stubborn to try. He knew what was happening but only became more and more agitated until by the time Hugh rounded off that third attempt—"*MAY ALL BEINGS BE PEACEFUL!!??*"—the Hermit was scurrying up and down the walls in a kind of squeaking rodent antithesis and we all realized, Perhaps not... perhaps not....

The Acid Test
A. Nonny Moose

At the Watts Acid Test, after the Watts Riots, police came and hung around all night long and looked into the building, which was maybe a place where some kind of training to learn auto mechanics occurred. There was a room or alcove that had some windows facing the side-walk out front. Cops stood out there and watched the scene in that room. A woman there was freaking out, saying, "Who cares?" over and over.

Wavy Gravy was being nurse-like and trying to soothe her. Ken Babbs brought a microphone that was hooked to a reverb and we had loud booming reverbs of "Whoooo cares? Who *careeees?*" The woman was lying on the floor in black light in a pool of piss. In the main room where the Grateful Dead were playing was a plastic garbage can with about 20 gallons of electric Kool-Aid.

I don't know whether Kool-Aid even exists anymore, but it is or was sugar and flavoring in a little 3"x 5" flat packet that was easy to rip open and mix the contents with a stated amount of water and it would make a flavored drink.

At some point during the night two detectives in plain clothes walked into the center of this main room and stopped in the beams of the movie and slide projectors. There was a young participant from Santa Cruz who was called The Ox. He was big. He walked up to the two cops and put his face right next to theirs and said, "I'm so high, where my consciousness is, is so far beyond anything you can imagine." I thought that in translation was something like. "Way to go Ox, they'll sweep us up like dust." The two cops turned without a word and left. The night proceeded without further untoward incident.

With the coming of dawn we carried the garbage can of leftover Kool-Aid out and dumped it in the gutter and began loading up our gear. There were still police cars stationed up and down the street as they had been all night long. We didn't know what to expect.

At some point a police car pulled up and Paige, the halves of whose face were painted two colors like a harlequin, and Paul, whose body was totally wrapped with electrician's tape, were arrested for being drunk or disorderly, and taken away. They were later released. We went back to wherever we were staying at the time and crashed into exhausted high slumber.

The blessing of the psychedelic experience is being immersed in the fantastic beauty of all life that constantly surrounds us. It is the state called rapture. In our normal consciousness we are subsumed in the rational mind-space of plans, thoughts, fantasies and so on. Our involvement with the rational causes us to hurry through life and this inhibits and prevents us from seeing and living every second in beauty and harmony.

The Electric Kool-Aid Softball Game
Wavy Gravy

After our extended family, the Hog Farm, returned from Woodstock, we were challenged to a game of softball by two neighboring communes. We figure to mix it. Put their names and our names in the same hat and let chance do the choosin'. They appreciate our cosmic intentions but just wanna play softball. Them against us.

We figure on losin', but hope to stay high. So before the game we proceeded to take the last of the green acid that we had retrieved from Woodstock and mix up a punch. And then we began to make up new rules.

The Gonk Family Theater is home and that telephone pole right across the road will be first base. First base is far out and you had to hit a double to get there. To get to second it was necessary to run into our bus, the Road Hog, jacked up on blocks without wheels, jump out the back door and touch the bumper. From second to third meant running like hell to our house, up a rickety ladder, dash through the attic and stick your head out the window, let your fingers touch the ledge. To get from third to fourth base, you had to slide down a rope into a bucket of water. In order to score, somebody else had to advance to fourth base, then piggyback carry you home.

When you got home, you knew you were home, 'cause home was a big pillow, sorta sexy and soft, surmounted by my sleeping bag, a very special sleeping bag, made of many patches, all nifty and new. They'd lay you down on the sleeping bag. And also, what was there waiting for you was a TV set, a cheeseburger and a glass of carrot juice, and, oh yes, a joint and friends to massage you. You were *home*.

First couple innings were really intense. A series of strikeouts. They had two guys on their team with one eye apiece. We gave them six strikes. Still they struck out. Anyway, we won the softball game, 5-1. And just for the record, that one run was unearned. I mean the guy's feet were dry, so he couldn't have touched fourth base. The great softball game dissolved into dancin' and dinner.

When the Hog Farm got thrown into the slammer for pot, all the charges were dropped, and the only thing actually arrested was my sleeping bag, which was taken by the FBI for analysis. They thought it perhaps contained portions of an American flag which turned out to be bunting. It was later released, and was last seen hanging in the Rock and Roll Hall of Fame. The sleeping bag's name is now Home Plate.

Zapping Nixon
Roy E. Tuckman

1. The Question
"The problem with psychedelics is that the person expands awareness so quickly that he gets 'there' with his ego intact." That was the point of view of Jack Gariss, one of my mentors and a master of meditation and hypnosis, among other things. He did a radio program on meditation and allied subjects for KPFK. I was an avid listener, then a volunteer for him and for the station.

"How could an intact ego be a problem?" I felt. After all, as a young man in his early '30's, I was eager to make my mark on the world, and after hundreds of trips, eager to make my mark on the universe. And one aspect of the psychedelic experience was the alliance with power. Real power. Power greater than all the armies and navies and greater than the A-bomb and the H-bomb. And I was convinced that this power could be brought to bear against the enemy. And the enemy leader was—Richard M. Nixon. And now he was the President of the United States and Commander in Chief of the war in Vietnam.

I had managed to avoid being sent to Vietnam. First there were a series of student deferments of one year each. Then LSD experience demonstrated to me the futility and foolishness of my "career" in anthropology and I quit graduate school. Having been shown through the psychedelic experience again and again the beauty of the world and the miracle of life, I could not tolerate academia. I could not tolerate reading more books I didn't want to read and writing more learned papers I didn't want to write. This was obviously not part of the miracle.

After I quit graduate school, in the middle of my Ph.D. exams, the draft board sent me a note which started with "Greeting," not the expected "Greetings." I had been drafted; out of the frying pan and into the fire. For advice, I turned again to LSD which constantly taught, somehow, that everything is perfect in existence, down to the position of every single atom. This information was difficult to translate into daily life in the world, and building this bridge became my *raison d'étre*. And going to Vietnam in a perfect universe did not seem to compute in this instance. The draft board was wrong! I had to show them that. I appealed my induction and was given an appointment to meet with them.

The night before my meeting with the board, Ravi Shankar, a future mentor, gave a concert in Los Angeles. It was the fulfillment of a dream. But despite the music, I seethed with anger and fear. We had attacked Vietnam! We had stifled their elections because the wrong person was about to be elected. The Japanese had kicked out the French from Vietnam in World War II. The Vietnamese had kicked out the Japanese who signed a separate peace treaty with them. The French then invaded to get "their'" country back, and the Vietnamese resisted recolonization. We picked up the cudgel when the Vietnamese beat the French. We were fighting against freedom and democracy, and the American people were being lied to in general and in detail. And my country was trying to make me participate in this crime as a soldier. The spirituality of the sitar and the tabla assaulted my anger and the situation became intolerable. I left in the middle of the concert and went home to concentrate on my upcoming meeting with the gentlemen of the draft board.

I carefully explained the political facts to the draft board, and how, as an American, it was impossible to fight against forces whose constitution was based on ours. That if I were to fight for American values, I would have to join the Vietnamese Army (called North Vietnamese here). But the only way I could be "excused" was by being a conscientious objector. And the only way to be a conscientious objector was to sign a statement that I believed in "a supreme being."

Well, this statement was obviously written before the discovery of LSD! I carefully explained to the draft board that God is not a being, but a process, a consciousness. That their statement was Aristotelian and we were living in a post-Einsteinian world. I was sure that they would understand.

Then I suggested that they should all take LSD and consider, with their expanded minds, why one would not want to travel 10,000 miles to kill people who were fighting for their freedom.

The gentlemen of the draft board then summarized my position. That, based on my own experience and my own "religion," I was conscientiously objecting to my participation in the war. That explanation seemed okay to me. They excused me and said they'd send me a letter with their decision. I jumped on my motorcycle and rode home, wondering how and why this table of old men could be given the power over my existence.

A few weeks later I got the letter from the draft board. It said that I had been granted a "1-O" which is Conscientious Objector! I had won. That night I took more LSD and, in a private ceremony before my sacred fireplace in Venice, I burned the card.

2. The Design

Our brainwaves have been divided into four types, according to their speed. Delta waves are the slowest, 1-3 cycles per second, characterized by sleep. Then theta waves, 4-6 cycles per second, characterized by "imagery." Alpha waves, 6-12 cycles, are relaxed awakening, quietude, meditation. Above alpha are the beta waves—from concentration up to frenzy to madness at 18 or so cycles. The average person lives in beta consciousness in daily life.

The LSD experience is a beta experience. High excitement, ecstasy, paranoid fear; all an experience of the brain seeing and reacting to itself. We experience the firing of our neurons. (Pardon the clinical coldness.) What is left out here is the fact that a few minutes of this experience can be the absolute height of a lifetime; memories sharp, clear and inspiring for decades. Minutes or hours of experience, in value equal to years of normal life consciousness.

It's called "getting high" but that doesn't communicate the transcendent nature of the experience. I always liked to think that God is the highest, as many hymns say. We get high, and God is the highest. *That* is the meaning of "high." A movement toward the highest.

"But it doesn't do any good to just go up and come down," said Dr. Smith, Professor of Anthropology and another main mentor, after I had poured out my heart and described my post-LSD visionary confusions. He was perhaps the wisest man I had ever met. "You have to take something up with you, and bring something down." Consciousness is not the goal, but "prehension." To learn and keep the learning for your daily life.

And so this became the program. LSD can take you to the library of the universe called by some the "Akashic Records," wherein is stored all the information and knowledge that exist or will exist. I had the library card in these little vials buried in the back of the apartment in

Venice, California.

The program became to write down questions before tripping, and while in the state of total knowledge, to remember to refer to the questions on the paper.

Sometimes there were answers from the cosmos. Sometimes the questions seemed so pathetic that I would laugh and laugh uproariously at them. Sometimes I would forget the paper, along with the rest of the daily world. But when I did remember the questions, I learned to respond with directions. Do this! Do that! There was no use for a philosophical discourse or explanations. They would probably make no sense to the earthly mind, and besides, who wants to write about these things when the world of music and nature await the expanded consciousness?

Of course, these directions were not always easy to follow. When the end of a trip would reveal the scrawled note stating "sell your motorcycle" or "go to Russia"—well, one could question one's sanity. Akashic Records or no, life can be hard enough without having to obey such inconvenient directions.

But then a miraculous discovery appeared at the end of the 1960s, described in detail over several years by Jack Gariss on the radio. The discovery was brainwave biofeedback! Biofeedback enabled a person to see, via electronic instruments, the functioning of one's brainwaves and then to alter them. So you could learn to turn Beta waves into Alpha waves and Alpha waves into Theta waves, etc. The process was a kind of meditation. But with an electronic guru monitoring the inside of your head, and directing you toward the desired state. No religion, no rituals, no mythologies, no authoritarian prelates, no services, no books. Here was a spirituality based on science and self-knowledge and the exactitude of neurons and electrodes and transistors.

The biofeedback meditation consisted of pasting two electrodes on your skull, plugging them into an electronic instrument, and meditating. When reaching the desired brainwave pattern, the instrument would respond with a pleasant beep and/or a blue light. Then you might get excited and lose it, and have to relax again into the meditative state. Or you might just sit and sit and sit and wait for the damned thing to respond; wondering whether it was your brain or the electronics that were not working well.

Jack designed an instrument for meditators called the "Bioscope" and offered it for sale to interested listeners for a little over $200. After seeing the first demonstration in a gathering at the YWCA in Glendale, I sped home, grabbed my checkbook, sped back and made my payment. It would take months before my Bioscope was delivered. But finally it came. My ticket to eternity!

In this pioneering effort, my goal was to combine biofeedback with psychedelics. First I wanted to see the effect the drugs or herbs had on the brainwaves. Then I wanted to see the effect the brainwaves had on the effect of the drugs. The two most interesting effects were:

1. With Peyote, I was not allowed to do the experiment. After ingesting the six buttons, plugging into the Bioscope and meditating in my wooden hut overlooking Silverlake, the Peyote Spirit told me directly and convincingly to not fuck around with it; to unplug and do my "biofeedback" with the Earth and the trees and the rocks and insects and whatever animals came around. There was no choice and I followed orders.

2. With LSD, I found the most interesting area was to bring the LSD beta wave experience down to alpha waves; to take the mind over-whelmed with intense excitement and to relax it, to view the LSD effects from quietude and peacefulness. This was new territory to explore. And a new "power" to use.

Our country was bombing Cambodia and Laos. The lie of the Gulf of Tonkin was exposed and it didn't matter to the war effort. The infamy of the My Lai massacre was exposed and the war continued. The lies of the generals and the politicians and the media continued. Demonstrators were being jailed and then shot and killed on campus and the war continued.

But I had found a way to hold hands with God and I planned to use spiritual power against earthly power to stop the madness. Of course, to the reader, the location of the madness might be an apt question—in the country or in my mind. But I had no question, just a plan.

3. Execution of the Plan

Looking back 30 years to that time of the early '70's, I marvel at the ignorance of the plan but at the courage in willingness to attempt it. There was no knowledge of the Metta Meditation of Theravada Bud-dhists, conquering through loving-kindness meditation. There was not a hint of Tonglin meditation, eradicating evil through absorption and transformation. No Native Peoples' prayer "if it is to be" and none of their recognition of "all my relations." In fact, the plan was an act of war, no less than the war our country was committing. It was simply another act in the "kill for peace" vein, but it was also a noble and/or foolhardy experiment. In short, do not try this at home!

The Bioscope served as a sort of homing beam, keeping me sure in the alpha state. For purification, three days of fasting, and for helping release the mind from habitual programming, the skipping of a night of sleep. Maybe more than one night. This practice does not aid in memory retention.

Of course, bountiful helpings of Nature's Herb. One of the delight-ful discoveries in experimentation with brainwave biofeedback was that marijuana helped alpha wave functioning immeasurably. No wonder the "establishment" is so intensely against the use of marijuana. Imagine a society not addicted to hurry, worry, hypercontrol, aggressiveness, needless acquisitiveness, and other types of adrenaline addiction.

And finally, when things seemed right and the time seemed right, a vial of LSD was added to the mix, and a couple of hours of waiting. Not to be ignored, of course, was a constant soundtrack of "Blonde on Blonde" and "Sergeant Pepper," the Byrds and the Stones and Judy Collins and Beethoven. Or maybe it was provided by KPCC, which might have been still on the air at the time, providing reliable rock radio.

How can one describe the onset, the voyage, the arrival? I look back nearly 30 years, through a non-psychedelic, earthbound 21st century existence to back then where, even at the time, words would fail. They will always fail, as they always have.

Great and then overwhelming feelings of energy sweep through. The music connects directly to the brain so that the listener becomes the singer and the writer and then the process of sound itself. The external world becomes sharper to the eye. It seems as though detail becomes so exquisite that you can see a hair on the floor across the room. The little dots in the fabric of my Wharfdale Speakers start to glow with jewelled radiance and, all about me, the room glows with a beauty too overwhelming to recall or explain. Things "break the light in colors that no one knows the names of," sing the Byrds in "I Wasn't Born to Follow." Yes, they knew this vision too.

Then an intensely complex fabric, like a doily, puts the entire visual field into its pattern and it moves in an achingly sinuous motion which shows that everything we see is actually a kind of projection onto these doily patterns. And the patterns are moving and the colors are moving and the whole vision is coming from *us.* And this is the universe, and we are alone in it.

The cat walks in, little Pidro Bravo later to be known as the First. And she has her own energy center apart from the doilies, but merging with them. And she knows this territory as her daily world and welcomes me to the knowledge.

As a child I used to think my grandmother, Anna Tuckman, was pretty dumb. She had worked as a seamstress. Her English was poor, although in retrospect, I am sure her Yiddish and Russian were better. She didn't even know how to read. At one point I offered to teach her the alphabet and made a chart of capital and small letters, written and printed, to memorize.

Then came the fateful day when I learned the secret of sex (in the Victorian '40s, it was a secret). I realized that my grandmother knew all these things! That she had also experienced them and that I had never known her. And suddenly I felt a new respect for her, and a recognition of my poor judgment.

And the same with Pidro the cat, and Thumper and Somekitty I, II and III, and the Smokies and Napoleons—the cats of my life—and all the animals and the trees and the plants. They lived daily within this expanded reality and in this relation. Rolling Thunder, Cherokee medicine man, had said that all the two-leggeds, all the four-leggeds, all the winged ones know of this relationship except human beings.

And there is exultant happiness at the beauty of life, in every second of existence. And there is heartbreaking sadness at the suffering of those who suffer and the pain of those who feel pain. And the tears flow for them and for the beauty as even the very rocks cry for all of us.

And the doily patterns become stronger and the projections upon them—the walls, the furniture, and even oneself—fade and fade into non-being and there are only the patterns in ever-changing geometrical designs dancing and flowing. These are the atoms and molecules, this is the energy of being which makes up all of us. And in them a knowledge upon which we reflect our lives and make our judgments, not as positive and negative, but simply from the clear point of view of the pattern of us and our lives, and this changes focus as the myths of our lives change their story. And we ache for our childhood and we forgive and we grow from the avalanche of insights.

And the geometric forms themselves begin to fade and there is only a hugely pulsating brightness, beyond brightness and beyond light with an explosiveness that is beyond sound and silence. The core!

But wait! Am I in alpha? My ears search for the beeping of the Bioscope to make sure I am on the beam. This territory is known, and everything is, after all, perfect, but this is a mission.

I have become electricity itself! And I am I, who is still and again Roy! And I focus on Nixon with all my power, like an angry God shooting lightning bolts from his pointing fingers toward Washington, DC against the war, against the lies, against a lifetime of criminality and against a leadership tainted by corruption from the beginning.

Crucial to this entire effort was my earthly contact with Richard Nixon. We had met and had spent an hour just feet apart. Energies had been exchanged and the relationship between us was real as two human beings.

Nixon was running for governor of California. He spoke at Royce Hall at UCLA and, as a KPFK volunteer, I helped programmer Carlos Hagen record him. He stood on the Royce Hall stage, and Carlos and I were in front of the front row, Ampex set up and plugged in, recording his words.

And when Nixon lost the governorship to Edmund G. "Pat" Brown, I went to the Republican rally at the Beverly Hilton Hotel to gloat at him in his defeat. But he didn't come downstairs. Gladly we heard the next day that the press "wouldn't have Nixon to kick around any more."

But he came back and he won and he became President over the bodies of the two slain Kennedys. The Phoenix nightmare arose and took the oval office. And the secret plan he campaigned under to end the war was another lie.

Now, however, I commanded the very electricity of life and I summoned these memories and frustrations against him. The Bioscope became an altimeter, keeping balance amid the cosmic energies. And wave after wave of energy was released from Silverlake to Washington, DC.

After hours and eternities, darkness regained its place and the shapes and objects of daily life returned. The speakers became speakers and the walls became walls. I was again in a house, on a couch, above Silverlake in Los Angeles, and I was Roy, and I slumped, exhausted and victorious.

4. Denouement

Halloween night, 1965, the time of my first LSD trip. I was sitting in the digs of an artist friend, Lang Bowen. He was a painter who used sand rather than paint, and the sand came from Mexico. White sand, brown sand and black sand, shipped across the border to be glued onto board canvasses. Some had rocks or semiprecious stones embedded in them. Some were just sand, incised with shapes and figures, many of Mexican-Indian origin. Now, 35 years later, I still have one black and tan Aztec dancer or priest, incised in brown sand on a black sand background; a witness to the night, and a reminder, maybe even a partner of sorts.

Lang was a friend of my cousin, and we had met for a couple of hours some year in San Francisco. But we met coincidentally in Oaxaca, Mexico, where I was studying anthropology, hoping to be hired for an Oaxacan project. Lang was making another of his frequent trips to Mexico to play. I was planning to stay in Oaxaca to work toward my doctoral degree somehow, but Lang said, "Come on with me to Yucatan," and so we went. And I found out more about Mexico in those two weeks' vacation than I had in six weeks trying to be an anthropologist. It was an unforgettable lesson. We climbed El Castillo, the famous Mayan pyramid, where Lang cowered inside, frightened by the spirits abiding there while I brashly surveyed Chichen Itza. We went to Isla Mujeres and on to Veracruz and Mexico City.

My spoken Spanish was fair; Lang's was practically nonexistent. But I had great difficulty understanding theirs, and Lang had no trouble with that. A strange contrast. But I would talk, Lang would listen, and between the two of us, we could communicate pretty well with everyone. And, armed with a traveling medicine chest of codeine, penicillin and Bacardi Rum, we felt we could eat anywhere. (I shudder in retrospect.)

We traveled for a while with a 6'4" Yucatecan whose family had lived there for 400 years, and who bragged about his "pure Spanish blood." And we were a trio: a blond native from Yucatan with a complete knowledge of language and customs; a tall and very dark black man whose presence constantly provoked warm expressions of solidarity from the people (he told me that Mexicans thought that all blacks in the US were in jail, and that they felt a sense of brotherhood with him); and me, a 6-footer in a 5-foot world, mistaken for an Indian from the north of Mexico. Walking down the street, we literally stopped traffic!

Lang and I disagreed on many things, but he also taught me to look with an artist's eye rather than the objective and intellectual, almost cynical view which my education and upbringing had instilled in me. And at one point, he said, "Would you like to try some LSD?" I thoughtlessly agreed to do so, and a future date in the US was vaguely agreed upon.

In 1964, LSD was still legal and pretty well unknown. All I knew was from a TV show in Los Angeles with Paul Coates, a journalist who used to regularly spar with Zsa Zsa Gabor. He had an artist on the show whose accomplished work was shown. Then the artist was given some LSD and asked to paint. The result was a childish scrawl and splash canvas. But the artist thought it was great. This LSD stuff was weird. But I was willing to try it for curiosity's sake.

About a year later, the time came. I went to El Grenada, a little nest just south of San Francisco. I still have a repetitive dream of flying airplanes from the El Grenada Airport, right off Highway 1.

There, sitting in this room surrounded by sand paintings, I had the first visual art experience of my life. I had never been truly moved by paintings. Music, yes. Poetry, yes. Film, yes. But paintings had never communicated anything to me, and now they did, and they also moved themselves, forming a dance with the molecular patterns of the space between my eyes and their shimmering sands, each grain arranged with absolute perfection. And I realized that the purpose of life was to make something beautiful. This became my purpose, and it also spelled the end of my academic career, although I didn't realize it at the time.

I must add that, in addition to a newfound appreciation for art, came a newfound appreciation for music and my own prejudices. While the LSD effects were beginning to manifest, the stereo was playing Bob Dylan's "Mr. Tambourine Man." I had been a big fan for the first three albums, the "folk-oriented" albums. But everyone among the folk-purist group knew that Dylan had "sold out" and gone electric. I hadn't heard a thing of his for quite a while, and was forcefully brought face to face with my own uptight prejudice to the great extent that I was inspired by that anthem.

After that amazing night of tears, ecstasy, profound amazement, discovery and re-dedication, I asked about books I could read to explain all this. Fortunately there was *The Joyous Cosmology* by Alan Watts and *The Doors of Perception* by Aldous Huxley. A good start to lay the foundations of my new life.

"Don't do too much trippin'," Lang said, as I jumped into my faithful 1963 VW Bug. "Don't do too much trippin'." "Yeah, sure," I responded, knowing that too much could not possibly be enough.

And now, about seven years later, here I was, poring over the *Los Angeles Times* for a trace of my experiment. And there it was: Richard Nixon had been stuck in an elevator in the White House. Victory! Victory?

I could never take any credit for this coincidental electrical failure. Not until now. And not until here. But I think I did it. Four days of mind-bending, mind-numbing, energy-exhausting travail to result in an inconvenience for the enemy. But it worked, or at least something worked. Back to the drawing boards!

I'm sorry I didn't end the war and I didn't eliminate the leader. But he was at least inconvenienced, and maybe I had indeed made electricity his enemy, if only for a short time.

So maybe Jack was right. The trouble with psychedelics is that they take you up so fast that your ego is still intact. Molecular consciousness is no place for politics, for anger and hatred and feuds. It is no place for memories or battle or other plans. It is a space-time for receptivity and growth and maybe for building that sacred bridge between the absolutely perfect universe and our imperfect world of poverty and pain, suffering and ignorance. And maybe Jim Morrison was right too. "You can't petition the Lord with prayer!"

The Conspiracy Trial
Paul Krassner

I was scheduled to testify at the Chicago Conspiracy Trial in January 1970. The evening before, Abbie Hoffman coached me with a chronology of Yippie [Youth International Party] meetings, but trying to memorize all those dates and places made me nervous. It was like being unprepared for an important history exam.

And Abbie gave me mixed messages. On one hand, he told me, "There's nothing you can do to help us, you can only harm us." On the other hand, he told me, "I want you to give the judge a heart attack." I assured him I would do my best. I didn't sleep much that night.

I had brought a stash of LSD with me, but things were too tense for a party. Instead I decided to take a tab of acid before I took the witness stand. Call me a sentimental fool. But it wasn't simply to enhance the experience. I had a more functional reason.

My purpose was twofold. I knew that if I ingested 300 micrograms of LSD after eating a big meal, I would throw up in court. That would be my theatrical statement on the injustice of the trial. Also, I wouldn't need to memorize so much information that way.

I had to psych myself up, to imagine it actually happening. The prosecutor would ask, "Now where did this meeting take place?" And I would go "*Waughhhhhppp!*" They couldn't charge me with contempt of court because they wouldn't know I had done it on purpose. The judge would say, "Bailiff, get him out of here!"

But just as he was dragging me away, I would get off one more projectile upchuck, right on the judge's podium—"*Waughhhhhppp!*" And, although there would be no photographic record of this incident because cameras weren't allowed, courtroom artists would capture my vomit with green and gold charcoal crayons for the eleven o'clock news.

Next day at lunch, while the others were passing around a chunk of hash, I took out a tab of LSD.

Abbie said, "What's that, acid? I don't think that's a good idea."

Jerry said, "I think he should do it."

I swallowed it despite what *both* of them said.

The acid began to hit while I was waiting in the witness room. A few volunteers were watching film footage of veteran protester Dave Dellinger pleading with a crowd at the convention: "Stay calm! Stay calm!"

"Boy," I said, "when the jury sees this, it'll really be clear that Dave was doing anything *but* trying to start a riot."

"Are you kidding?" said a volunteer. "They're never gonna allow that to be admitted as evidence."

Then suddenly I was thrust into the middle of a Looney Toons cartoon. It happened at the precise moment that I was escorted into the courtroom by Tom Hayden and Jerry Rubin—or, as I perceived them, Tom and Jerry. The furniture started dancing merrily.

Judge Julius Hoffman looked exactly like Elmer Fudd. I expected him to proclaim, "Let's get them pesky wadicals!"

The court clerk looked exactly like Goofy. It didn't matter that a Disney character was making a guest appearance in a Looney Toons cartoon—one learns to accept such discrepancies in a dreamlike state. Now I was being instructed by Goofy to raise my right hand and place my left hand on a Bible that was positively vibrating.

"Do you hereby swear," said Goofy, "that the testimony you are about to give in the case now on trial before this court and jury shall be the truth, the whole truth, and nothing but the truth, so help you God?"

The truth for me was that LSD—or any other catalyst for getting in touch with your subconscious, whether it be meditation, Zen, yoga—served as a reminder that choices are being made every moment. So naturally I assumed that Goofy was offering me a choice.

"No," I replied.

Although I hadn't planned to say that, I realized it was a first in American jurisprudence. Ordinarily, the more heinous a crime, the more eagerly will a defendant take the oath. However, my refusal to swear on the Bible was a leap of faith.

Everything was swirling around in pastel colors, but there was still a core of reality I was able to grasp, and somehow I managed to flash back to a civics class in junior high school when we had studied the Bill of Rights in general and the First Amendment in particular. Now I found myself passing that lesson on to Goofy.

"I believe in the constitutional provision for the separation of church and state," I declared, "so I will choose to *affirm* to tell the truth."

"Let 'im affirm," said Elmer Fudd—begrudgingly, it seemed to me, as if to say, "Let 'im resort to the goddam Constitution."

I had seen only artists' charcoal renditions of the missing defendant, Bobby Seale, on TV newscasts, and now I was hallucinating a generic courtroom sketch of Seale, shackled to his chair with a gag stuffed in his mouth.

Defense attorney William Kunstler looked exactly like the Wise Old Owl. Prosecutor Thomas Foran looked exactly like the Big Bad Wolf. And I felt exactly like Alice in Wonderland. The Wise Old Owl was questioning me about the original Yippie meeting.

Q. And which one is Jerry Rubin at this table?

A. The man trying to hide behind Mr. Dellinger.

Q. Can you identify Abbie Hoffman at this table?

A. [Pointing] He looks familiar. Yes, I would say that would be Abbie Hoffman.

Elmer Fudd: Would it be or is it?

A. It definitely is. It *would* be him too, but he *is*.

Q. Can you identify Anita Hoffman?

A. Yes, the young lady who is standing.

Q. What about Nancy Kurshan?

A. The young lady who is *now* standing.

The Big Bad Wolf: I object to this, Your Honor.

Elmer Fudd: Yes, I think it is inappropriate that the spectators here be identified by witnesses.

The Wise Old Owl: Your Honor, they were at the meeting. He has just stated they were at the meeting. I am asking him to identify them.

Elmer Fudd: He hasn't been identifying them. They stood up when their names were mentioned. He hasn't gone down there and identified them.

Alice in Wonderland: Do you want me to go down there and identify them?

Elmer Fudd: No, I don't want you to do anything but to answer questions properly.

The Wise Old Owl: Your Honor, I am going to object to his not being able to identify these two women. If they had been men, they would probably be indicted here as defendants because they have been in every one of the meetings. They have been stated by witness after witness as being present.

Elmer Fudd: "If they had been men, they probably would have been indicted here," and anything else that followed these words, are stricken from the record and the jury is directed to disregard them. I will say that if there is anyone else that this witness identifies, I would ask them not to wave back at the witness.

Alice in Wonderland: Now, look, *I'm* a man and *I* wasn't indicted.

The Big Bad Wolf: May we have that comment stricken, Your Honor?

During a brief recess, I started fiddling around with a gavel that was on the witness stand, and the bailiff took it away from me. I recalled the time that Jerry was busted for pot, and Abbie and I got the giggles in court because there was a letter missing from the motto on the wall behind the judge so that it now read IN GOD WE RUST.

And I recalled the time that Abbie got busted for throwing a baggie of cow's blood during a demonstration, but I testified that I had flashed the V-sign to him and he was simply returning it. The judge asked me what the V-sign meant, and I explained that it had different meanings. It could mean *hello* or it could mean *victory*.

"Well," asked the judge, "what did it mean to you on this occasion?"

"It meant, *Hello, victory*."

Recess was over and the Conspiracy Trial resumed. Although I felt myself being sucked into some kind of psychic whirlpool, I was still able to speak with lucidity. But then, as the questions continued, I became increasingly nonlinear about the dates and locations of various meetings. I had really wanted to throw up, but now I didn't feel the slightest bit queasy. I just couldn't remember the chronology of Yippie meetings.

The Big Bad Wolf: One of the ways you test the credibility of a witness under the law, Your Honor, is with his memory....

The Wise Old Owl: Now, I will call your attention to Sunday, August 25, at approximately 4 p.m. on that day. Do you know where you were?

Alice in Wonderland: Sunday, August 25. May I respond to his comment about credibility and memory?

Elmer Fudd: No. Just answer this question if you can. If you can't answer the question, you may say, "I can't answer it."

Alice in Wonderland: Well, I was upset by what he said, and that affects my answer, see. You are pretending this is not an emotional situation.

When my testimony was completed, in order to get centered, I asked myself, "All right, now, why did you take LSD before you testified?"

"Because," I answered myself, "I'm the reincarnation of Gurdjieff."

This was slightly confusing, inasmuch as I didn't believe in reincarnation—I thought the concept was a massive ego trip—and besides, I had never even *read* anything by Gurdjieff. Then I flashed back to a conversation with Ram Dass (then Dick Alpert) during my first visit to Millbrook. I had been curious about Timothy Leary.

"Do you think," I had asked, "that Tim ever gets so involved he forgets he's playing a game?"

"Well, you know, he's an old Irish-Catholic boozehound, and he tends to get caught up in his own game sometimes, but Tim's a very skillful game player, and he knows what he's doing."

"Well, who would you say—among all the seekers you've ever known of—who would you say was always aware of playing a game, even the game of playing a game?"

Alpert thought for a moment and then said, "Gurdjieff."

So *that's* why I had taken the LSD, because the Conspiracy Trial was just another game. But not to Abbie Hoffman. He was furious. He felt that I had been totally irresponsible.

"You were *creamed* on the stand," he shouted. "You were *mean* to the judge."

I couldn't explain to him that somehow my original courtroom scenario had been short-circuited. Try as I might, I just hadn't been able to vomit.

"You're not a *leader*," Abbie yelled. "You're a fuckin' *social gadfly*. You don't urge people to *do* things. You never make *demands*. That's what organizing *is*."

From Abbie's point of view, I was guilty of self-indulgent betrayal. As penance, he wanted me to turn *The Realist* into a Yippie organ. I refused, and Abbie broke off our friendship. It was almost a year before we had a reconciliation.

Originally published in HIGH TIMES.

A New Religion
Steven Hager

I grew up in Urbana, Illinois, a college town surrounded by cornfields 120 miles south of Chicago. I entered high school in 1965, an arrogant, trouble-making, underachiever with low grades and high IQ. I was raised in the Lutheran church, and was scheduled to be confirmed when I turned 15. Before that happened, I'd already lost faith in what the ministers were telling me. I didn't believe my Jewish relatives were going to hell, or that millions of Asians, Africans or non-Christians were also doomed. Once the big lie of "one way to heaven" was exposed, it left a big gaping hole with nothing to plug into. I was deal-ing with a lot of pent-up anger against my parents and society for the lies I'd been gullible enough to get suckered into.

Then I discovered Jack Kerouac, Henry Miller, Aldous Huxley and George Orwell. The door to a different spirituality opened. When *The Electric Kool-Aid Acid Test* by Tom Wolfe was published in 1966, it offered a new vision to plug into. At the time, I was running away from home a lot and attending school infrequently. My main interests were reading and rock music. I played bass guitar for a local garage band. I'd read about LSD, and considered the Merry Pranksters my most important role models, but the mind-altering substances readily available in Urbana were limited to alcohol, glue and roadside hemp plants that never had any effect, even though we spent a lot of time harvesting immature plants and trying get high.

Sometime in 1967, a friend returned from a trip to San Francisco with several hundred green capsules, which supposedly contained LSD. I was crashing in someone's room at the University of Illinois, sleeping in a crawlspace in the attic. My roommate came home one night with two capsules he'd purchased for $30.

Our first plan was that he would take half a capsule and I would stay straight in case a problem developed. Tripping was a big first step and I didn't feel sufficiently prepared. After watching him swallow some powder, I changed my mind and decided I had to board the bus with him. I took about 1/4 of the hit. We sat quietly, waiting anxiously. Every five or ten minutes, we would take more. Eventually, we downed it all.

It got depressing and boring to think we might have been cheated with fake LSD, so we went to the Illinois Union basement lounge, the heart of the campus counterculture. After five minutes in the room, things got strange. We started laughing, then got real quiet and self-conscious. We bailed out of that public space because we were sud-denly blasting off much faster than we could handle indoors. So we scurried back to the safety of his room. After listening to the Velvet Underground and a few other albums, my friend went for a walk, while I called a girl I had a crush on and spent hours on the phone, rambling and talking about the hallucinations I was seeing when I closed my eyes. I pretended I needed "babysitting" in case of a "freak-out," but really just wanted an excuse to talk endlessly to her. She was half-asleep and turned on a tape recorder periodically so she could lis-ten to my "revelations" later.

When my friend returned, I brightened up, happy to have my fel-low tripper back. I handed him the phone, but the girl was long asleep. I'd been talking to myself on a phone for some time.

The sky started to lighten. The first pangs of hunger appeared. I decided to walk to my parents' house and raid the pantry before they woke up. Sneaking into the house and stocking up on supplies was something I did pretty regularly.

At dawn, as I was leaving the house with a big bag of groceries, I had a mind-blowing experience. I remembered something that had happened when I was about 10 years old: I had an older brother, who sometimes tormented me, and a younger sister, who I tormented in return. I had been in one of those weird states of mind, the evil autopilot had taken over, and I was about to do something unkind to my sister for no particular reason.

I'd mindlessly done stuff like that many times. But this time I'd stopped and stepped outside myself and analyzed the motivation behind what I was about to do. I'd realized, "Wow, this is not right and I don't have to do this. And if I do it, I'll probably just regret it later." After that day, I never went after my sister without some sort of justification. I'd broken a cycle of abuse. The memory and importance of breaking that cycle came forward.

Then I had a similar revelation about my parents. I realized I was creating and participating in the problem by being so angry with them. I thought my parents were wrong about everything, and I was right. But LSD teaches you about the subjective nature of experience. People can have profoundly different points of view, and each one can be "right." Years of anger, resentment and hatred melted away in seconds. I never felt so happy and liberated. I no longer felt obligated to change my parents or anyone else. I wanted to wake my parents and explain that I wasn't angry anymore, I just wanted to love and respect them, and we never had to agree about anything, but that didn't mean we couldn't stay together.

Within a few weeks, I ended up moving back to my parents' house, getting a part-time job and going back to high school. I also started an underground newspaper. Something else happened. I'd had a serious stuttering problem my entire life, and I knew it was real embarrassing to my father. But the stuttering suddenly disappeared. After an LSD experience, my friends and I knew what getting "high" really meant. Then we discovered real marijuana. We figured out that getting "stoned" was different from getting "fucked-up." Substances like glue or alcohol didn't have the attraction of mind-expanding psychedelics.

I look back at all this today and realize we were participating in the creation of a new religion, a religion so new it doesn't even have a name. It may take another hundred years before people figure out what to call it. I've also learned that one of the most enlightened figures of this religion is Neal Cassady. Neal taught a form of enlightenment based on living in the moment, having as much fun as possible (without hurting others), and celebrating life's little ceremonies. We all know the big ceremonies, like birth, marriage, and death. I'm sure Neal excelled at those, but he was also a master at the everyday celebration. Neal knew how to live it; Jack knew how to write it down.

Ken Kesey's magic bus ride across the country in 1964 was an important development in the creation of this new religion. The Pranksters taught us how to make an Exodus from Babylon. It seems so magical that Neal emerged to take control of the steering wheel. Stephen Gaskin amplified the concept by going on the road with a caravan of buses six years later. The Grateful Dead scene amplified the concept even further. There's an important lesson here somewhere. Maybe it's that we're supposed to evolve into a migratory community. Maybe the real Exodus has yet to happen.

It's only in the last few years that I've learned enough about the history of cannabis to realize Hinduism and Buddhism would not have happened without cannabis. The Soma referred to in the *Rig-Veda* (the oldest living religious document in the world) is cannabis, and cannabis probably played an important role in the development of many major religions. (Moses' "burning bush," for example.) It seems profoundly unfair that for the past 50 years, this peaceful, loving culture, this infant baby religion, has been on the run, with most of its leaders thrown in jail for possession of a sacred plant. Cassady, Kesey, Leary, Gaskin, all jailed and hounded for cannabis possession.

Millions of people run through the criminal justice system just for cannabis possession. How could we be expected to turn our backs on this sacrament? Suppose all alcohol was made illegal tomorrow. Wouldn't a few Catholic priests keep some wine and use it for underground ceremonies? Would they be jailed for possession? Would their property be confiscated, would their lives be destroyed? Would society let something that outrageous take place? But which is worse, stomping on the thousand-year-old religion, or stomping on the baby infant religion? I mean, both are terrible, but it has to be worse to hit the baby because the baby is defenseless.

Cannabis and other psychedelics have played a central role in creating a new spirituality that has been embraced by millions of people around the world. There will never be freedom of religion until this culture is recognized. This is not some trivial pursuit; it is the very core of what we are about. The counterculture peaked after Woodstock. That's when the repression really started to kick in. Woodstock scared people. But Woodstock was our Sermon on the Mount.

Being from a college town, I came back from Woodstock and watched all the young grad students and professors with counterculture ideals get chased out of the universities and denied tenure, even though they were among the best and brightest teachers around. I watched the whole scene get co-opted, while our leaders were assassinated or jailed. Today it's really just a fragment of what could have been. We shouldn't be angry about this. Anger and violence are not what our culture is about. But we do need to figure out a way to pass what we have learned on down.

I'm saddened when I meet supposedly hip college kids who don't know who Ken Kesey is. Our culture isn't that strong. It could disappear. We've amassed a lot of knowledge about the nature of enlightenment. We have much to offer future generations. I just hope our baby infant religion can hold together and wait out this Great Drug War. What could have been, will someday come to pass.

Chapter 2

The Leary Papers

In Reverse Order
Stanley Krippner

I was with Tim in the post-Harvard days. I would visit him at IFIF (International Federation of Internal Freedom) and I was there one night when there were two graduate students from MIT, and they were trying to get Tim to try marijuana. They were trying to convince him that marijuana had a long and glorious history, in medicine and in spirituality, and they had found it of great use in their graduate work, also for their spiritual development. Tim was extremely skeptical, and they were trying to bring him around.

I didn't know what the outcome of that was, but a few months later, I was invited by Tim and his group to a party in New York City—this was a party with all the familiar suspects of those days—and somebody rolled a joint and was passing it around, and I saw Tim smoking a joint and I thought, "Well, those MIT students convinced him." So he came late to marijuana in terms of his drug history. This was *after* the LSD experiments at Harvard, long before Millbrook [Leary's acid research center in upstate New York].

During the Millbrook days, I got up there to see Tim several times. One time I went up with my wife and my two stepchildren, and there was a workshop going that weekend. I participated in the workshop. They did some very original things there—I don't think they invented them—but they're now standard in the so-called growth movement workshops, like blind walks and role-playing. There was a pet ocelot, and one of my friends who came up there was virtually blind. I remember she woke up in the morning and the ocelot was in bed with her and she screamed in panic.

We came up and reassured her, "It's only the pet ocelot, it's not a bat, it's not a vampire, it's not a snake." We spent the better part of an hour tracking the ocelot down, and putting it back in its cage. And then, after that experience, my stepson, Bob, was bouncing on the trampoline. It was his first experience on a trampoline, so he didn't quite have the technique down, and he bounced up and he fell and he hit his head on the metal railing, and a gash opened his head. His mother was panicked, and I came running over, and somebody went running for Tim, saying, "He'll know what to do."

"That is a pretty bad cut," I said. "We might have to go to a hospital and have some stitches. If Tim can get us a car to the local hospital, that's the best we can do."

Well, Tim came out, and this was very uncharacteristic. He was extremely calm, and Bob was crying, and Tim took a look at his head, and he just held his hand over Bob's head, and Bob calms down, and Tim says, "You know, this cut isn't very big, it's just a

scratch. If you just breathe deeply and calm down, it'll be all right."
And Tim took off his hand—the bleeding had stopped—and within
10 minutes, Bob had stopped crying and he was off playing, and
we didn't have to go to the hospital.

So that's my one experience with Tim as a lay-on-of-hands heal-
er, and as I said, very uncharacteristic. I'd never seen him, in all the
roles that he has played, come out knowing just what to do on
such an occasion and, instead of panicking and calling an ambu-
lance, making a big production of it, doing something very low-key
but something that was quite effective.

"Look at That Freak Visiting Leary!"
Michael Horowitz

Except for the four-way hit I mistook for a single dose at the
1979 Tribal Stomp, taking LSD spontaneously has usually worked
out well for me. But on one other occasion I indeed played psychedelic roulette with the magic molecule.

It happened in July 1970 when I visited Timothy Leary in
prison—c ur first meeting. In a sequence of events that began at
the Om Orgy benefit for Tim in May, Rosemary Leary turned over
his archives to me and my friend for safekeeping, and soon after
told me that Tim wanted me to visit him. I was no longer a hippie
minding his own business; I was now a member of the
entourage/support team of the High Priest, the Disgraced Harvard
Professor, the Pied Piper, the Acid Martyr—the world's best known
advocate of "better living through chemistry."

Like many other LSD enthusiasts of the time, I saw Leary as
someone on the front lines of the struggle to establish a model of
higher consciousness that would evolve the human race. I was
ready to help him get released from prison where he was doing 10
years for the crime of possessing two roaches of marijuana.

That morning, before my friend came to my Berkeley apartment
to drive me to the airport, I went to my stash for a 250-mic dose of
LSD embedded in a tiny green square of "windowpane" aka
"clearlight." It had recently hit the streets in that form. I sliced it in
half with a razor blade, and placed one half under my thumbnail
to offer Tim if he had no objection. I started to waver about taking
any myself, but as my friend honked his car horn, the desire to be
tripping on acid while meeting the High Priest of LSD got the better of me, and I slipped the other half under my tongue.

Less than an hour later I was the only passenger in a Navaho
Piper Cub flying to the California Men's Colony in San Luis Obispo
where Tim was incarcerated. It was the first time I'd flown Trans-
High Airlines, and in that tiny aircraft I felt one with the white

fluffy clouds, completely oblivious to where I was going.

About an hour later, as my taxi turned into the prison grounds, a massive Reality Check came in the form of a giant sign in front of the gate, warning that the penalty for bringing "narcotics" or weapons into prison was 20 years. That tiny thing under my thumbnail began to feel uncomfortable.

I walked into a building where visitors checked in, thinking, *Please let this acid stop coming on.* The uniformed guards all turned to stare at me as I walked up to the main desk. I tried not to look at them, but felt their collective gaze, and my paranoia grew.

My hippie garb—though toned down a bit from my everyday San Francisco look—had never felt more unfashionable. Beginning with my far-gone 'fro, the purple-tinted glasses, the patches on my fringe-leather jacket ("Zap" on a bolt of lightning on one sleeve, the peace sign on the other), the embroidered shoulder bag with the "Tim Leary for Governor" button, bell-bottomed jeans and boots—what was I thinking? That this was something other than a *fucking prison*?

The guard behind the desk asked me whom I was visiting.

"Doctor Leary," I said, softly—but not softly enough.

"Look at that freak visiting Leary!" one of guards hissed from across the room. My heart began to race.

While the clerk looked at the visitors' list for my name, the other guards in the room—seven or eight big burly men in grey and khaki uniforms—sidled up, surrounding me. I was handed forms to fill out. The words were swimming on the page! The miniscule contraband throbbed on the tip of my writing hand as I gripped the ballpoint pen. I could feel the eyes of the guards laser-beaming me. Could they see that dark green dot that glowed like a radioactive fungus under my fingernail?

I had not expected a questionnaire. By sheer force of will I made my eyes focus and began answering the questions. I agonized over what street address to use—why hadn't I thought in advance about these things? "Purpose of visit?" I wrote, "Editorial and archival matters," bearing down with the pen. When I was done, the admission guard looked long and hard at my application.

"It says here you're an archivist. That right?"

"Uh-huh."

"What's that mean—archivist?"

"I keep track of Doctor Leary's professional papers. His contributions to science. Family photo albums."

The guard sneered but nonetheless passed me on: "Awright. Go to that gate." One of the other guards said "It looks like he's on something, don't it?" And they all cracked up as I walked away, not looking back.

A huge electronic gate opened and I walked through; it clanged shut behind me, and then a second security gate opened and closed. Emerging into a kind of courtyard, I saw a figure in the window of a shabby one-story building. It was a tall, silver-haired man dressed in blue denims. He was waving his arm, giving the peace sign, grinning broadly.

"Perfect!" said Timothy Leary, embracing me. Now I was glad I looked like the hardcore freak I was. I bought us coffee and candy bars from the vending machines and we adjourned to a little side room off the main visiting area. I felt incredibly relieved to have survived the guards. I no longer felt like Josef K visiting the Castle, but like a swaggering Merry Prankster. I was with the Hedonic Psychologist himself, and I was on acid!

As it turned out, I'd celebrated a little too soon. A minute later

Tim jumped to his feet to confront me.

"*You're on acid*? Shit! What do you think this is? Fillmore East? I'm looking at ten years! I desperately need your help—and you show up on acid!"

"I have some for you."

"Great. I just can't wait to trip in this place! Look around—it's the perfect set and setting, isn't it?"

"Sorry," I said, downcast, feeling I had totally blown it.

Timothy sized up the situation and did a complete about-face. "Okay. We're gonna have a good time. You can't do good unless you feel good. What do you want to talk about? Listen: I'm writing a book about LSD and DNA. There are seven stages of evolution, and each is preceded by a revolution. The evolution of the species is recapitulated in each terrestrial life form. A different drug discovery triggers the next stage. The first drug was oxygen. Early amphibians had oxygen parties on the shoreline. The latest drug is the one you're on. How many hours do we have?"

I looked at a wall clock. "I guess about five."

"When did you drop?"

"About two, three hours ago."

"What did you bring?"

"Half a hit of clearlight."

"Okay. Wait till the guard turns away."

Fantastic! He was going to get high with me! I was going to get the lowdown on DNA and LSD, the keys to evolution and revolution. I looked down at my fingernail.

It wasn't there!

"Um, Tim..."

The Road to Algiers
Stew Albert

If Tim Leary really had the day off—free from meetings with fugitive Eldridge Cleaver—maybe I could accept his generous offer of the world's purest LSD, to be imbibed for many pleasant hours on an Algerian beach.

"I could take a small dose."

"Definitely," Leary said. "This acid has powerful and good effects even with a small ingestion. Naturally I'll take more than you."

"When?"

"Right now would be an excellent moment. We haven't had anything to eat, and the white light will go immediately into our bloodstreams."

We sat on a beach blanket. Waves were breaking soundly on the Algerian shore, and the Mediterranean sun was turning up its fire. I thought about how every Yippie in New York City would envy me, beach-tripping with Tim Leary after his prison escape and in his secret exile.

Tim handed me a bottle which once contained aftershave lotion. I took a tasteless sip and returned the container. Tim took two large gulps and big-smiled himself.

Time passes. The waves keep coming. The sun gets hotter. I think of Camus' antihero strolling along this same beach and shooting an Arab because he was blinded by the sun. But these Arab women in their French-style bathing suits with their round muscular Semitic bellies, why would anyone shoot them? Why shoot anyone on a day like this?

No veils.

Must be university students. Warm bellies with curving lines like ancient codes, memories and great secrets hiding in their glistening flesh. How could that literary absurdity, that Mersault, open fire just because he had bad sunburn?

Am I getting fried? Leary's beaming face is just like the sun and its white sand. Not gray Coney Islandish sand, but snow white, and when you lie face down, acid Algerian sand has waves like the ocean. The sky is filled with green rubies, sweet blue flashes and bending space.

The Russian tourists have bellies without coding.

Smooth.

Harmless bodies with nothing to say. All they can do is pound the ball over the net and pretend they don't see Leary standing on his head.

Where is Leary? Big shiny hot sunny smile and white sandy-toothed Leary.

Serious Leary?

"I just spoke to Eldridge on the hotel lobby phone," he says. "He's nervous about some reports he's getting. People calling from the States warning him. I think we should go back to my room and have some wine. I want to talk with you about something important. Important to both of us."

The sand is taking me every place I ever wanted to go, so why is Tim helping me stand up? Maybe he is launching me into the curving sky? Past the Russians we go, and Arab grocery stores with their mysterious ancient advertisements for Coca-Cola. The apparently stone-sober Leary smiles at the hotel clerk as we enter his ancient mosque.

"The sun," Leary explains, "and a little too much to drink."

"Yes, *monsieur*, a bit ill." And he goes back to watching television.

Red wine is good and warming.

Below Tim's balcony I saw donkeys and wagons and old peasants, just like thousands of years ago when even the Bible was young.

"I'm okay, the wine is bringing me down. What did Eldridge say?"

"People are trying to associate me with criminal activities. They don't understand the Brotherhood."

"Tell me about it."

"Later."

"I'll bet you're really out of it," I said. "All that acid you took."

"Just a mild buzz, like having a martini. I've taken so much acid that it has very little effect on me."

Later, sitting in his apartment, feeling relaxed, Eldridge Cleaver bogarts the hash pipe.

"The Algerians all assume Tim is black. Maybe he should go for a deeper suntan."

I was surprised to see Cleaver in such a lighthearted Leary mood.

"Don't get me wrong," he continued "I like Tim. The way he keeps moving all the time, getting out of his chair and walking right up to you and smiling and talking. I guess he's up to something, but I don't care."

"How does Huey [Newton] feel?"

"Tim's okay with Huey, but he's hearing some heavy stuff about the good doctor."

"Like?"

"Mostly loose sort of shit, like Leary having some kind of illegal organization that sells the stuff. I thought he gave it away, but Huey says the word is they sell it. And Huey wants to make sure the Black Panther Party gets its fair share."

"You gonna talk to Tim?"

"I intend to. Our operation here is very expensive and Tim will pay his proper dues. And that goes for the LSD that you guys have been drinking at the beach, tripping out before the vacationing Russian secret police. The Black Panther International Section definitely wants a piece of that."

"Eldridge, are you gonna trip with Leary?"

"Ah, no. I like Tim but I don't trust him. He might try to program me."

"He has the best stuff."

"We Panthers have a scientific interest in acid. We might want to perform experiments. Perhaps we will confiscate Dr. Leary's acid."

"And trip alone."

"Maybe I'll trip with you."

"Hey, Eldridge, I'm honored."

"One thing, Stew, I need my guns. If I'm taking acid I still have to wear my guns...."

Tim Leary eats in a hotel restaurant and wonders if the Arab waiter recognizes him like he was some big French movie star. But the waiter never heard of Haight-Ashbury. He only knows Tim as a very (disguised) bald American who calls him *boy*.

Leary decides that he will introduce acid to Algeria by converting to Islam.

Stew Albert is the author of Who The Hell Is Stew Albert?

Duffel Bag #38
Uri Horowitz

Somewhere in the deep recesses of my psyche, in the vicinity of my smoldering serotonin receptors, my fried memory circuit stores multiple duffel bags of LSD trips. Mostly hazy images of being acid-drunk in dark rooms, listening to blistering Hendrix solos, and being drenched by the swelling angst of my brooding, emotionally stunted peers who will fight the drug to the teeth and in the end just get fucking leveled by the shit. I've been the baby and the babysitter in the midst of these tragic psychedelic blunders. No matter what precautions you may take, LSD can always bite you back.

Each memory bag has its share of sparkling cosmic jewels, but nothing like the one hidden at the bottom of duffel bag #38. This is my memory of tripping with Doctor Leary.

I had been cooped up at my sister's house drinking heavily with a buddy of mine. We hadn't been out all day, and our binge was reaching heights of unchartered treachery. "Machine Gun" was thumping hard, and I could feel the tension blossoming between us. He'd been drinking whiskey in my sister's musky bar since dawn and he had yet to say a word. His disposition was rankle and his gaze menacing. I feared he was falling into a state of alcoholic psychosis.

I cracked my seventh Anchor Steam and looked up in horror as I saw my drunken friend standing in the doorway waving a fire-poker at me. He had a mad look in his eye and his skin had turned blotchy with a combination of rage and dehydration. I had clearly subjected him to too many lengthy versions of "Machine Gun" and he had become a definite threat. We must get out now, I thought, if only for reasons of personal safety.

"We're going to Tim Leary's," I said. My friend dropped the fire-poker and looked at me like a frightened animal. "Bring all your drugs," I added, and we were off.

Tim's house wasn't far and, being very ill, he was doubtless home and partying hard. Even at death's door, he never failed to cheer me up.

While we were perched at a stoplight, my friend took a vial of liquid from his pocket and quickly squeezed two drops on my neck. I slapped him hard, but it was too late. The chemical had already seeped into a pocket of flesh near my collarbone.

We were greeted by the house freaks who led us to Tim's bedroom. We lurked in his doorway for several minutes and watched as a particularly bizarre-looking cat shot the old man up with ketamine as he writhed in his wheelchair.

As he drifted back, the old doc saw me and motioned me to get a balloon. I glided past a band of faded oddballs on the floor, arriving at a tank in his closet the size of a small human. I filled two massive balloons with nitrous oxide and offered one to my friend, who began sucking at it like an infant on a breast. An hour later, after a multitude of deep pulls of the gas had revved up my brain to lysergic overdrive, I found myself on the edge of Tim's bed staring at his carpet, becoming consumed with the paranoid fear of never coming down.

My friend was holed up in Tim's closet, silently drinking. I was surrounded by strangers, and the thought of attempting small talk with any of them was painful. So I continued staring helplessly at the carpet, listening to high-strung techno, sweating from the inside out, and just waiting for some dolt to make me more self-conscious by asking if anything was wrong.

I was growing desperate and finally looked over at Tim sitting in his wheelchair beside me. Despite his legendary tolerance for parties, even *he* seemed uneasy from the sheer number of freaks and drug-induced chaos in his bedroom. Someone passed me yet another balloon. At first I was inclined to reject it, but instead found myself muttering those now famous words, "Why not?" I sucked half of it down and passed it to the doctor, who sucked down the rest.

Then something glorious happened. Someone had put on a concert version of "Are You Experienced?" The first note crackled as if a lightning bolt had hit the room. Titanic electricity—like the birth of some new and alien cosmos. An acid shiver ran up my spine and thrust my slumped body upwards. I glanced at Timothy. Our exchange was of a rare and riveting kind. Like a pair of lysergicized yogis, we looked long and deep into each other's eyes, mutually possessed by a fearless understanding. Thought and judgment stopped, time and space were obliterated. This singular potent exchange was my strongest connection with Tim in all the years I knew him.

Star Struck
Robert Altman

It all happened in 1969 when I was a novitiate photojournalist given the opportunity to get up close and personal with my favorite maverick of the day—Dr. Timothy Leary.

To some Tim was perceived to be a genius. To President Nixon he was "the most dangerous man in America." You might get the scoundrel Tim or the visionary good doctor; the excommunicated Harvard professor or the international luminary. The man had many facets.

The Timothy Leary I got to know was the sunny and charismatic pied piper Tim. He was simply and always a joy to be around. How did I get there? Early on, fortune smiled my way. With a pinch of God-given talent and some extra hard work I became an accomplished photojournalist. And my camera became my passport. This cachet enabled me to meet some of the remarkable movers and shakers of the '60s.

Once in a while I was granted even greater intimate access to these *wunderkind* and let me tell you, it was downright intoxicating hanging with these guys. And for me Timothy Francis Leary topped them all.

Tim possessed a great and original intellect. But that was just the beginning. This guy knew his way around people. He was a charmer *cum laude*. Socially, the sun always shone when Tim Leary was around. You might say that when he entered a room the air was sucked out and replaced by pure oxygen. Being in Tim's constellation was a unique experience.

One day in 1969, Tim decided to run for governor of California. Is it any wonder that Nixon didn't know what to do with him? His campaign slogan was "Come Together—Join the Party." Tim and his lovely wife Rosemary kicked off the campaign with a press conference in Berkeley, California, which was the ground-zero epicenter of the counterculture.

I was there to record the affair for the media. After the event ended we lingered. Tim and Rosemary needed a ride to San Francisco. I was happy to oblige. I did the driving while my pal Barbara Mauritz rode shotgun. Tim and Rosemary occupied the back seat. Somewhere in the middle of the San Francisco Bay Bridge, Tim's arm reached over. I spotted a powdered residue in his palm.

"Want some?"

It could only be one substance, no explanation necessary.

Wow! I thought. This is an occasion.

Sharing acid with the great Tim Leary. I needed no second invite and immediately accepted my guest's granular overture. Physically restricted at this "moving" moment the only thing I could do was stick out my tongue and lap it up. I was thrilled. Indeed I trilled inwardly: "Hey, I just licked acid off Tim Leary's palm!" This would be one of those great moments I'd share with my grandchildren.

Some time now passes. Lively conversation ensues and soon we decide to go out for dinner. A medium-priced Chinese restaurant was chosen and we merry four finally sat down to eat. Once again I was beaming. A young fella of 23 delighted to be in my mentor's company. *Bon mots* flowed as we reviewed the genial nature of the day's events. Tim and Rosemary's future looked promising.

So much was going on that by this time I completely and absolutely forgot that I had just imbibed a powerful psychedelic. This absurd amnesia became the kernel of my next shocking flash.

We were now in the middle of dinner when I found myself gazing at the good doctor's face. "Hey, what's going on?" I asked myself. All of a sudden I see Tim's physiognomy in a brand new light. Here it was suddenly respirating, undulating, almost liquefying right in front of me!

My God... the only time I've ever seen this kind of thing was when I was tripping! This guy is the real deal. He must have taken so much acid and evolved so far that his presence alone was enough to raise a psychedelic experience in others. No money down. No chemicals necessary. Talk about "Tune In. Turn on." Holy shit!

Couldn't take my eyes off him. Amazing. What a presence! This kept on for a good 10 minutes... indeed it was stupefying and most profound. Finally the mental tapes of the palm lick got replayed in my—well, let's face it—addled brain. Uh-oh. How embarrassing.

Ah, the '60s decade. If you remember it you weren't there. Seems I couldn't even remember it as it was happening.

The Master Musicians
Rosemary Woodruff Leary

Pan, Bou Jeloud, the Father of Skins, dances through the moonlight nights in his hill village, Joujouka, to the wailing of his hundred Master Musicians. Down in the towns, far away by the seaside, you can hear the wild whimper of his oboe-like raitas; a faint breath of panic borne on the wind.

—Brion Gysin
Liner notes from the album Brian Jones Presents The Pipes of Pan at Joujouka

Timothy and I spent September of 1969 in Tangier. One night Paul Bowles and Brion Gysin told us about the musicians of Joujouka who lived high in the Rif Mountains. The Master Musicians were priests of Pan, who celebrated the ancient rites of the goat god and the local goddess, Aisha, the beautiful, the blue-faced one. Brion told us that his friend, the Moroccan artist Hamri, could take us to the Master Musicians, the Ahl Serif, as they were the tribe of his mother.

We started from the sea, at Tangier, on a clear fall afternoon. In a succession of taxicabs, each more decrepit than the last, we headed toward the Rif Mountains. When one driver had gone as far as he would go, we'd find another. In villages, Hamri disappeared into crowded marketplaces and reappeared within a few minutes laden with oranges and packages, and trailed by the owner of the taxi that would take us to the next outpost.

We reached a checkpoint at a dusty fort on the barren plain where Hamri's "cousin," the local Commandante, allowed our passage. We were in the middle of nowhere, and our driver was reluctant to continue, but Hamri harangued and cajoled him until at last he agreed to take us into the foothills of the mountains. After miles of jouncing on a steep rutted road, the driver stopped and would not continue. We gathered our packages, paid the driver, and started on foot up the mountain path in the early evening light.

From across the slope of the mountain a shepherd boy watched us. He stood on one leg, the other leg bent and resting on his thigh, his arm crooked around his staff. Hamri called out to him. The boy leapt into the air, waved his staff, and took off running up the mountain. "A cousin," Hamri told us. "He'll tell the village and perhaps they'll send the animals. We'll rest here." We waited, and soon a group of villagers descended to meet us. A woman offered golden apricots from a fold in her cloak. Hamri exchanged greetings with everyone, waving his arms to include us. The villagers insisted on carrying our bundles and packages up the mountain.

The sun lit the distant peaks. Soon we saw the village, the whitewashed walls of low houses turning blue in the darkening light. A few dim lamps glowed from the doorways. Hamri led us to a long and low white building with a porch. He said it was the schoolhouse, built with funds that he and Brion had given to the village.

We left our shoes on the porch as the men did and ducked our heads to enter the schoolhouse. Hamri introduced the men but it was impossible to keep up with their names. The last man stepped from behind a taller companion. "Berdu," Hamri said with emphasis. Berdu, the smallest and surely the poorest among the village men, shambled forward. He reached up and took off an imaginary plumed hat and made a sweeping, courtly bow to me. I curtsied, and everyone laughed. The village idiot, I presumed. I thought he looked simple.

We were invited to be seated in a corner of the room that was heaped with embroidered pillows. The kerosene stove hissed in the far corner, and shortly we were served sweet mint tea in small glasses. Hamri talked quietly with the men. Their clothing was simple: shirts and pants with a mix of European and handmade, always a ragged cloak, and one could occasionally glimpse the embroidered bags the men wore beneath their cloaks.

Eggs and flat bread were served all around. After we'd eaten and the tin dishes were collected and cigarettes exchanged, the men opened the embroidered bags and pulled out simple reed-stem pipes and, to our delight, packages of finely-cut kif. Hamri and Berdu shared their pipes with us. The kif was fresher and greener than any I'd had in Morocco.

A man took a violin from its case and placed it upright with the point on his knee. Hamri told us the man had been a sailor, and that he'd brought the violin back from England. The violinist smiled and began to pluck a reel. Penny whistles joined the violin and Berdu stepped into the aisle. He hitched up his cloak and held it with one arm. With the other arm behind his back he danced a sailor's jig until the violinist turned the reel into Flamenco. Berdu became a self-important *torero* who, with a twitch of his cloak then became an imperious woman trailing flounces as the music became a Gypsy wail.

She opened her mouth to sing an impassioned lament, the violinist rose, swaying to accompany her; then the violinist interrupted the voiceless song to correct the glowering opera singer who stood before us. The violinist was now Paderewski, enraptured by his own music. Berdu snapped the baton in disgust and stalked away. He returned as an old woman carrying an invisible heavy bucket. With great effort, he lifted the bucket and dashed the contents onto the head of the violinist who continued to ignore him and finished the real and wonderful music. The violinist then wiped his brow and sat down to everyone's laughter and applause.

Tim and I looked at one another. I reached into my own embroidered bag and discreetly took out two tabs of LSD. I placed one into his mouth as though I were placing a kissed fingertip onto his lips, and I put one into my own mouth. We swallowed the LSD with sweet green tea.

Berdu, with a surprisingly deep and resonant voice, began a prayer. "La Illah Allah Allah." The men responded, "Mohamadu Akbar."

In a conversational tone, the prayers continued, Berdu commenting, it seemed, on the village, the animals, and Hamri, who bowed his head to gentle laughter. Berdu directed us through prayer to laughter to a sense of closeness. There was a time of silence. We heard a few gentle coughs, a distant tinkle of bells. People stirred, shifting positions, and Berdu sat down among us. We could no longer see him.

"Who is he?" I asked Hamri.

"Berdu, the Master," Hamri replied.

"The Master?"

"The Master Musician of Joujouka."

I needed to step outside. I found my boots on the porch lined up with the men's backless leather slippers. I started to put on my boots, but a man I had not noticed before waved his hand dismissively and pointed to the men's slippers. I nodded my thanks and put on the nearest pair of slippers. He motioned to my left and I followed a path out onto a gently sloping field. I was facing a star-filled sky. There were no electric lights to dim the stars. Everything I saw was as it had always been, timeless.

I could hear the goats' bells, and their strong smell told me they were nearby. I pulled a cluster of white wool that had been caught on a bush. As I walked back to the long house I rolled it between my fingers, effortlessly drawing the silky tuft of wool into a fine strand of thread. When I returned to the long house I was reluctant to go back inside to the room of men, to the air heavy with kif and tobacco smoke and kerosene. I wondered what the village women and children were doing.

Hamri stood in the doorway, backlit by the kerosene lamps inside. He beckoned to me to join him and the men. He led us out over a slight rise to a small clearing between the hills where brush was being piled onto a crackling fire. "Stand here," Hamri said, placing us 10 or so feet from the fire. To our left, a row of hooded men took long wooden horns from patchwork bags. Behind them stood a group of men with drums, each drum aslant across the chest, held with thongs. They carried curved slender rods in their right hands, and in their left hands, heavier wooden sticks, the top ends carved in relief spirals like rams' horns.

The night was still except for the fire which threw sparks into the darkness. The hooded men lifted their horns, and a thin piercing sound from the oboe-like instruments was sustained for an incredibly long time, maintained by the subtle joining of one horn to another, as no single breath could be that long. I traveled the reedy seamless breath to a distant star that seemed to grow brighter, larger, and then the horns went higher, taking me almost to the point of pain, then the music swirled into a skirling bagpipe sound whose rhythm the wind had torn away.

The drums, silent until then, boomed into being, a thudding heartbeat of rhythm. My breath was caught by the horns; my pulses by the drums. Was this music, or was it the thunder of mammoth hooves, screams of birds of prey? It seemed the very tempo of life in my body. Eardrums could be shattered. Hearts could burst from these sounds. The drums built a wall that contained the reed instruments. The reeds descended into a weaving ribbon of silver notes, playful to the drums' assertive tempo, seductive, cajoling, demanding rhythms.

A creature leapt over the fire to confront the musicians. He was tall, powerful, barely covered by tattered clothing. His face was concealed by a deep straw basket adorned with antler-like branches. He pounded his feet to the drums, caught by their rhythms, his arches curved so high that his feet were hooves. Trailing branches in his hands, flailing the air, his pelvis thrusting, he was goaded by the music. He whirled around the fire, pausing once to glare at me with a goat's horizontal eyes. The creature struck me with the branches. Struck me or anointed me, I don't know which.

"Bou Jeloud," Hamri said.

Pan lives, I thought.

A slender figure in a blue-spangled dress came from the shadows. Arms curved, veils aswirl, her hips swaying with seduction, she turned before the Bou Jeloud. He followed her dancing form, leaping before her as she teased him with her veils. She played with him, turning him around and around, mocking him. Abruptly she was gone and the creature confronted the musicians, but they taunted him with their rhythms. He danced before them, controlled by them. The drums reverberated through the mountains. The horns' high notes seemed to come from everywhere. Bou

Jeloud bucked convulsively, howling in anguish that Aisha had left him. The drums slowed; the horns were one pure fading note. Bou Jeloud scattered the fire with his flails and disappeared into the black night.

Later, at the schoolhouse, Berdu brought former Bou Jelouds and Aishas to the center of the floor to demonstrate and mime their styles. He made fun of all of them, showing how one of them had grown too stout, another too clumsy. Hamri said they were chosen while very young for training, and that characteristics they showed as children determined which role they would play.

And then I danced for them. Not that I wanted to, or even thought that I could, but my usual inhibitions were lessened by LSD, and there seemed to be silken threads tied to my ankles and wrists that Berdu controlled ever so surely. And the music was irresistible. Penny whistles, violin, and softly tapped drums drew me to my feet. For a few moments I was Aisha to Berdu's gently mocking Bou Jeloud. There were shouts of "Musicienne!" and "Encore!" when I sat down. I rose again, but the magic that had descended upon me was fading and I had become self-conscious. I pretended to stumble, and fell back into Tim's lap, and we all laughed.

We left on muleback the next morning. All the way down the mountain I could still hear the drums in my head, and I could hear them at will for many years. The memory of the music that night reminds me that for a brief, magical time, I was a "musicienne" among the Master Musicians of Joujouka.

Excerpted from The Magician's Daughter, *a work-in-progress.*

Acid Factory
Jerry Hopkins

As *Rolling Stone's* European correspondent in 1972, my wife Jane and I spent most of a week visiting Tim Leary in Lugano, Switzerland, where he was in exile after escaping from a jail in California. He met me and my wife and young daughter at the train station in his Porsche and whisked us away to the villa where he was staying, and as soon as we entered he offered us some acid in tablet form.

By now I'd tried a variety of natural psychedelic substances—psilocybin, peyote, hash—and somewhere along the way I decided not to eat any chemicals. Yeah, yeah, I know: boring. But that's what I decided. And now, on top of that, I didn't want to lose control. I mean, this was Tim Leary, right? And I was the guy from *Rolling Stone*. So I said, "No, thanks."

"Well, then," Tim said, "try this instead." He produced a small brown bottle with a screw-on top and glass dropper, which he filled with the sticky liquid inside. "Open," he said, opening his mouth. We did as he said and he dropped some hash oil on our tongues. This was the first time I'd seen liquid hash; much later, Tim would be accused of being a part of The Brotherhood importing the stuff to the US.

The next day, we joined a local commune in building an Indian sweat-house from tree limbs (which we cut) and plastic, in anticipation of the arrival of a busload of other heads who were described as the European branch of the Hog Farm. The guys did all the heavy work, while the women were in the kitchen trying to organize spaghetti. After a while, when the sweat-house was well underway, Tim pulled us aside.

"Look," he said, "it's going to take hours for these people to get that spaghetti together, and I know a nice little place where we can get a decent piece of fish and a good bottle of wine." So that's what we did.

The next morning, Tim was sitting on the balcony reading *Life* magazine, which he regularly had air-mailed in along with a number of other American periodicals. In it there was a review of a new book by Andrew Weil, who was, as I recall, described by the reviewer as the natural successor to Tim Leary. Tim laughed and stood up and told us that he knew this guy when he was a student at Harvard University, back when Tim was a professor there and was tossed out when it was revealed that he'd been giving his students LSD. That was the first time he'd been busted, in an article in the *Harvard Crimson* written by... you guessed it... Andrew Weil.

Soon after our visit, Tim was arrested and returned to the San Luis Obispo prison, and the following spring, Jane and I wrote him what we hoped would be a cheering letter. About a month later, I was in Los Angeles researching a book about Jim Morrison when 15 county, state, and federal police entered our Mendocino farmhouse by every door and a few windows. It was Friday night, and my wife was preparing supper for several neighbors.

The cops said they were looking for an acid factory, but found only a lid of grass, some roach-clips, and four tiny pot plants in a window box—a big disappointment for the police, I'm sure, but enough to book Jane for possession of an illegal substance and paraphernalia (misdemeanors) and cultivation (a felony). They also said they had a warrant for my arrest.

It was after midnight before I returned to my motel (one that Morrison had lived in) and found a message from a Mendocino neighbor. In the morning, I returned to Mendocino to raise a thousand dollars for bail (Jane's and mine; my plan was to turn myself in and bail myself out at the same time: $500 apiece).

It was Saturday—of course; police always made arrests on Friday night to keep miscreants in jail through the weekend—and by the time I got to the country store in town to cash a check (a friendly service offered by the owner) I was told there was only $600 left in the kitty. One of the oldtimers in the community, a retired logger who had befriended us, went to a friend of his, a fisherman, and borrowed the other $400, kept in a sock under his mattress, we were told.

We then hired a lawyer named Leo Cook in the Mendocino County seat, Ukiah, where we were to be tried. Police told him that we had put acid on our letter to Tim and, believing there was an acid factory in our neighborhood, figured we were running it. (In fact, there was one about a mile away on the same country road.)

He also learned that the field lab in San Luis Obispo that claimed LSD was on the letter had asked that their preliminary findings be confirmed by a state lab in Sacramento. The police didn't wait, however, and when the state tests came back negative some weeks later—Jane and I finally decided the spot on the letter was spilled chablis—the lawyer said our defense would be that wonderful old standby, Illegal Search & Seizure. So far, so good.

Of course, the story of our arrest appeared on the front page of the Mendocino weekly the following Thursday. I went to the owner of the country store and said yes, it was true about the marijuana, but we didn't send LSD to Tim Leary. If I hadn't known why I'd moved my family to Mendocino before that, his response then made it clear.

"I don't care what you do in your own home," he said, "that's none of my business. You're a good customer and your checks don't bounce."

On judgment day, Leo, our legal lion, addressed the court, saying that if his clients had sent a file in a cake to Tim Leary, that wasn't grounds for thinking we had a file factory in our home. Later, I'd see the humor in this, but at the time I panicked. I turned to Jane and asked what happened to the Not Waiting for Sacramento Defense?

Well, Leo got around to that, too, and argued, I thought quite persuasively, that by visiting our home before seeing the state test results, which had been requested by the field lab, the police had overstepped their authority.

The judge made his ruling right away. He said that if the letter in question had gone to anyone other than the dreaded acid king, the lawyer's plea might hold some weight. However, in this case, he said, he was finding the defendants guilty and a higher court could correct him if it wished. Which it did, taking one look at the evidence and the dates of the lab tests and the raid, dismissing all charges.

A little while later we saw Tim's companion, Joanna, and told her what happened. She passed our tale along to Tim on the next visiting day and reported back that he thought the story was hilarious. So far as I know, the cops never did find the acid factory.

The Topic of Cancer
Todd McCormick

Editor's note: Todd McCormick has been a victim of cancer since childhood. When he was nine, his mother started giving him medical marijuana to prevent the nausea of chemotherapy and radiation. He would later become an expert grower, working to determine which strains of marijuana were most effective for specific medical conditions. He had exiled himself to Amsterdam and was living there in 1996 when California publisher Peter McWilliams, who had strongly supported Proposition 215, traveled to Amsterdam after the initiative passed, in search of an author to write a book on the cultivation and use of medical marijuana. Todd, then the editor of Hemp Life *magazine, was perfect for the job, and he returned to California with a large advance from Peter to finance his research.*

Todd grew 4,000 plants and got busted by DEA agents, claiming that federal law supercedes state law. He pleaded guilty to avoid a mandatory 10-year minimum sentence, and is currently serving five years in prison while his case is on appeal. Although he's eligible for an appeal bond, Federal Judge George King disallowed it. He's the same judge who forbade both Todd and Peter McWilliams from using a medical-marijuana defense in their trials. Furthermore, he denied Peter the right, while awaiting trial, to smoke pot in order to offset the nausea caused by his anti-AIDS medicine. Ironically, when he threw up his lunch, he would also regurgitate those very same pills that were keeping him alive. Peter died from choking on his own vomit, resulting in heart failure. He was, in effect, murdered by a federal judge.

Meanwhile, Todd received no medical treatment since his imprisonment in January 2000. When the pain in his neck and back became unbearable in August, he asked the prison doctor for Marinol. Instead, he was required to take a urine test. Although he hadn't smoked any pot, the result showed traces of cannabinoids in his system. But, when he was incarcerated, he hadn't been tested to provide a basis for comparison. Moreover, in June 1998, Todd won at a hearing to determine whether current testing procedures were inadequate to differentiate between marijuana and Marinol. Nevertheless, he was put "in the hole"—solitary confinement—for a month, where he wrote the story below. He would be pleased to hear from readers. Write to Todd McCormick, #11071-112, P.O. Box 3007, Terminal Island, CA 90731.

I remember the evening quite well. I had just come home from the hospital and endured yet another radiation treatment on my left arm. It was my last such treatment, and because of that milestone I planned to party, a rather private party, one where my friend Glen and I would play the board game Risk, consume about an ounce of high-quality, sticky-green, resin-covered cannabis, and place the buds in the center of the board, which would fill the Atlantic Ocean very nicely. As we played, we would each pack long bong hits for the other. You couldn't pack your own, nor could you refuse one offered. You see, we would strategically try to win by getting the other baked.

To complement the fine cannabis, we would also ingest at the fine hour of 11 p.m., three hits each of LSD, rather strong hits at that. It was called White Lightning because of the blotter art on the sheet of paper. I would guess each hit to be in the 300-mic range; one hit was really more than most people needed, and often friends would split a hit and find half a hit quite enough. But tonight was the first night of the rest of my life, post-cancer, or so I hoped. I had been living with the reality of cancer since age two.

It first began in my spine and spread to my skull, right ear, left hip (which placed me in a wheelchair for quite some time), and then moved up to a space between my left lung and my heart, and in that space brought me closer to the final exit than I had ever been before. By that time I was nine years old. I battled the cancer near my heart into my tenth year of life, and with the help of cannabis defeated the sinister growth and went into spontaneous remission! Yes, I was sick no more. I set out to explore the world, conquer new lands, make new friends, ride my dirt-bike into the proverbial sunset. That's when I met Glen.

I was 12 years old, and for my birthday received a Suzuki RM 125 off-road motorcycle. Lucky for me I turned 12 in October, right at the beginning of the school year, lucky in the sense that I began to skip school at the beginning of my school year. I went on to avoid 98-1/2 days of their brainwashing bullshit. I was too busy for school. At 12, I was riding trails, exploring the forests, meeting kids much older than me, since most kids didn't get to blow off school and ride their motorcycle while smoking pot until at least 16. As always, I was the exception.

It was because of pot that I met Glen. He was playing basketball at a court off Broadway Avenue, and I was hanging out, hustling a few dime bags to make the cash to support my own pot-smoking and buy gas for my bike. We met through some common friends and in an odd match bonded like fast friends. He was 17, a jock, very much concerned with where he would attend college. I was 12, wearing a leather jacket, faded Levi's, steel-toed boots and a T-shirt I had printed in psychedelic letters that said "Death Is Definite—Life Is Not." I loved that shirt, my own creation and always a conversation starter. In the back of my mind, it is why I saw such little need for school, or school as the industrial-strength, bore-you-to-death mill that I was supposed to be attending. I liked to learn—education is still my favorite pastime—but there was something too shallow in typical schools.

I sold Glen a bag and gave him a ride home. We got stoned at his place and talked for hours, but not about my past. I hid my cancer like it was some kind of disease. I yearned for friends that didn't know about my childhood sickness. I wanted to be normal. I did, however, like to talk about human mortality, hence the T-shirt. I loved to see people squirm at the thought of this week being your last and how would you live if you knew when that day, your day, would come?

I liked Glen because he was not afraid of the subject—it actually interested him—and he pondered with me who he would say goodbye to, who he would go spend time with, who he would try to fuck. After all, we were teenagers, or at least he was. I was 12, pushing a mid-life crisis. I had been cancer-free for two years straight, by far the longest time cancer-free since I was two. I hid from him what I felt was a weakness, as if I were a leper in disguise. I looked healthy, I acted healthy, I rode a motorcycle, I took karate, I smoked the finest grass, I had girlfriends. But I secretly feared each healthy day might be my last.

For years, I skated through life like I was a normal, healthy teenager. My friends were all four or five years older than me, but accepted me even though I was young and small. I certainly looked my age, but I did not act my age. In most respects I actually acted older than them. I always had money, wheels, bags of grass, sheets of acid, mescaline and, on a good day, some mushrooms. I was definitely into tripping but frowned upon hard drugs—you know, coke, speed, PCP, heroin—the shit that provides no insight into life.

I didn't even like butts and booze—cheap trash, worse than the "hard" drugs and practically force-fed into society. So when my friends got drunk, it was me, the tripping pothead, that saw to it they got home and didn't drown in the toilet puking out oh-so-legal alcohol. Not that I thought alcohol should be illegal, but in contrast to my drugs of choice, alcohol looked good in its bottle but smelled like shit, went down like shit, made you shit-faced and caused people to have the social skills of an asshole—none of the qualities one would find in the highs of acid, 'shrooms, mescaline, grass or hash. Never.

My facade lasted until I was 15. Then one day at karate I thought I fractured my left upper arm kick-boxing. If only I had... When I went to the doctor, I went with Glen. He had a car, and the hospital I visited was a 30-minute drive down the highway. I always liked the highway ride because we always got high-on-the-way. When we got there, Glen was a little taken aback at the recognition

I received from the staff at Pediatric Oncology. I remember him asking me what did "pediatric" mean? Why were we going here for my arm? I told him it meant "the study of disease in children." That sure didn't clear up the question of why we were here, though.

Glen went in with me to the hospital room. When my doctor arrived, he carried with him a four-inch-thick folder with my name on it. Glen noticed. He was quiet. He watched. My pediatrician felt my arms and seemed concerned, so off to X-ray. Glen stopped to ask the lady at the desk where it was, but I already knew. On the elevator, I began my practical confession, that I'd had cancer. "Once?" he asked. More like from age two to 10. I began showing him scars from surgery. He'd noticed them before at the beach but didn't ask.

At X-ray they knew me too. I went in, got the films and brought them back to my doctor, on the way reading them myself. Instantly I could see the problem. My arm's bone was fractured, all right, not from being kicked, but from something inside the marrow swelling and causing the bone to blow apart, fracturing out like an egg was growing inside and the bone was not strong enough to stop it. I could see it myself. Cancer had returned. That feeling of constant worry. If today was my last healthy day, well, here it was, clear as a picture could be in black and white.

Glen couldn't really grasp what it meant. I on the other hand was flashing back to chemotherapy, IV's—being fed by a liquid drip—and sleeping with one arm tied to the hospital bed so I wouldn't pull out my IV in the middle of the night when I would try to roll over. And radiation treatments—oh, how I hated radiation treatments—in 30 seconds, *zap*, all your energy was gone and, boy, what a headache.

The elevator doors hadn't even opened and I was holding back tears. Here we go, welcome to my nightmare! Time to smoke a joint, a *fat* joint. I took Glen out to an open space just outside my pediatrician's office. I had gotten high there before and, just being there then, the smell of marijuana brought me back to being 10 and smoking with my mom, right there, that very spot. Now here I was, five years later. Never did I expect to be back again, but here I was.

After the joint, I brought the X-ray films to my doctor. "It's back," I said, and he knew that I knew what I was looking at. I practically had a master's degree in medicine by the time I was nine. When you live with something as long as I did, being involved *becomes* you. He threw the films up onto the light-box and confirmed my reading. "Yes, you're right," he said, "it's back." Immediately I began to bargain. "I'll do radiation therapy, but not chemo." My doctor laughed. "You've not changed much," he said with a smile. "Come back tomorrow and I'll have our treatment plan worked out."

Glen and I talked all the way home. It was a whole new world, the world of cancer, a world he had never seen, only heard about on TV or in the news. That night, almost all my friends came over. I had to let them know. Most couldn't believe I'd kept quiet about it for so long. I hung around with a tough crowd. Most of my friends were black-leather-jacket, wannabe tough guys. We were noisy, definitely not the nice quiet kids of the neighborhood. As thick-skinned as a kid could be, my having cancer reduced my friend Kevin to tears. He was by far the toughest kid I knew, he could kick ass like an army of one, and no one in our area would fight Kevin. He hurt people and didn't care. But that night Kevin hugged me in front of everyone. He held me like I was his little brother and he didn't know how to be my bodyguard. He felt weak, he felt helpless.

The effect Kevin had on all the other guys was profound. Suddenly the toughest one of us went from hard to soft. I watched my friends change that night. All our stoned conversations of what-would-you-do-if were here. Right here, right now. What would you do if your best friend was sick? What would you do if something was hurting someone you loved and you could do nothing about it? When the typical response of a teenage boy faced with a situation he fears is either fight or flight, here they were. There was nobody to fight and no way to run away. Facing reality was now their hardest challenge. Every one of them went home and talked to their parents—or parent—not something that happened much at that stage in their life. They talked to each other. They cried in front of each other, another no-no-for guys.

They wanted to go with me to the hospital, and I let them. The experience was heavy. I brought them to the children's section of the hospital where kids go bald and cry all night. Where parents weep and IVs drip. This is where I grew up. As I watched them see it for the first time, I saw the impact it had on them, the compassion that poured out of them. They held back tears over a child they did not even know. My friends would never be the same. I was beginning to be glad I had gotten cancer again.

My friends were growing up and doing so in a very honest, very caring way. I was proud of them. We were closer not just to each other but to strangers, children, our families. As if overnight, they went from harsh and cruel toward strangers, to warm and empathetic toward everyone. Glen really stuck by me the closest. He quit his job to be with me practically all the time during my treatment. He learned a lot about my disease, radiation, recovery. He was positive it was back only this once. His optimism could have floated the Titanic through an iceberg.

So, the last night of my treatment, we were hanging out to celebrate the new beginning. We clinked tabs and dosed. Ah, we should be tripping by midnight, and the sunrise would be poetic. As we began to play Risk and smoke each other out, the LSD kicked in. We started talking about how cancer was like a psychedelic experience, that if you made it through, it brought you closer to life. That until you really realize how fragile life is, you take the trip of life for granted, never really appreciating it for the gift it truly is. How he thought I had gotten it one last time for everyone else to experience it. Like cancer was the tab of acid and typically I brought it to the party so naturally I had to have it, but everyone else got off on my stuff.

Glen rationalized it as cancer being the best, most reflective experience we ever had and, more so, it being necessary to human evolution. Cancer was better than LSD or any drug, for that matter. It was life itself. Here we are alive on the planet, just like cancer in a human is alive by eroding the very substance that gives us life. When the human that has cancer dies, the cancer dies too, but that doesn't stop it from poisoning the system from which it feeds.

We're polluting the air, water, land, even the food we eat. We're killing the forests that clean the air we breathe, so maybe cancer in humans is only a microcosm of what we are to the Earth. We were happy now that I had cancer. How great an experience! We're all going to die somewhere, some way, so wouldn't it be better to take this trip and have the meaning of life or one of the many meanings of life exposed to you before you go? So many of the people you meet that had cancer and survived are glad to have gone through it because of what it had taught them. What it shows you is hard to put into words, but some of the time is so precious as to be worth all the agony.

Years later, my girlfriend and I were in San Diego at a Whole Life Convention. Tim Leary was giving a workshop, so naturally we arrived early to meet a hero to us both. I was wearing hemp clothes as I always do and a T-shirt that we had made up for the 1994 California Hemp and Health Initiative. It had a peace sign entwined with a hemp leaf on a background of an American flag. Tim noticed it. A week earlier, he gave a party for hemp activist Jack Herer and many of the petition-gatherers, so when he looked at me he thought he knew me. To our surprise, as soon as he saw us enter the room, he stopped a conversation with someone and said, quite loud, "Oh, a friend just walked in who I must talk to. Excuse me."

We thought someone was behind us, but Tim walked up to me and gave me a hug like he had known me for eons. My girlfriend was just as surprised as I was. "You didn't tell me you knew Tim Leary," she remarked. "I don't," I replied. Tim then proceeded with conversation. "How ya been? You look well. Why haven't you been up to the house?" "Because we've never met," I said, "but I'm a huge fan of your work." He looked at my girlfriend and said, "Always the joker, isn't he?" As she said my name in utter surprise, Tim chimed in, "Aren't you going to introduce me to your lady?" And they exchanged names.

The people were now arriving for his speech. He held our hands and sat us in the front and said, "I have bad news I have to tell you after this is over." So we sat. I was still in awe, and so was my girlfriend. "He really believes he knows you," she kept saying. The entire hour, Tim sat on a chair and spoke directly to us two as if the room didn't exist. Only the three of us were there, he spoke to me, he was teaching and we were his chosen students. For a few moments, he even held our hands while he conveyed his thoughts on life's meaning and explored the limits of our minds' genius.

After the seminar, we went out onto the patio. I had some very good Moroccan hashish we smoked. Tim was most concerned with telling us he had just been diagnosed with cancer. He said this between tokes. Then he looked at me, waiting for that horrified gasp. When I remarked, "That's great," he choked on his toke.

I hugged him to both tap him on the back but also to tell him that cancer was the best trip I'd ever taken. That of all the mind-expanding drugs I'd ever done, none has come close to the insight derived from living with cancer. He got it instantly. He understood what I was getting to. I showed him some scars from cancer treatment, and he pondered life. I told him of doing LSD on the evening of my last radiation treatment, the conclusions we came to, and how glad I was to have been fortunate enough to experience that "trip." We smoked and talked for quite a while.

The next time I got to see him was at his home in Beverly Hills. It was his 75th birthday, in October 1995. My girlfriend and I had just gotten out of jail in Ohio on a medical-marijuana case that became national news, so he knew why we had not been over earlier to visit. He knew where we had been.

I presented him with a joint for his birthday. He smiled and said, "Don't I get a lighter too?" We smoked, we laughed. He remembered me. He remembered what I had told him about cancer being one hell of a trip. And he told me I was right.

That was the last night I saw my friend. My girlfriend and I moved to Amsterdam a month later. While I was there, Tim left for the Great Unknown. While here, he experienced all that life had to offer, from the lowest lows to the highest highs. I still see him in my dreams. He still makes me laugh, he still makes me think. He was right the first time we met. He *did* know me. It was I that forgot to look deeper. We all know each other, we're all connected. Alive eternally, in each other's heart and in each other's mind. Enjoy!

A Game of Mind Tennis
Paul Krassner

This dialogue with the ailing Timothy Leary was taped in September 1995, several months before he died.

"So, Tim, here's a toast to thirty years of friendship."

"And still counting. We've been playing mind tennis for thirty years. Isn't that great?"

"The one thing in countless conversations we've had that sticks out in my mind is something you once said, that no matter what scientists do—they can decodify the DNA code, layer after layer—but underneath it all, there's still that mystery. And I've enjoyed playing with the mystery. Are you any closer to understanding the mystery, or further from it?"

"Well, Paul, I watch words now. It's an obsession. I learned it from Marshall McLuhan, of course. A terrible vice. Had it for years, but not actually telling people about it. I watch the words that people use. The medium is the message, you recall. The brain creates the realities she wants. When we see the prisms of these words that come through, we can understand. Do I understand the mystery?"

"I guess the ultimate mystery is inconceivable by definition. But have you come any closer to understanding it?"

"Understand? Stand under! I'm overstood, I'm understood."

"The older I get, the deeper the mystery becomes."

"The faster."

"Let's get to a specific mystery. The mystery of you. Because everybody sees you through their own perceptions. How do you think you have been most misunderstood?"

"Well, everyone gets the Timothy Leary they deserve. Everyone has their point of view. And everyone's point of view is absolutely valid for them. To track me, you have to keep moving the camera, or you'll have just one tunnel point of view. Sermonizing there. Don't impale yourself on your point of view."

"Some people know you only through that Sixties slogan, "Turn on, tune in, drop out." I think a lot of people don't really understand what you meant by dropping out."

"Everybody understood. Just look at the source."

"All right, here's words. Fifteen years ago, at a futurist conference, you called yourself a Neo-Technological Pagan. What did you mean by that?"

"*Neo* has all the connotations of the futurist stuff that's coming along. *Technological* denotes using machines, using electricity or light to create reality. There are two kinds of technology. The machine—diesel, oil, metal, industrial technology. And then the neo-technology, which uses light. Electricity. Photons. Electrons. *Pagan* is great. I love the word. Pagan is basically humanist. I grew up in a Catholic zone, and pagan was the worst thing you could say. Of course, I'd never met a pagan in Springfield, Massachusetts, going to a Catholic school. 'Where do these pagans hang out? I wanna be one.'"

"Was there any specific thing that made you turn from Catholicism?"

"Yeah, there was a period, I know exactly what it was, I was fifteen or sixteen, I was being sexually molested in my high school and actually seduced by a wonderful sexy girl, much more experienced than I. And, *whew*! She opened it up! The great mystery of sex. *Wow*! At that time I was going routinely to confession on Saturday afternoon. But I had a date with Rosemary that night. Sitting there in the dark church. Then you go in and say, 'Bless me, father, for I have sinned.' Absolutely, totally hypocritical! They want you to confess and repent while I have every intention in the world of being seduced by this girl tonight."

"The glands overshadowed the philosophy."

"The glands? Shit, Paul, that statement is very mechanical."

"I'm a recovering romantic."

"Because you used the word *gland*? Glands are very interesting. People don't talk about glands very much."

"Talk about machines, then. What's the relationship you see between acid and technology?"

"Well, LSD is one of the many drugs which are based on neuroactive plants. Peyote, and fungus on rye. Those crazed experiences which happened in the Middle Ages, what did they call them?—"the madness of crowds"—simply because of some plant they had chewed. The point is that the human brain is equipped with these receptor sites for various kinds of vegetables that alter consciousness. So our brains evolving over fifty million years have these receptor sites. The reason why certain people like to take these drugs is because these receptor sites activate pleasure centers. Now this was not a mistake. The DNA didn't fuck up. The devil didn't do it. There was obviously some reason for those receptor sites that would get you off on peyote, psilocybin. And there are dozens of compelling receptor sites and drugs we don't even know about."

"In the changing counterculture, then, do you see a continuity from psychoactive drugs to cyberspace?"

"Of course. It's a fact. Every generation developed a new counterculture. In the Roaring Twenties, jazz, liquor. In the Sixties, the hippies with psychedelics."

"The counterculture now, it's not either/or, it's not necessarily drugs or computers. I'm sure some do them simultaneously. But how do you think that that the drug experience has changed the computer experience?"

"I did not imply that you can't do both. The brain is equipped to be altered by these receptor sites. So we can see these receptor sites overwhelm the mind. The word-processing system. Then suddenly you can take psychedelic plants that put you in different places. I'm being too technical. But there's an analogy between receptor sites for marijuana and for LSD or opium, which activate the brain, and the way we can boot up different areas of our computers. Back in the 1960s we didn't know much about the brain. I was saying back in 1968, 'You have to go out of your mind to use your head.' But *head* simply is an old-fashioned way of saying *brain*. We didn't know about brain-receptor sites. But now, we can use bio-chemicals to boot up the kind of altered realities you want in your brain. So you smoke marijuana because it gets you in a mellow mood. Grass is good for the appetite. That's operating your brain. But now it's specific: 'Use your head by *operating* your brain.' That's the new concept. Use your head! That's hot. Operate your brain because the brain designs realities."

"Do you see a connection between the War on Drugs and the attempt to censor the Internet?"

"Oh, absolutely, yes. The censors want to control. We have to have people to impose to keep society going. I don't knock rules, rituals. We have to have them. The controllers censor anything that gives the power to change reality to the individual. You can't have *that* happen."

"My theory is that the UFO sightings and all the people who claim to have been abducted by aliens, that this is really just a cover-up for secret government experiments in mind control."

"That's a very popular theory, Paul. I get like ten mimeograph letters a day about UFOs and the government. Boy, the governments are really fucking busy, trying to program our minds."

"And of course those UN soldiers in Bosnia can hardly wait to get back in their black helicopters so they can attack Michigan and Arizona."

"I'm happy about UFO rumors. I'm glad because at least people are doing something on their own. The sixty-year-old farm wife in Dakota thinks she's been taken up and serially raped by UFO people. *Wow*! They came all the way from another planet a thousand light years away to get this lovely grandmother and pull her socks off and have an orgy with her. *Wow*!"

"Or at least an anal probe. To your knowledge, is the government still doing experiments in mind control? We know they used to, with the MK-ULTRA programs and all. Do you know if they're still at it? I can't imagine they would've stopped."

"G. Gordon Liddy would give you the current CIA line. Liddy

says: 'Yes, it is true. When we learned that the Chinese Communists were using LSD, the CIA naturally cornered the whole world market for Sandoz LSD. They didn't realize that LSD comes in a millionth of a gram. The CIA found LSD to be unpredictable.' Well, no shit, Gordon! Can you name one accurate prediction? The fall of the Shah? The rise of the Ayatollah?"

"What did you think of Liddy getting that free speech award from the National Association of Talk Show Hosts after he said that if the ATF [the Bureau of Alcohol, Tobacco and Firearms] comes after you, they're wearing bulletproof vests, so you should aim for the head or groin?"

"That's pure Liddy. He's basically a romantic comedian."

"When you were debating him, if you had listened to his advice retroactively when he led the raid on Millbrook [16 years previously], then later you would've been on stage debating yourself, because he would've been shot in the head and groin by somebody, if his advice had been followed."

"He was a government agent entering our bedroom at midnight. We had every right to shoot him. But I've never owned a weapon in my life, and I have no intention of owning a weapon, although I was a master sharpshooter at West Point on both the Garand, the Springfield rifle and the machine gun. I was a Howitzer expert. I know how to operate these lethal gadgets, but I have never had and never will have a gun around."

"But when you escaped from prison, you said, 'Arm yourselves and shoot to live. To shoot a genocidal robot policeman in the defense of life is a sacred act.'"

"Yeah! I also said, 'I'm armed and dangerous.' I got that directly from [black militant] Angela Davis. I thought it was just funny to say that."

"I thought it was the party line from the Weather Underground [the radical New Left organization that helped him escape, funded by the LSD-dealing International Brotherhood of Love]."

"Well, yeah, I had a lot of arguments with [Weather Underground leader] Bernadine Dohrn."

"They had their own rhetoric. She even praised Charles Manson."

"The Weather Underground was amusing. They were brilliant, brilliant Jewish Chicago kids. They had class and dash and flash and smash. Bernadine was praising Manson for sticking a fork in a victim's stomach. She was just being naughty."

"She was obviously violating a taboo. What are the taboos that are waiting to be violated today?"

"There is one taboo, the oldest and most powerful—I've been writing and thinking about it for thirty years. The concept of *death* is something that people do not want to face. The doctors and the priests and the politicians have made it into something terrible, terrible, terrible. You're a victim! If you accept the notion of death, you've signed up to be the ultimate victim."

"Is that why you announced publicly that you have inoperable prostate cancer? Friends knew it but—"

"I actually have been planning my terminal graduation party for like twenty years. Of course, I'm a follower of Socrates, who was one of the greatest counterculture comic philosophers in history. He took hemlock."

"The Hemlock Society was named after that—"

"I've been a member of the Hemlock Society for many years. They talk about self-deliverance. That's the biggest decision you can make. You couldn't choose how and when and with whom you were *born*."

"Although there are people who say you can."

"All right, well, go for it. But for those of us who don't have that option..."

"Ram Dass even once said that a fetus that gets aborted *knew* it didn't want to be born so it chose parents who wouldn't carry it to term."

"Richard's so politically correct. Isn't that fabulous?"

"Are you planning to do what Aldous Huxley did, which was to make the journey on acid?"

"That's an option, yeah."

"Do you believe in any kind of afterlife?"

"Well, I have an enormous archive covering sixty years of writing, around three hundred audio-videos. It's being stored away. And I belong to two cryonics groups, so I have the option of freezing my brain."

"By afterlife, I didn't mean the products of your consciousness so much as your consciousness itself."

"My consciousness is a product of my brain. How can I know about my mind until I express thought?"

"Obviously there are people who believe in the standard Heaven and Hell and Purgatory. I'm assuming that you don't believe in *that* kind of afterlife."

"They're useful metaphors. I must be in Purgatory now, huh? Occasionally I have a pop of Heaven. That's not a bad metaphor. Of course, we realize that Hell is totally self-induced."

"On Earth, you mean."

"Well, wherever you are. What do *you* think about that? Do you believe in life after death and all that? What's your theory?"

"That you are eaten by worms and just disappear, or you're cremated and your ashes—"

"Wait, now, you have your choice of being eaten by worms or barbecued. Or you can be frozen. You don't have to be eaten by worms. You don't have to be microwaved. I'm going to leave some drops of my blood, which has my DNA, in a lot of places. I'll leave my brain with them. Why not try all these things? Not that I *care*, Paul, believe me. I have no desperate desire to come back to planet Earth. I think that I have lived one of the most incredibly funny, interesting lives. I'm fascinated to see what's gonna happen in the next steps. But I have no desire to come back. Most non-scientists don't realize that in scientific experiments, you learn more from your mistakes. So I hope that I will leave a track record of making blunders about the most important thing in life. How to preserve your DNA. I hope someone will learn from my mistakes."

"Are there regrets that you have? Things that you would've done differently, knowing what you know now?"

"I'd play the whole game differently, sure. About a third of the things I've done have been absolutely stupid, vulgar and gross. About a third have been just banal. But a third have been brilliant. Like baseball, one out of three, you lead the league. MVP. Most Valuable Philosopher."

"When I first met you in 1965, you were talking about baseball—and games in general—as a metaphor. How would you describe your game in life? It's been a conscious game. You didn't just fall into a pinball machine and get knocked around. Although that happened too."

"Well, I identified with Socrates at a very young age. The aim in human life is to find out about yourself and know who you are. The purpose in life is to discover yourself."

"With these big media mergers going on now, giants—Time-Warner-Turner here, Disney-Capital Cities-ABC there, how do you think the individual can fight that best?"

"Why fight it? Like Southern Pacific merges with Pennsylvania Railroad, so what?"

"But you said before, they're trying to control, so aren't they trying to control the information?"

"You can't control information if it's packaged in light. In photons and electrons. You simply can't control digital messages. *Zoom*, I can go to my Website and put some stuff up there. Immediately my messages are accessed by people around the world. Not just now but later. The nice thing about cyber-communication is that counterculture philosophers who learn about technology can work together, can be faster than committees, politicians and the like. So I have great confidence. You have to learn to play their game. That's why I went to West Point and that's why I went to the Jesuit school, and learned enough so I could play that mind-fuck game. I understood. And I moved on."

"Do you mean you knew before you went to West Point, before you went to Jesuit school, that you wanted to learn their tools?"

"I didn't want to go to either. My parents insisted on that."

"But you went with that attitude."

"Yeah. They took me around to about ten Catholic universities and colleges in New England. None of them would accept me because of my high school track record. I was the editor of the newspaper in high school and I made it a scandal sheet exposing the principal. I had a great-uncle who was a big shot in the Catholic Church. He had pull in the Vatican, and he pulled some strings, so I got into a Jesuit school. I just watched, repelled but fascinated."

"I don't believe in reincarnation, but if I did, I would think I knew you in a previous life. But that's only a metaphor, I don't believe in it. Do you believe in that concept?"

"In the time of Emerson, the 1830s, there was a counterculture very similar to ours. Self-reliance. Individuality. Emerson took drugs with David Thoreau. Margaret Fuller went to Italy and got the drugs. Later, William James started another counterculture at Harvard. Same thing. Nitrous oxide. Hashish. *The Varieties of Religious Experience.*"

"Well, have the medical people given you a prognosis on *this* life, of how many years you have left?"

"I'm 75, and I've smoked [cigarettes] and lived an active life, but not the most healthy life. So my prognosis would be like two to five years. Jeez, I'll be 80 then."

"Are there specific things that you want to accomplish during this period?"

"Our World Wide Web site is a big thing. We're putting books up there on the screen. You can actually play or perform my books. You read the first page and my notes. And you can revise my text. We call them living books. As many versions as there are people that want to perform 'book' with me. True freedom of the press! The average person can't publish a book. This way they can."

"Do you think it's destiny or chance that one becomes in a leadership position—a change agent, as you call it?"

"Well, destiny implies that you were created that way. No, I think that the individual person has a lot to do with it. Thousands of decisions you make growing up in high school and college to get to a point where you have constructed your reality. You can be a judge or—"

"A defendant."

"I think one of the good side effects of the [O.J.] Simpson trial is that people understand how totally evil lawyers are."

"You mean defense lawyers *and* prosecutors?"

"Yes."

"A friend of mind was scheduled to be on jury duty and they asked him what he thought of prosecutors, and he said, 'Cops in suits.' Are you optimistic about the future, even though there's creeping fascism?"

"The future is measured in terms of individual liberation. You have politicians—and the military people want to hurt other people. That's all about control. They have to devise excuses for victimizing people. I do think that the new generations growing up now use electronic media. A twelve-year-old kid now, in Tokyo or Paris or here, can move more stuff around on screen. She is exposed to more RPM, Realities Per Minute! A thousand times more than her great-grandfather. There's gonna be a big change. The greatest thing that's happening now is the World Wide Web. Sign-ups zoom up like *this*. The telephone is the connection. *The modem is the message!* You can explore around. If you're a left-handed, dyslexic, Lithuanian lesbian, you can get in touch with people in Yugoslavia or China who are left-handed, dyslexic lesbians. It's great! It's gonna break down barriers, create new language. More and more graphic language. And neon grammatics. Anything that's in print will be in neon."

"Well, that really brings us full cycle. We started talking about words, and now they've become neonized."

"Consider, Paul, death with dignity, dying with elegance. It's wonderful to see it happening. I talk about orchestrating, managing and directing my death as a celebration of a wonderful life! That has touched a lot of people. They say, 'My father went through this whole thing. He wanted to die.' Amazing."

"So the response has been that people are glad to now that they aren't the only ones who are thinking about death?"

"Yeah. People are thinking about dying with class, but were afraid to talk about it."

"What do you want your epitaph to be?"

"What do *you* think? You write it."

"Here lies Timothy Leary. A pioneer of inner space. And an Irish leprechaun to the end."

"Irish leprechaun! You're being racist! Can't I be a Jewish leprechaun? What is this Irish leprechaun shit?"

"Okay. Here lies Timothy Leary, a pioneer of inner space, and a Jewish leprechaun to the end."

* * *

Postscript: Although Leary had decided in 1988 to have his head frozen posthumously, he became disillusioned with cryonics officials shortly before his death, and changed his mind.

"They have no sense of humor," he said. "I was worried I would wake up in fifty years surrounded by people with clipboards."

Instead, he chose to be cremated and have a small portion of his ashes rocketed into outer space to orbit the Earth. I asked him if the remainder of his ashes could be mixed with marijuana and rolled into joints so that his friends and family could smoke him.

"Yeah," he replied. "Just don't bogart me."

Originally published in The Realist.

Chapter 3

The Grateful Dead

Jerry Garcia Strikes Again
Mountain Girl

In 1972, when the Grateful Dead were young and sassy, and highly motivated to stand out and be weird, we were trekking across Europe in two big rent-a-buses. A very long haul from Germany down through Switzerland, over das Alps mountains and ober dem valleys, oop und doon, oop und doon, so everyone dropped acid (natcherly) for the ride to Paris. A 12-hour trip stretched into the infinite, wheeled along by two nice rent-a-drivers, Kurt and Mick. Long, long day. Cows grazing the high mountains, shimmering vistas—and, inside the buses, giggling and goofing.

At the very tip-top of the highest pass in Switzerland, in view of the mountains and skiers' paradise, the pressure relief valve on the butane tank blew out in a long horrible howling hiss, somewhere just behind our seat. The bus driver slammed on the brakes, sliding to a halt, as we panicked and leaped for the exits. But before the doors could open, Jerry rose from our seat, waving a box of matches and shouting, "Gas leak? I know what to do to find a gas leak! Strike a match! I'll find it!" And he began lighting matches and tossing them into the rear of the bus. And that is a true story.

Group Hallucination
Curtis

San Francisco, 1967, the Human Be-In.

Something odd happened at this Gathering of the Tribes that still permeates my mind. I have confirmed that I was not the only one who experienced this.

Right before the Grateful Dead played, there was a "gentleperson" from India who offered blessings from the stage. While this was occurring, a group of folks in the back of the crowd started screaming, "Fuck you, bring on the band," and other derogatory comments.

The person on stage stopped for a moment, kind of gazed in the general direction of the comments, bowed, and something that looked like a lightning bolt left him and struck in that general area, illuminating it with light. This in turn seemed to swell the energy to even greater heights, and I heard the words "Don't freak with a freak" come from the Cosmic Kitchen.

It was only a matter of moments before the Dead were (chuckle) tuned up and playing. This is when the oddity took place. I think the band was playing a song called "Alligator." The audience energy was swirling in what appeared to be a circle and gave the impression of being on a gigantic carousel. This swirling re-formed into this incredible egg-like shape of light that appeared above the stage, and everyone's body seemed to dissolve.

What happened next is hard to describe. It was like the light had joined everyone there together, and the realm of individuality was gone. There was a mutual chill of excitement that filled the air, and I began to hear comments like: "I think we made it." "Are we here?" "This is it!" And "God, isn't it beautiful?" For a moment there was absolute silence. We were all stuck in this "egg of light," and it was beyond any beauty that I could describe in words.

It was at this point I heard the words "Where do we go from here?" come from the Cosmic Kitchen. Almost instantaneously, I heard hundreds of responses come from the crowd, and very few were identical. The light began to fade, and in a flash we were back to the stage and crowd. I did hear folks asking one another, "Did you experience that?" among other questions, and the answer was yes.

When everything came back together, something new was present. It no longer seemed that we were this one big family. It appeared that we somehow had resettled into smaller groups that were perhaps now driven by ego. Coincidentally, this sort of shows up in successive events pertaining to the history of Haight/Ashbury and that culture.

This experience at the Be-In kept running through my mind. In the early '70s, Ram Dass and I discussed this at length, while sitting on the roof of the Palace Heights Hotel in Delhi, India. We came to the conclusion that this incident, which occurred in Golden Gate Park, was the beginning of what we termed the "Social Karma Ego-Dharma Games," or a point where people started growing apart, rather than growing together.

Mysterious Stranger
Todd Bauer

I was still fairly wet behind the neurotransmitters when this story took place. Finding the freedom which accompanies college too addictive to kick—even for a summer—I had enlisted in summer courses between my freshman and sophomore years. During that summer of 1985, the two guys I lived with were strict vegetarians—marijuana and/or mushrooms being the mainstays of their diet.

It was also this summer that a little band called the Grateful Dead were playing about an hour away at the local outdoor music venue. We all got tickets and, having been to plenty of concerts, listened to plenty of Dead albums and taken plenty of mushrooms, I thought I was practically a pro. Little did I know I was about to be taken to school.

My two buddies had arranged a ride for us, and I showed up at the rendezvous point all decked out in my iron-on decal Dead T-shirt thinking I was the shit; I even had a couple of joints! We were fresh out of the veggies but figured we could pick them up at the show.

About 10 minutes later, this VW microbus pulls up, and we pile into a van utterly devoid of contents except for five long-haired, tie-dyed hard-cores and a boom box. I didn't know any of them, but they were completely friendly and we were just having a good ol' time until, as we were pulling into the parking lot, the bus ran out of gas. No one seemed phased by this, and as there was nothing I could do without imposing, I didn't worry either.

We pushed our thirsty heap to a parking space and then went about our search for the precious mushrooms. Much to our regret we found that it had been a bad harvest in this particular lot, but the crop of blotter acid was banner. After much contemplation we decided to take the plunge and had a great show.

We were still flying high when we returned to the van and recalled that it needed that one special ingredient in order to run. I set about watching the images emerge from the puddles on the blacktop while others went off to score some gas.

By the time they returned with that automobile ambrosia, we were about the only vehicle left in the lot. As we were pulling out, we spotted a guy with no shoes or shirt dancing around the intersection. Being the naturally curious people we were, we pulled over and inquired if we could be of any assistance.

"I've got to get to Pittsburgh!" our half-clad hitchhiker kept repeating. "I've got to get to Pittsburgh!"

"Well, we're headed to Oxford, Ohio, but you can get in if you want."

"Sure, sure."

Now let it be noted that I am strictly an observer in these events, taking no active role in the policies implemented while on this mission. And as strange as the experience of my first trip and my first show were, up until this point I had no trouble discerning whether it was the drug or reality that was escorting my perception of a walk on the weird side.

As we drove, our animated interloper hopped about the cramped quarters, seemingly filling every empty space with an appendage of his body while regaling us with his heroic quest. This oratory was delivered with lightning speed and was earnest and covered every bodily function (in great detail), several species of various vermin, thalidomide babies, boxers vs. briefs, P.M. Gladstone and tetherball championships. None of us said a word—half out of not having the chance, half out of being intrigued and half out of being terrified. He never did get around to how he lost his shoes and shirt.

After a while, someone decided that we needed something to eat, so we pulled into an all-night 7-11. Promptly upon entering, our oracle from Del-High started screaming, "You've got to buy mouthwash! You've got to buy mouthwash! They can smell it on your breath!" He then shockingly sprinted out of the store and down the road. Even more shocking, though, was that one of my newfound friends sprinted after him and brought him back.

Thus we endured tales of slaughterhouses, portable toilets and cabbage farming, until we reached our destination. Immediately after opening the door, our Pittsburgh-seeking Galahad raced off again, presumably for that ever-elusive mouthwash. This time, though, no one went after him.

Over the years, I attended quite a few more Dead shows and embarked on quite a few more trips, and have thus come to the conclusion that it was not the drug, but the stream-of-conscious-ness-spouting streaker which made the evening one of my most strange.

I truly hope he made it back to Pittsburgh.

Epiphany in the John
The Modesto Kid

July 1995, a warm day in Pittsburgh. The Grateful Dead are in town for a concert at Three Rivers Stadium, home of the once-champion Pirates and Steelers.

I hadn't planned on going to the concert, too many people, so much hassle just to get a ticket. A buddy from grade school, Jason—now a successful downtown lawyer following his dad's path, second wife, two kids, big house, nice cars—had gotten four tickets through the Duquesne Club, the posh, up until just a few years ago solely WASP, hangout downtown where the well-con-nected rolled the big deals. Jason had two extra tickets; I bought them and sold one to another pal.

Concert day rolls around on a beautiful Friday, the weather gor-geous, warm but not too warm, rain in the forecast but nothing imminent. Somewhere around three o'clock I finish up all my crum-my crew details and drop a piece of acid-laced paper about a quar-ter-inch square onto my tongue, fully aware that the rest of the day is quite likely to be special, remembering my dear dead (from stomach cancer, not drugs, though for too many years he was a cigarette smoker) buddy's drug admonition: "When you are on a drug, just remember you are on a drug."

I went into my garage, pumped up the tires and oiled the chain of my 21-speed road bike. Next, I fired up a joint and took a few deep pulls of some righteous weed to get things rolling. Then I got on my bike for the approximately eight-mile trip to the stadium. Laser-like, I zipped by and through the swollen swarm of noxious traffic with ease, crossed a pot-holed bridge over the Allegheny and headed west on a trail along the river to the stadium.

There was nothing quite like the Dead parking-lot scene; perhaps Arab souks or the gathering of Phish phans come to mind. Through two generations, the Dead parking lots were an anthropological treasure, a sociologically satisfying source and a visually voluptuous active volcano. My buzz escalated among the gentle, fuzzy, bearded and longhaired and colorful lot. I eased through the crowd on my bike and got to the ring road surrounding the huge carved-out concrete mountain, found where the police were headquartered and then locked my bike and helmet to a traffic sign close to the heat. On foot I meandered through the Biblical-like gathering.

Before the concert started, I had to take a leak, so I left the carnival-like scene and entered the stadium. After going through the gate, I was in a big corridor that circled the huge edifice's orifice. Every so often on the inside of the circular corridor were the bathrooms, concrete-block walled-off areas tucked under the ascending seats. Lots of cold density, but the people were not like a sports crowd, no huge amounts of beer-released testosterone invested in victory, but rather gentle souls anticipating Jerry Garcia's golden licks and the Dead's mesmerizing melodies. The lights in most people's eyes were powered by grass and psychedelics.

I headed for the Men's Room, through a big metal door with a panel of stainless steel screwed onto its face, into a painted concrete-block rectangle. Long hair, tie-dyed T-shirts, beards, ponytails, shorts, some with no shirts, sneakers, Birkenstocks or bare feet, all milling toward the urinals and commodes, a loose bunch waiting to relieve themselves and get back out into the open air.

I had just shaken the dew from my lily and was heading toward the exit. In the entrance comes a young couple, a baby-faced pair, he maybe 15 or 16 and she 14 or 15, both blistered out of their heads, chemical joy welled-up behind their eyeballs, faces deliriously happy, but her face also indicated that though she was in the Men's Room, there was no way she was going to let go of her boyfriend, despite his need to be there.

One tall, outgoing, bare-chested dude in blue jeans and a ponytail held together with beaded elastic was heading past them. He stopped and goodnaturedly said to her, "Hey, you're not supposed to be in here," and then moved on to the exit. She smiled sheepishly. The crowd in the john quietly and calmly noticed the presence of the young woman, heard the gentle admonition, and accepted her presence as no big thing and went about the business

of doing their business. I walked on out of the john without stopping to see the outcome of his, the boyfriend's, outgo.

Too Much
Steve Parish

When we were over in Europe [note: Parish was the road manager for the Grateful Dead], we had made a mistake—all the acid
was 10 times stronger than we thought—and we saved it for a special time. We took it in Heidelberg, and found those laughing
skulls, and we all just laid around on the bus playing with laughing
skulls all day.

The Grateful Dead Play the Pyramids
Paul Krassner

There was a concert in Pittsburgh in 1967 with the Grateful
Dead, the Velvet Underground, the Fugs, and me doing stand-up.
There were two shows, both completely sold out, and this was the
first time anybody had realized how many hippies actually lived in
Pittsburgh.

Backstage between shows, a man sidled up to me.

"Call me Bear," he said.

"Okay, you're Bear."

"Don't you recognize me?"

"You look familiar but—"

"I'm Owsley."

Of course—Owsley acid! He presented me with a tab of Mon-
terey Purple. Not wishing to carry around an illegal drug in my
pocket, I swallowed it instead. Soon I found myself in the lobby
talking with Jerry Garcia. As people from the audience wandered
past us, he whimsically stuck out his hand, palm up.

"Got any spare change?"

A passerby gave him a dime, and Garcia said thanks.

"He didn't recognize you," I said.

"See, we all look alike."

In the course of our conversation, I used the word evil to
describe somebody.

"There are no evil people," Garcia said, just as the LSD was set-
tling into my psyche. "There are only victims."

"What does that mean? If a rapist is a victim, you should have
compassion when you kick him in the balls?"

I did the second show while the Dead were setting up behind
me. Then they began to play, softly, and as they built up their presence, I faded out and left the stage.

Later, some local folks brought me to a restaurant which, they told me, catered to Mafia clientele. With my long brown curly hair underneath my Mexican cowboy hat, I didn't quite fit in. The manager came and asked me to kindly remove my hat. I was still tripping. I hardly ate any of my spaghetti after I noticed how it was wiggling on my plate.

I glanced around at the various Mafia figures, wondering if they had killed anybody. Then I remembered what Garcia had said about evil. So these guys might be executioners, but they were also victims. The spaghetti was still wiggling on my plate, but then I realized it wasn't really spaghetti, it was actually worms in tomato sauce. The other people at my table were all pretending not to notice.

* * *

In 1978, the Grateful Dead scored a gig in Egypt. Bob Weir looked up at the Great Pyramid and cried out, "What is it?" Actually, it was the place for locals to go on a cheap date. The Pyramids were surrounded by moats of discarded bottlecaps. The Dead were scheduled to play on three successive nights at an open-air theater in front of the Pyramids, with the Sphinx looking on.

A bootleg tape of Dean Martin and Jerry Lewis doing filthy schtick was being used for a preliminary sound check. Later, an American general complained to stage manager Steve Parrish that the decadence of a rock and roll band performing here was a sacrilege to 5,000 years of history. Parrish said, "I lost two brothers in 'Nam, and I don't wanna hear this crap." The general retreated in the face of those imaginary brothers.

But there were a couple of *real* injured veterans. Drummer Bill Kreutzmann had fallen off a horse and broken his arm. But he would still be playing with the band, using *one* drumstick. Or, as an Arabian fortune cookie might point out, *In the land of the limbless, a one-armed drummer is king.* Basketball star and faithful Deadhead Bill Walton's buttocks had been used as a pincushion by the Portland Trailblazers so that he could continue to perform on court even though the bones of his foot were being shattered with pain he couldn't feel. Having been injected with painkilling drugs to hide the owners' greed rather than heal his injury, he now had to walk around with crutches and one foot in a cast under his extra-long *galabia*. Maybe Kreutzmann and Walton could team up and enter the half-upside-down sack-race event.

An air of incredible excitement permeated the first night. Never had the Dead been so inspired. Backstage, Jerry Garcia was passing along final instructions to the band: "Remember, play in tune." The music began with Egyptian oudist Hamza el-Din, backed up by a group tapping out ancient rhythms on their 14-inch-diameter tars, soon joined by Mickey Hart, a butterfly with drumsticks. Then Garcia ambled on with a gentle guitar riff, then the rest of the band, and as the Dead meshed with the percussion ensemble, basking in total mutual respect, Bob Weir suddenly segued into Buddy Holly's "Not Fade Away."

"Did you see that?" Ken Kesey said. "The Sphinx's *jaw* just dropped."

Every morning, my roommate, Merry Prankster George Walker, climbed to the top of the Pyramid. He was in training. It would be his honor to plant a Grateful Dead skull-and-lightning-bolt flag on top of the Great Pyramid. This was *our* Iwo Jima.

In preparation for the final concert, I was sitting in the tub-like sarcophagus at the center of gravity inside the Great Pyramid, after ingesting LSD that a Prankster had smuggled into Egypt in a plastic Visine bottle. I had heard that the sound of the universe was D-flat, so that was the note I chanted. It was only as I breathed in deeply before each extended *Om* that I was forced to ponder the mystery of those who urinate there.

I had a strong feeling that I was involved in a *lesson*. It was as though the secret of the Dead would finally be revealed to me, if only I paid proper attention. There was a full eclipse of the moon, and Egyptian kids were running through the streets shaking tin cans filled with rocks in order to bring it back.

"It's okay," I assured them. "The Grateful Dead will bring back the moon."

And, sure enough, a rousing rendition of "Ramble On Rose" would accomplish that feat. The moon returned just as the marijuana cookie that rock impresario Bill Graham gave me started blending in with the acid. Graham used to wear two wristwatches, one for each coast. Now he wore one wristwatch with two faces.

This was a totally outrageous event. The line between incongruity and appropriateness had disappeared along with the moon. The music was so powerful that the only way to go was ecstasy. That night, when the Dead played "Fire On the Mountain," I danced my ass off with all the others on that outdoor stage as if I had no choice. Ordinarily, I belonged to a vast army of secret dancers who only dance when they're alone.

The next day, a dozen of us had a farewell party on a *felucca*—an ancient, roundish boat, a kind of covered wagon that floats along the river. Garcia was carrying his attache case, just in case he suddenly got any new song ideas. There were three guides who came with our rented *felucca*: an old man whose skin was like corrugated leather, a younger man who was his assistant, and a kid whose job was to light the "hubbly-bubbly"—a giant water pipe which uses hot coals to keep the hashish burning.

Now we were all completely zonked out of our minds in the middle of the Nile. The Egyptians kept us dizzy on hash and we in turn gave them acid. The old man mumbled something—our translator explained, "He says he's seeing strange things"—and gave *me* the handle of the rudder to steer, which I managed to do even in my stoned stupor. The *felucca* was a vehicle of our cultural exchange.

"You know," Bill Graham confessed, "last night was the first time I ever danced in public."

"Me too," I said.

That was the lesson.

Originally published in The Realist.

Chapter 4

Disneyland

You Want Fries With That Disco Hit?
Nancy Cain

No, I have nothing to say about acid. Well, maybe one thing—no meat for me, thank you. Because long ago I dropped Orange Sunshine at Disneyland and I saw humans eating hamburgers there and it was damned impressive. It was indelible. It was understood. *Arrrgggghhh*! I think kids today wonder what the big deal is about dropping acid, but back in the 20th century, when you let blotter paper dissolve on your tongue, there was a good possibility that you would never return to the world as you knew it. And even if you did come back, you might randomly return to that acid eternity of simultaneous universes upon universes of infinity flashing forever no matter where you are or what you're doing. I can still see it all on the head of a pin if I look carefully. Yep, there it is. That pesky infinity. Kids today may not know about that. Acid is nothing to them.

Yippie Day at Disneyland
Snakebite

Excerpt from CIA files, Unnumbered Memorandum, 19 July, 1970:

Subject: Hippie Action in Los Angeles. 6 August 1970 is the anniversary of the US bombing of Hiroshima. On this date the Hippies plan to "take over Disneyland" and do their thing. The local police and security authorities are watching the situation closely.

David Sacks and friends organized a Yippie invasion of Disneyland on August 6, 1970. The word went out on "underground" FM stations. Organizers mailed more than 100,000 flyers calling for the "First International Yippie Pow Wow," promising a Women's Liberation rally to free Tinker Bell, a pancake breakfast at Aunt Jemima's for the Black Panthers, and more.

We got one of the flyers showing Mickey Mouse waving a machine gun. We were going. Mickey needed us. We loaded up my old Ford Econoline van. It was painted primer brown, with a bunch of windows. We called it *The Brown & Clear* after the amphetamine Dexamil. Seven of us left the "Castle" in Modjeska Canyon singing, "Who's the leader of the club..." Most of us dropped some Orange Sunshine. Yum! The air in the van was green. We'd rolled a whole lid to last the day. "...that's made for you and meee?"

It was only now, 1970, that Disney would allow long-haired freaks into their park, let alone work there. The Disney staff were banned from wearing any facial hair at all (despite old Walt having a mustache). A few years back, a group of us picketed them with signs at their front gate, such as "Disney Is Mickey Mouse About Haircuts" and "Jesus Isn't Allowed Into Disneyland." Who could blame them for caving in to that kind of pressure?

Disney officials and local authorities were freaked out. Their estimates ranged from 20,000 to 200,000 Yippies who might converge at their "Happiest Place on Earth (there were 200 or 300 of us among a crowd of 50,000 "normal" visitors that day). Authorities contacted the National Guard. Riot gear was issued and extra staff were employed. An average work day at the Matterhorn called for 17 or 18 employees. On this day, Disney had 50 on that ride alone.

It was a beautiful summer day full of promise. We arrived as the Sunshine was forcing silly grins on all our faces. "M-I-C-K-E-Y..." What a scene!

We were massively outnumbered, but we were there in style. As the day progressed, more freaks rolled in and rolled up. Security was everywhere, mostly in plainclothes. They tried to look unobtrusive and blend in. Fat chance of that. Disney had a 6-foot minimum height rule for their security guards, and these guys were *not* having fun. Not even close. They looked like Amish folks at a Rastafarian picnic. When we spotted them, we pointed them out to all within earshot. Nervous police from virtually every city in Orange County packed the backstage areas.

Our first ride had to be Adventure Through Inner Space as we started to peak on that acid. We were being shrunk down to molecule size inside the human body. *Oh my gawd*! Do not try this at home. "M-O-U-S-Eeee..."

We needed a drink. Had to tone down that high. The park itself was "dry," so we took the monorail to the Disneyland Hotel for a belt, then returned to the party.

Families were on vacation. Parents were cursing us. "Dirty hippies!" Their kids behind them were flashing peace signs. The daily Disney Parade down Main Street had a few freaks join in chanting, "Ho, Ho, Ho Chi Minh. The Viet Cong Is Gonna Win."

There was rebellion among the ride operators. They thought we were cool. After all, we were a great change of pace from the families from Ohio. Employees at Pirates of the Caribbean let us on for free. They didn't want our "E" coupons. "We're with you," they said. One of them hid in the shadows of the ride and jumped out at us. One of my hallucinating partners screamed and almost fell in the water.

We smoked dope on most of the rides. I remember looking down from the Skyway and blowing smoke toward the plainclothes cops.

Pass the word: There's gonna be a smoke-in on Tom Sawyer's

Island. We're gonna liberate Tom! We board the rafts like George Washington crossing the Delaware.

Somebody made a speech. We smoked a joint in Injun Joe's Cave. Joe would have been proud of us. About 4:30, somebody raised the Viet Cong flag over the Wilderness Fort. *YeeeeeeeeeeHa*! We have staked out our territory.

Meanwhile, back on Main Street, a scuffle about another flag is raised, this one with a big marijuana leaf. It was flying over Town Hall. That didn't sit well with some patriotic visitors and park security. All this time we thought Disney had a sense of humor. We found out how wrong we were when police in riot gear appeared from every back lot in the park. They'd had enough. There were hundreds of cops! Helmets, visors, shields, bulletproof vests and batons, all new. It was surreal.

Imagine Main Street lined with riot police. Helicopters in the air behind them. This was the largest assemblage of police forces to that date in Orange County's history. Disneyland is shutting down! It's only 6 p.m. We hadn't ridden the Matterhorn yet. To usher everyone out, they had to "sweep" the park clockwise from Adventureland. One of our group was an ex-employee who knew their routine, so we stayed ahead of them to prolong the fun. They offered everyone full refunds (we took 'em).

A headline in the *Los Angeles Times* the next day read, "Disneyland Closed 6 Hours Early by Longhair Invasion." (The only other time Disneyland closed early was the day JFK was shot.) Disneyland's ban on long hair was back. See what happens when they relax their standards?

We went to Disneyland that day hopeful, perhaps, that if straights could just see us at play in the park like all the other children—posing no threat and having no violent intent—just maybe our lifestyles might be more accepted and understood a little better. The officials didn't see it that way, but a few people did. As we were leaving, some "citizens" asked us why. "You people weren't doing anything but having fun. Why are they doing this?" For those people, it brought home the message we hoped to impart. If they had watched TV or read that *Times* article, they would have thought differently.

How Uncle Walt Acid-Washed My Brain
Dawna Kaufmann

In the mid-'70s when I was a wide-eyed young hippie, my favorite place to get high was Disneyland, which was a short hop from my Hollywood pad. My then-boyfriend and I would hightail it to Fantasyland, taking the Skyway gondola across the park, a ride just long enough for us to share a doobie in privacy, with only the employees on the Tomorrowland end the wiser. Fortified by our Vitamin M, Rick and I would enjoy the rest of our visit in the theme park that calls itself "The Happiest Place on Earth." Usually, we agreed with that opinion.

Unlike today, when an all-inclusive passport to the park allows you to float from ride to ride unfettered except for long lines of people, in those days the rides had tickets in denominations of A, B, C, D and E—with E being the best. If you wanted more E's, you had to buy them. Our precious big-deal tickets were always earmarked for the Haunted House and the Pirates of the Caribbean, both relatively new and top-of-the-line rides in New Orleans Square.

We certainly never would've squandered an E on Fantasyland's It's a Small World, the "living commercial" for Bank of America in which you rode a track car through rooms of costumed puppets from foreign lands singing the sappy anthem in their native tongues. Knowing the park's layout as well as we did, we would hit all the niftiest spots and, many hours later, head home with tired feet and a pocket of lower-end tickets, grumbling because we couldn't afford to buy additional E's to ride our faves again and again. Or maybe we were just pissed that we'd worn the wrong shoes and the reefer had worn off. Whatever.

We learned that on December 31, there'd be a special celebration. Disneyland would operate as usual until 6 p.m., then close down and empty the park, reopening at 8 p.m. for a New Year's Eve party that would last until 3 a.m. For a fixed price, attendees would be able to ride anything to their heart's content. *This was for us*! But however much the fixed price, it was over our budget.

Still we decided we'd not only find a way in, but would cheer the occasion with LSD we'd received as a Christmas gift. The plan was to go to Disneyland early in the day, pay only the cheapo general admission price (no ride tickets included), find a place to hide for the two hours, take our acid, then come out at 8 p.m. and partay all night into the new year.

Arriving around 4 p.m., we set about finding a hiding place—surely an easy task for habitues such as us. Well, *Bzztt*! When we tried to go behind buildings or rides, we were met with barbedwire fences, attack dogs or armed security guards. There was no secret haven for us on Main Street, in any of the "Lands," near the Swiss Family Treehouse or even on Tom Sawyer's Island.

On yet another pass through Fantasyland, we spied a tiny white gate we hadn't seen before and, desperate, we ran through it, surprised there were no impediments. It led to a grassy knoll directly behind It's a Small World, and under the track for the Mine Train. It was now six o'clock and workers were clearing the park of patrons, so we had no choice but to curl up on the wet grass and hope we wouldn't be spotted.

We dropped the acid and sat under bushes about three feet apart, whispering that soon the horrible Small World music would be turned off, and maybe we could catch a few Z's. But the Spirit of Walt Disney had another plan for us—one as cold as the ice his corpse is allegedly frozen in today.

Turned out the park didn't really close for those two hours. It was designated play time for employees, so they could have their own "free rides party" before working the night shift. The music never ended: "It's a world of laughter/A world of tears/It's a world of hopes/And a world of fears/There's so much that we share/That it's time we're aware/It's a small world after all/It's a small world after all/It's a small world after all/It's a small world after all/It's a small, small world."

In English, Spanish, French, German, Italian, Japanese, Samoan and who knows what else. Repeating and hypnotic. And, for two damp acid-heads, brain-bending and demonic. In fetal positions, with cigarette butts as useless earplugs, we lay there utterly paralyzed. The insidious tune tortured us until, like victims of Stockholm syndrome, we actually began to sing along. The LSD blazed mind pictures that taunted and haunted us, but we couldn't fight back.

To make things worse, the Mine Train whizzed by us regularly, and when employees on it noticed us, they pelted us with soft drinks and ice. Their aim got better with each cycle. I suppose we should've been pleased that they didn't turn us in and have us arrested. Having to go to the underground police station in our stony condition, and risking the chance of seeing Mickey and Minnie Mouse carrying their giant heads in their hands, would have surely caused lifelong trauma.

So for two hours we endured. At eight o'clock, we rose up, brushed the ants and grass off ourselves, sneaked back through the white gate and joined the crowd. We ran to the front of the park to collect our party hats and noisemakers, then scampered to the Skyway for a much-needed joint. The rest of the night was as good as it gets, the ultimate Disneyland experience, and my most memorable acid trip.

Chapter 5

Bummers

Family Values
Steve Parish

It made me remember when I was 16 years old, in 1966, and I was hanging out with a couple of friends, and we get ahold of some real Sandoz acid, with the S on it and everything. So we each take a tab of it, and we go out for the whole day. We're in New York City, and we're tripping around and we start really getting out there.

And so we find this friend of ours who has a car, and we all pile in the car with this guy. Now this guy was bigger than a house, and a madman, and he liked to fight. So we go out with him, and we convinced him somehow—we were crazy, we were all coming on to this Sandoz, a real strong trip—and we convinced him he should drive his car onto a bicycle track.

It's wintertime, and it starts snowing. We're driving this car into this bicycle track—it was a 1958 Chevy Impala—and we drive it on the track and we get it going faster and faster, and the car halfway rolls over onto its side and slides down, because it had been snow-ing, really heavy snow, and it was getting really wet.

So it slides down, and this car is stuck on this track. I open the door—the car is at a deep angle—I'm getting out of the back seat and I push the big heavy door up and it swings back and *boom*, hits me right in the face. I thought I broke my nose or something, it almost knocked me out.

So I get out of there, and I'm okay. The four of us get out of the car, and he starts going, "I'm gonna kill you guys! I'm gonna kill you guys! My car! My car!" So we go out and we find a guy who's driving a wrecker, and we stop him out on the street. We're com-ing on to this acid now really heavy, hallucinating out of our minds, we could barely hold it.

We convince this guy that he's gotta help us get this car. We jump in the wrecker with this straight guy, and it's all hot in there, we're really coming on, we're convincing him to go on further and further into this park, and the guy goes, "I'm not driving in there." He tricks us into getting out, and he leaves us.

By this time, the driver of the car is out of his mind and wants to kill us, so we take him up to this apartment where there was always a party going on—the kid's parents were gone—they're partying and he's going nuts, just talking about how he's gonna kill somebody, and steamin' up the place.

Everybody says, "You gotta get this guy outta here."

I can't deal with it and I leave. I go to my house where my mother lives, and I think I can just put this trip away right now—I was totally peaking—I'm just gonna forget about this whole nightmare. So I go in there, my mother is watching Johnny Carson. I sit down and I try to be just as normal as I can be.

I go, "Yeah, I was just hanging out with the guys, I'm gonna go to sleep now."

I almost had it, trying to maintain, and I glance at the TV out of the corner of my eye, and there was Johnny Carson, and he looked as small as Charlie McCarthy—remember, the ventriloquist's dummy—and he was sitting on the table with his legs crossed, in a really strange manner, talking to whoever he was interviewing, and I thought, no, I didn't see it like that, he didn't look like a midget, and the person he was talking to was normal size.

I looked again, my God, it was the strongest hallucination I've ever had—he was *tiny*—and so I start getting really weird. I say, "I'm going to bed," so I get in bed, pull the covers over my head. There was a radio that I had right by the bed there. Well, man, it's playing just as loud and clear as I could ever hear it, and I kept reaching for the knob, and the knob was turned off. I was having the strongest visual and auditory hallucinations.

I got up and walked into where my mother was and I said, "Mom, I've taken LSD, and I'm really having a strong time with it, I need to talk to you." Well, she starts coming unglued, *screaming*: "You're crazy! You've ruined yourself! You're never coming down!" She ran downstairs and for some reason comes up with bread and water, and starts trying to feed me this loaf of bread.

I said, "Why are you doing this?"

She goes, "Because I've heard that it'll make you come down, it'll bring you down to your senses."

So I just bolted. I just put my clothes on and ran out into the night and ended up walking it off.

Beginning to See the Light
Stephen Naron

A square, a square-inch of paper, dipped into a mixture of rat poison and anything else a fucked-up acid manufacturer wants to throw in. Me, a well-educated high school student knowing well that if I placed this piece of paper in my mouth, it would be either the most tremendous explosion of brain-cell-flying psychedelic visions not unlike those of the prophets of Israel in the desert of Sinai (false prophets, that is), or a suicidal death bringing paranoia. There I sat on my bed staring at the members of Devo Dance, an electric jigaloo on MTV. What kind of freak makes these videos, anyway?

I leaned back against my stuffed Bob Dobbs that I made in Home Ec class in 7th grade. I looked at him, his handsome face, his eloquent pipe. Who really was this guy, anyway? I own every book I can find on Bob and the Church of the SubGenius. I've paid my dues. I've passed on a well-watered-down but informative, unexplainable explanation to fellow Conspiracy haters, and I still only have a small inkling as to the personality of my superdupersavior.

Maybe that's the attraction—you know this guy, he's your savior, you like him, you do and believe what he says, but you don't really know who he is and you want to. But I guess if he was giving out his address to everybody, people would be busting down his door and kissing ass. And I don't like ass-kissing. I like respect. I'd rather just share a brew with him or shoot him, something like that.

I glanced at the acid in my palm and popped it in my mouth. I felt it dissolve on my tongue. It's better to regret something you have done than to regret something you haven't done. I lay there for 40 minutes, wondering what it would be like, if I'd lose my shit and scrape my eyeballs out with a toothbrush or not.

It came on slow at first. Lights seemed bright and I felt kinda funky. Then boom! I was screwed. My body caved in and became a puddle of flesh on my bed. I grinned a perma-smile and thought, this is nice. I put on some tunes, quiet, hands shaking. The volume knob was on 1, but the music pounded away in my head.

The Velvet Underground, slammin' away on the guitar, Lou Reed, singin' in his usual dire tone. I knew every word, pulled out the air Stratocaster and jammed with Lou and the band. I was there on stage, people were cheerin', I was dancin' all over the place. All right, these shenanigans lasted for three hours and when I was done, let me tell you, I was plumb tuckered out, 2 o'clock in the morning, time to crash and crash hard.

I curled up in my warm comforter and closed my eyes. Why can't I sleep? I flipped and flopped. What if I trip forever? Never come down. What if my parents find out? Fuck my parents. That's kind of trivial compared to an eternal existence of strange paranoid delusions. The minutes that I awaited slumber seemed like hours. I ran to the bathroom. My face looked all wet and distorted in the mirror.

Down the stairs into the hallway of my parents' room, the pictures on the wall were talking: "You're gonna burn, die, die, die—*Bob* can't help, you know, asshole!" Tears dripped from my eyes. I slipped into my parents' bed. I grabbed my dad's back in fear. He shrugged me off, as in saying, "I don't care if you're wiggin' out, I gotta go to work tomorrow." The pictures were right. I am gonna die.

I went up the stairs to my room. When would it end? Patterns and patterns flew over my head. I turned on the TV. It was Dave Letterman, my late-night friend. Make me laugh, Dave. Please be a show on how to relax on scary LSD trips. No such luck.

"Tonight's guest is Gene Shanagelman, horror effects specialist."

"Hello, Dave," Gene said.

"So, Gene, what are you gonna do for us first?"

"Well, I thought I'd show you the exploding head of Arnold Palmer from *The Night of the Bleeding Head*."

I don't need this. I turned off the tube and leaned back. Goodbye, cruel world, I'm leaving you today, goodbye, goodbye. I reached for anything sharp to slit my wrists. Darkness engulfed me. Fear reached its ultimate intensity, and that's when I smelled it, an aroma, I've smelled it before in my dreams, not marijuana, not tobacco, something strange. A thin pipe parted my lips, its flavor perked my senses, a euphoric feeling came over me. My vision blurred, but a face smiled warmly at me, something gripped between its teeth, its strong hand on my shoulder.

"Bob, is that you?"

"Sshhh, go to sleep now. I hope you've learned your lesson, my friend. Slack be with you!" My eyes became heavy. I heard a loud thud—"Ow, shit!"—and he disappeared into the void of my room.

"Goodnight, Bob."

With that I drifted into happy slumber. I awoke the next morning sore all over. Was it all a drugged-out hallucination, or did I really smoke a bowl with Bob? I never dropped acid again. I recommend a much better drug, that will get you just as high. Get addicted to *Bob*. It's the greatest thing you'll ever try.

Smoking Brains
John Berndt

I met Rich in Baltimore during the summer of 1985. It was hot, and I was hallucinating, because I had just given blood, was very tired, and had taken some LSD. Rich was a tall, scruffy, junkie punk from Tennessee who lived in the apartment next to a friend of mine. I met him sitting on the roof, talking into a portable tape recorder, recording his own voice—which was quite soft, but intense—and then playing it back, and lip-synching to it. This interested me, as it was the only talking he seemed willing to do—communicating by playing back this tape while looking at you, and moving his lips.

I ended up in Rich's apartment, which was filled with cats but was otherwise almost empty. He played loud psychedelic music, and kept looking at me and dilating his eyes. When I began to act disturbed, he did "werewolf" impersonations for me, which evolved into somehow altering the bones in his hands and face. Also, he told me that he used to eat a lot of magic mushrooms and then climb apartment building exteriors at night. Finally, he opened a cabinet behind a bunch of speakers in his room and showed me his collection of skulls which he had dug up from an all-black cemetery, most of which were bloody and fleshy. I left.

The next morning, I naturally assumed that I had hallucinated everything. I went back to the site, this time unintoxicated, met Rich again, and found that I had hallucinated nothing. Rich showed me how he took the rotting brains out of the skulls and used them to cut marijuana he was selling to the punks in Baltimore. I watched him smoke human brains; he offered me some, but I declined, remembering the disease that cannibals get from eating brains. This is apparently ongoing, and I have heard from friends still living in Baltimore that he excavated a corpse from the graveyard and has it on his couch. I'm not sure if its brains are intact.

Farewell to Normality
Wentworth Scrogging III

It was the summer after my freshman year of college. I was in a smelly dormitory room on the campus of a prominent Southern university. It was the mid-1970s, which was actually still the '60s because it took a few years for the '60s to reach the South.

Someone had given me a couple of hits of acid. I took one and waited, with some trepidation, for about half an hour. Nothing happened, so I took the other one. A friend came over and played guitar for a while. Things were starting to be slightly strange. I told him I'd taken two hits, and he said, "Uh-oh." I wondered, "Does that mean something *bad* is going to happen? Like maybe I should've only taken one?"

I went outside and encountered a tree in the courtyard. This was by far the most three-dimensional tree I'd ever seen in my life. It was very cartoon-like. The trunk was right in my face, right out in front of everything, like in a View-Master slide.

Then I sat in the courtyard and read a Zen koan—this seemed like the type of thing a person should do on LSD. I picked the first one from *The Gateless Gate*. It was something like, "Why did the master reply 'Mu' (meaning 'No') when asked whether or not a dog has the Buddha-nature?" That was a tough one. You would expect Buddhism to teach that all beings, even dogs, have the Buddha-nature. The book went on to say that you shouldn't take the word "Mu" as a negative answer to the question, but I didn't know how else to take it.

Each word burned right off the page and into my eyes, into my brain. The book said this question was the main barrier to enlightenment, and that to pass this barrier, every bone in my body, every pore in my skin, would have to be filled with "Mu." It said "Mu" should be like a red-hot ball of iron caught in my throat, so that I could neither swallow it nor spit it out, and it definitely was.

I knew if I could solve this problem I would become enlightened, but how? I struggled with it for a long time until finally, suddenly, the answer came to me. (I forget what it was—sorry.) I read the next few koans and these were transparent to me—the answers came instantly and seemed undeniably correct. Yes, I thought, maybe I *am* enlightened.

Then I looked up. I was in the middle of a large courtyard, surrounded by wonderfully picturesque Gothic buildings with gargoyles and upward-pointing spires and intricate details everywhere. Suddenly I noticed that the buildings were all starting to sway—everything was moving, with alternate layers of bricks going in different directions.

The swaying became more intense, until finally the buildings began violently shaking and crumbling, accompanied by extremely realistic sound effects. (This was a lot more convincing than those stupid simulations they have in museums, where you stand on the moving platform and pretend you're in an earthquake.)

The earthquake subsided. I got up and walked into the next courtyard and had an encounter with another tree. This one had big slick plastic leaves and bizarre-looking cone-like pods. (A magnolia?) I found it very frightening and sexually threatening. I began to think maybe I was having one of those bad trips I'd read about.

Then I had to walk across an overpass to get to a building where my girlfriend lived. I knew there was this big thing about how people who eat LSD were supposed to jump off of bridges and out of windows, so I proceeded very cautiously, reminding myself, "Don't jump. Don't jump."

Finally I made it to the other side, and I got to my girlfriend's dorm and told her about taking two hits and everything. She was really worried and told the dorm-mother and dorm-father, and they were really worried and thought I should go to Student Health. Instead of just assuring me that everything would be okay, they were all running around and panicking like they were on drugs or something. I felt like telling them, "Don't worry, everything will be all right," but I figured if they were panicking maybe I should panic too, so I did.

"You don't think they'll arrest me, do you?" I asked. They weren't sure. We went to Student Health, where I got to answer questions like, "How many of the tablets did you take?" and "What did the tablets look like?" The whole thing was very surreal. It was like getting stoned and going to the mall—you can tell you're not in the real world because everything is just a little too bright and shiny.

For some reason, I was terrified to have my girlfriend leave the room—I felt like a baby being abandoned by its mother. I asked if she could stay. Needless to say, she was very embarrassed by the whole thing. (She broke up with me the next day.)

Then the doctor came in. He was a nice guy, very professional and concerned, but a little hard to look at on acid. His nickname, I later learned, was "Lumpy." His face was covered with *huge*, horrible, globular, cancerous-looking growths, protruding from his forehead, his cheeks, his chin, his nose. I didn't know what they were, but I imagine they would have been frightening even under the best of circumstances, which these weren't. Under the influence of the drug, these facial imperfections were magnified to approximately a million times their usual size.

Lumpy insisted on injecting me with Thorazine. He stuck an enormous needle in my ass and told me I'd be normal soon. (He never asked whether I *wanted* to be normal.)

People took me back to the dorm. I sat outside for a while and played with a dog which had very electric-looking hair. I don't know whether the dog had the Buddha-nature or not, but I think maybe it did.

I was finally starting to enjoy the acid, but then the Thorazine began to kick in, and it was a real bitch. What a shitty drug! I was still tripping my brains out, but now I couldn't even sit up without fainting. I had to stay on my back for the next several hours. Everything seemed foggy and slow-motion.

The first part of the trip had been intense, and scary at times—I can't say it was a whole lot of fun—but this Thorazine stuff was a real bummer. I had no idea that being normal was such a drag. Fortunately it wore off the next day, and I've never been normal since.

The Needle Prick
Dead Joe Jones

It was '71 or '72 and I was a 16- or 17-year-old sprout who had run away from home and found myself in Washington DC's P Street Park for a free concert, where John Lennon was rumored to appear. I had an excellent herb buzz going when I was approached by a glassy-eyed gent with a baggie filled with little purple pills, which he was offering for a buck apiece.

I had a portrait of Lincoln in my pocket so I sez, "I'll take five." He handed them to me and I quickly gobbled them down. He sez, "You must be able to handle a lot." Cocky me replies, "All you can dish out." Reaching into his baggie, he said, "Open your mouth." I did, and he placed six or seven more of the little tabs 'pon my tongue, I swallowed and said, "Thanks." He said, "Good luck," and wandered off.

I was over by the stage, just getting into the music and starting to feel the acid come on, when the emcee delivered the news that Lennon wouldn't be showing after all and, "Oh, yeah, while I'm up here and have your attention, beware the purple acid, it is way too strong and may or may not be cut with belladonna."

First thing through my head is, "Oh, fuck, remember, the name of the game is maintain."

I forgot, went searching for my friend and found her by the creek. I told her that I had just eaten a mess of the purple stuff and, "I'd sure appreciate you trying to get us somewhere safe." She sez, "Let's head for the hostel." We hadn't walked more than a block before I was assailed by a vision of Chinese men and dragons everywhere I looked. Then I lost consciousness altogether.

I later found myself hovering over a group of people crowded around a body lying on the sofa. They were jabbering concernedly over whether the body was going to make it as its heart had just stopped beating. I realized at that moment that it was me lying on the couch and that I needed to get back there pretty soon. About that time one of the people sez, "Let me shoot it up with this speed and see if that doesn't bring it around."

I felt the needle prick and was bolt upright and freaking complete, there were people there from all different periods of history, and all I knew was that I had to get out fast. Told them I had to go for a walk. They tried to discourage me with, "It's late and we are in downtown DC, and if you go out the gangs will get you for sure."

I was still nonplussed and hearing none of it. As I exited the building I ran into... well, it was the Pope, or at least someone done up in pontiff drag. At any rate, he blessed me and I wandered off down the street headed for the Potomac Bridge. I had walked well into Virginia when a car full of Navy Seals pulled over and the driver got out and said, "Hey, there, fella, don't you know the cops will bust you for walking on the freeway in Virginia?"

I said, "No, but I've been walking for hours now and I didn't think anyone could see me, seeing as how I was dead and all."

He said, "You ain't dead, you just look like it. Get in."

I got in and rode about 60 miles with them, all the while discussing Martin Buber. They dropped me off at a truck-stop outside of Richmond. As I got out of the car, the driver asked me if I had any money. I said, "No," so he gives me a twenty and sez, "Take care now."

Well, I go into the truck-stop and I mean everybody in the joint stopped what they were doing to stare at me. I went to the counter and ordered a coffee-to-go and asked the waitress where the restroom was. She told me and I went there and looked at myself in the mirror. It was horrid. No wonder they were staring. I went back to the counter and paid for the coffee and left.

As I was leaving, the waitress sez, "Honey, I don't know where you come from or where you're going, but looking like you do, I wouldn't get near no people, they're likely to kill you."

I said, "Don't worry, I just checked in the bathroom, I'm already dead."

Before I could walk to the on-ramp, I was offered a ride by an old farmer who said he could get me to a better spot.

Several rides and the better part of a twisted day later, I found myself at a church in Virginia Beach. I told the padre my problem, he checked my pulse and said I didn't have one, that I had better lie down and rest while he meditated on my situation.

I lay down and fell asleep. When I awoke, I felt a little weird but fine. The priest told me that he had got the skinny on me and had contacted my mother, who had arranged for me to be flown back to Shreveport and directly into the hospital for uncontrollable loons.

Megabummer
Dennis Eichhorn

I had a megabummer back in 1974 when I was living in Moscow, Idaho. I was married with no kids and worked as an ID checker and bouncer at the Garden Lounge, a busy whiskey bar in the Moscow Hotel. I was a graduate (BA in sociology, 1968) of the University of Idaho and a former member of the varsity football team, and I liked getting stoned. A lot. And I dealt drugs (grass, acid, mescaline, peyote, hashish, psilocybin—all the nice stuff that used to be popular before speed, PCP, cocaine and heroin took over the fledgling drug culture) to supplement my meager income, while my wife worked as a lab technician for the university dairy.

Anyway, one afternoon I decided to drop acid for maybe the 200th time. I swallowed a couple of purple microdots and sat around a while in the living room of our rented house while it came on, listening to recorded music and smoking pot until my nose got numb and I began to hallucinate mildly. Then I decided to take a walk and get out among 'em. I went downtown and chanced upon some friends. They had just rented a "snake," one of those articulated devices used to unclog drains, and they were on their way home to root out a section of their plumbing that was plugged. I went along to help for no particular reason.

At their house we went into the basement and started working on a clogged pipe that led into a sump. I got into the mechanics of the operation and wound up doing most of the work. I was bent

over with my face close to the drain when the plug of shit and hair
in the pipe broke loose, spewing a geyser of scum all over my head
and shoulders. I was drenched with stinking crap, and my nose,
eyes and mouth were filled with filth. This happened while I was
beginning to peak on the acid, so I gave the incident a great deal
of thought.

I was gagging and spitting and trying to wipe myself clean
when the upstairs phone rang. Even though I'd only been in the
house once before, and that was months earlier, the call was for
me. One of my wife's friends had been frantically phoning all over
Moscow, trying to locate me. My wife had taken ill and been
rushed to the hospital in Pullman, Washington, just across the state
line. Her life was in danger. I was to go there at once.

Things were beginning to get out of control. I was hearing
satanic laughter and seeing strange little critters in nooks and cran-
nies. I borrowed a car and sped the eight or ten miles to the Pullman hospital, found my wife's room, and went to her bedside. She
was all doped up with tubes in her arms and nostrils. "They
removed one of my ovaries," she croaked. "I had a tubular preg-
nancy that ruptured. Promise me that you'll never leave me." We'd
been quarreling a lot and talking about divorce in recent weeks,
but of course I promised, even though I knew it was a lie the
moment I said it.

It was nearly six o'clock, time for my evening stint at the Garden
Lounge. I was still buzzed, but I drove back to Moscow and reported for work, reeking of *eau d'excrement*. I had a couple of Groupie
Specials (Chivas Regal and Coca-Cola, the drink that the Beatles
made famous in their early years) to dull the acid's edge, and settled in near the front door to check the ages of the hordes of students flocking to Moscow's trendiest watering hole.

I was disoriented and plenty worried about how we were going
to pay my wife's hospital bill, assuming she lived, but my shift was
going fairly smoothly. I could tell I was still stoned because the customers all looked very bizarre to me, like characters from the
Satyricon film. Then came the word from a barmaid: a group of
underage students had snuck into the downstairs room through
the back door.

This frequently happened, and as usual I went downstairs and
checked for their nonexistent IDs and then asked them to leave.
Normally that was all it took, but this time one of the young studs
took exception. He looked and acted like a freshman football player, probably from Washington State University in Pullman. His
friends slunk out, but he wouldn't take no for an answer and followed me upstairs to carry on a high-volume argument.

I didn't know what to do with the guy. He was bigger than I

and in tremendous physical condition, plus he was well-wired on booze and drugs. The longer I talked with him and tried to calm him down, the more he reminded me of someone. But who? I couldn't quite pin it down. Then it hit me: he reminded me of myself 10 years before, when I wasn't old enough to drink legally. I was arguing with a younger, potentially more hostile version of me. I remembered all the crazy ultraviolent things I'd done, the many bartenders and bouncers I'd beaten senseless in my formative years before I'd discovered drugs.

I wanted to reason with my younger self, tell him not to go off half-cocked and fuck things up. I also wanted to somehow get my younger self out the door before he killed me. And I kept thinking about my sewage shower and the tubes in my wife's nose. I didn't know what to do. I started to lose it. My knees began to quiver. That had never happened to me before. For the first time in my life I wasn't sure of my prowess in a one-on-one situation. There was still plenty of LSD in my system, and I was hallucinating my features onto my younger self's face. I was frightened—scared to the core. Afraid of myself. That's a horrible feeling.

A barmaid named Katie had been watching my plight. She knew how to handle my younger self. Katie stepped over and put a soft hand on his wrist and told him, "You just can't stay here without any ID. You'd better go before the police come. Come back when you're old enough and I'll buy you a pitcher of beer." That did it. I'd been saying the same things, but she could get away with it. My younger self would never punch out a petite, attractive woman who was smiling gently into his eyes, especially if there was a chance he might get to fuck her sometime.

So he left. And I had eight or 10 more Groupie Specials to calm my shattered nerves. The aftereffects of that trip lingered for a long time. I quit my job a few days later, and within months my wife and I were divorced. It was a real bummer.

Havasu High
Kenneth Lawrence

In 1971, Ferg, Jack, and I were studying theology just north of U.C., at the Graduate Theological Union in Berserkely, as we called it then. Free Speech, Mario Savio, Angela Davis, People's Park, ROTC, SDS, Black Panther Party... tear gas, police riots, Alameda County Sheriffs spraying pepper gas from police units racing along Telegraph Avenue.

We'd been steeped in Eldridge Cleaver, Martin Luther King, Kierkegaard, Tillich. What did God have to do with all of this? Where was God, anyway? What was God? Was it all an anthropomorphic illusion? I was doing my thesis on Robinson Jeffers, who said basically, chuck it all and go back to nature. The planet's never wrong.

But we managed to see God most every night, especially after Jon Herganruther came back from his Peace Corps stint with 14 pounds of hash strapped to the inside of his thighs. We were more restrained around LSD, having volunteered at a Fort Help outpost treating acid-heads who shuffled, lurched, mumbled, and drooled their way on and off campus.

Joel Fort, MD, savior of the psychedelically lost, enlisted people like us to counsel burnouts, some with toxic psychosis from bad acid laced with stuff like Strychnine and Drano. So we didn't particularly want to go there. A permanent, paranoid, cognitive funk was not my idea of a good time. And even though my roomie in our pad on Shattuck Avenue was working his way through his Ph.D. in biochemistry by making inorganic mescaline in a UC-Berkeley lab, hallucinogenics generally took a back seat to major papers, reading, and putting together a workable thesis.

It was April, and we'd had enough Reagan, Nixon, riots, and the feeling—as Steve Stills of Buffalo Springfield sang in "For What It's Worth"—that "There's something happening here... what it is ain't exactly clear..." We had to clear out, get some space, connect to the land again.

So we loaded up our backpacks and gear in my 1951 green Chevy panel truck, enlisted Sig and Gordy, and roared off on a Sunday morning for Paradise: Havasu Canyon, on the Havasupai Indian Reservation, near Peach Springs, Arizona, 24 hours away. Shadowfax, my truck, was named after Gandalf's trusty steed in Tolkien's *Hobbit*, and despite rusted floorboards so bad you could see the asphalt, it had a strong, big six-cylinder engine and plenty of room for us all.

My brand new Channel Master cassette deck, mounted under my seat, blasted out Hendrix, Dylan, the Dead, and Jefferson Airplane, while we smoked doobie after doobie through the night, trading driving stints and bumping the driver awake from the passenger side. At about 8 a.m., we rumbled up to the edge of the rim of Havasu Canyon, strapped on our packs, and lurched down the trail in the cool morning air, marveling at rimrock and shadows, colors in tone of blues and burnt sienna and yellow ochre, Maxfield Parish in desert paint.

Seven miles down, we stripped and lay face down in cool Havasu creek, rushing on its way down to the Colorado some 13 miles distant. Once refreshed, we hustled on to the reservation store, paid our fees, noted carefully the grim poverty of the locals, and headed down toward camping spots near Havasu and Mooney falls, the garden spot, the oasis. Havasu Canyon is breathtakingly beautiful, with the river shoring up into circular travertine mineral deposits.

From a distance, it looks like an endless series of hot tubs brimming with smoky turquoise water, like Southwest Indian jewels spread along the canyon floor. We frolicked nude and cavorted and joked and laughed and drank tequila and smoked along with the other trekkers, checking out the females just like good little graduate students in theology should do. Jesus would have loved our asses.

In a couple of days, we had to fill our adventure bags with something more, so Ferg, Jack, Gordy, and I decided to pack up enough camp gear and food to sustain us, and march down to the mighty Colorado, 10 miles downstream. Sig stayed to watch the camp. We arrived in late afternoon, and Gordy, a young 19-year-old unknown to me, an acquaintance of Ferg's, came down onto a large sandbar on the Colorado, right at the confluence, a tiny stream of water by that time, the stream's entry.

Across the great river, and up and down from where we bedded down, 2,000-foot sheer cliffs blocked the sky, and a bench about 40 feet high back from our sandbar. We ate dinner, and I soon realized that the only thing Gordy and I had in common was our height—about 6'6", both thin and strong. For lack of discussion, we soon drifted toward a deep sleep, the rushing river our lullaby, a thin slice of starlight cut in a narrow, brightly-ribboned swath above us.

Much later, I woke to distinct gurgling, and in a half-dream reached out with my right arm—into water! And rising fast. I literally jumped out of my bag, rolled onto Gordy, and yelled, "Gordy—get up!—the river's *on us*!" I'll never forget this kid's reaction: totally freaked out, he let out a seven-cycle scream: "*Eee-Yaa-Eee-Yaa-Eee-Yaa-Eee*!" I hit him twice—short, hard slaps to both sides of his face.

I was throwing my boots and clothes and sleeping bag into my backpack and slinging them over my shoulder, wading forward in knee-deep, rushing water, while yelling at Gordy to hurry. I waded toward the sheer rock wall leading up to the bench. It got deeper until, right at the wall, Gordy frantic and afraid beside me—trying to calm him in the middle of my own sheer panic—the water swirled and roared right up to our necks.

Then, like monkeys in the dim starlight, we scaled that wall like it was simple, rocketed by adrenaline, finding handholds and tiny ridges that weren't even there—suddenly up on top, astounded that we had not died.

I made a fire and watched the water rise another 15 feet. Glen Canyon dam engineers, we found out later, like to release at night. We might have been washed all the way to Lake Mead, 20 miles downstream, bloated cadavers bashed beyond recognition by rapids and boulders. Gordy couldn't handle it. He bitched constantly about being wet and cold. At 26, by contrast, I'd been through many scrapes and learned that it's all part of the topography. Shit-hole the rest, and look for the good. His griping began to drive me into a depression, which I resisted as I tried to doze.

At first light, still miserable and cold, but resolute, I packed my gear and headed up the trail toward camp. Goddamn it, no sour-puss kid or trial by water was going to spoil my party! Then, I remembered the hit of LSD in my pocket, fished it out of the plastic baggie, and washed it down with a swig of water. I'd survived, and I was going to find a place way off the "dead center" Ken Kesey described, that zero place where you're stuck in your perceptions and emotions, where your acculturated expectations nail you and your creativity down.

This was an initiation journey, no doubt about it. I could feel it. It was going to get good. About 40 minutes up the trail, this subtle, growing lift came on, and my body began to tingle. The sun lit up the high peaks and canyon walls above the Colorado, glowing reds and incandescent yellow, with patterns of stark black shadows serrated against a cobalt blue sky. I was sure of it: I was going to have a perceptual orgasm.

The day moon, floating above the far canyon walls, looked like an ivory button that I could just reach out and get, to fasten on my shirt. And the stream began to talk to me. I'd get down on all fours to study a tiny rivulet at length, or examine a frosty twig of sage, enraptured by its incredible beauty.

As I rounded another corner on the trail, I stared into a large cave cut into the rock, obviously part of the extensive silver mining that went on down there in the 1870s. I mean, the cave was really black. Inscrutable. I was drawn into that hole, and imagined it was really a black hole in the universe, and it was going to suck me up and spit me out into another dimension, mashed into a thin, long line. Minutes passed.

Suddenly, incredibly, two creatures slowly walked out of the blackness toward me with eyes like fractured dinner plates, set on red placemats. They were dirty, trembling, vacant. The Nobody Home look I'd seen before in Berkeley. Part of the rock. I answered their stares with, "I just about drowned on the Colorado back there, and I dropped acid about an hour ago."

They both smiled and relaxed. "Far out," the taller one added. "We've been on peyote for the past two weeks straight."

They hadn't eaten anything in three days. I gave them a candy bar, which they inhaled. Then I went on. Those two might still be there, ancient miners in the cave of Altered Consciousness.

Another hour passed, while I tripped on the warming heat of the morning, cactus, bugs, tiny fish, spiderwebs. A cornucopia of visual delights. I even slogged into the stream itself, wanting to merge with the stream, loving the cool wash on my ankles and legs. Then I heard it: "*Here, Kitty, Kitty, Kitty! Here, Kitty, Kitty, Kitty*!" The call was desperate, insistent, pained, on the verge of panic. I thought, "Okay—auditory hallucinations. Part of the topography of acid."

I rounded another corner and, after I trudged up the trail to the stream, came face to face with a middle-aged woman in a wispy, long red dress, a ridiculous flowered sunhat, and black heels. She immediately grabbed me by the front of my shirt and screamed, "*Have you seen my cat*?" The tears gushed, the mascara ran, the lipstick smeared in a grotesque, manic mask. "*Oh, my God! You've got to help me find my little kitty*!"

I couldn't even answer. I was stuck in a psychedelic rapture, just trying desperately to sort it out. Was this real? It couldn't be. Even in the most acetic of sober roll calls, this perception could not pass muster. My mouth just hung open.

"Oh, my God," she said, "I've scared you, haven't I? My guide just left me. *Just left me*!"

I was having great difficulty tracking the enormity of such an improbable happening on my mystical journey. Was she another gatekeeper, another sign in the wilderness for me? This woman, in her summer city best, had come down by mule and guide 15 miles through a demanding and harsh desert canyon—carrying a *cat*, for God's sake—which, predictably, had escaped from her almost immediately when she stopped and got off her mule.

I explained that I couldn't stop to help her, I was sorry, and after a very cursory look around, said I had to go. She wailed some more. I imagined her feline would soon be lunch or dinner for a fox or bobcat, and paused a moment to picture, in a vivid lysergic-acid moment, a wild animal eviscerating her tabby. I thought I could feel blood dripping from my mouth and the taste of fur. It was time to move on.

Another two miles, and I stopped in the growing heat to fill a canteen with water and purifiers, then headed for what appeared to be a long, canopied set of overarching desert eucalyptus, so that a vortex some 300 yards away poured out the silently moving Havasu toward me. It seemed endless, a slick tunnel of moving liquid, shining like a gaseous cloud, a pipe into the Earth without up, down or escape. A Chiaroscuro-like landscape, the river of Death. I was moving upstream seemingly without will, caught in what I suddenly imagined was a human vein. Then, suddenly, I was in a different place, in some intergalactic dimension, light-years away, sliding up a current of green, now purple froth, with some inscrutable, opaque, luminescent ceiling pulling me along. I just... gave in to it.

At the end of this mysterious funnel into the underworld, as I finally decided it was, I could just barely make out a figure standing in the water by a tree limb broken down into the stream. And as I neared, I discerned yet another apparition: a short, long-haired, scraggly figure in a worn Hell's Angels jacket, torn jeans, and one arm. Surely, I had left the planet for good.

I stopped dead in my tracks about 40 yards away, studying. Then, with no apparent threat, moved forward. I could see now missing teeth, a scarred, oddly-misshapen skull from which stared a fixed, milky-pale glass eye. So here it was. The Demonic, the Antichrist, ready to devour me. I might as well just offer myself up. Then the thing spoke, when I was about 10 feet away.

The thing said, "Hey, man, how's it goin'? You look like you're up on somethin' man. Come on over and sit here on this branch with me."

I relaxed as much as I could, complied, but fully believed an arm would come popping out of his empty leather sleeve, a sawed-off shotgun or a long knife surfacing from under the jacket. By now, I could barely hear him. My paranoia so removed me from the scene that it seemed as if he were speaking to me from the other side of the universe, in echoes.

He pulled out a can of Schlitz from his pocket, popped it, and offered me a swig, talking about his work as a male nurse at the reservation. Another guide on the journey, after all? We talked about last night's little surprise on the Colorado, his motorcycle accident 10 years ago, and as I relaxed, I could talk and hear more. Then, as we parted, I had the distinct impression that we hadn't really talked at all, it was telepathy. Another arcane movie clip of the absurd. Was he real? Was he not? Does it make any difference?

I had somehow come to the conclusion that there was something terribly, deeply tragic about it all, and although I couldn't account for this feeling, I began to cry. I cried for the Cat Woman and the Hell's Angels Nurse, for the Peyote Pals, for Gordy, the sorry nature of society, Vietnam, for me, for the rocks and the trees, all of it. And just as suddenly, my innards churning and uncontrollable, I broke into uproarious laughter, almost falling down. The whole thing. Funny, pitiful, weird.

I gathered myself together for the last two miles, trudged into camp laughing and then sobbing, pouring out a stream-of-consciousness version of the events of my bizarre day, explaining I'd dropped acid. After an hour of Sig listening and supporting, pouring me some hot tea, I went to my tent in total exhaustion and zipped up the door. Still unable to close my eyes for any time, the images spinning, I just sat and zoned. After some time, I heard voices and Ferguson, my good friend, outside my tent.

"Hey, Kenneth! Open Up! I've got something for you."

Without saying a word, I unzipped the tent and he flipped a tarantula in, the size of a large fist. It landed just in front of me, brown and furry and terrible, flexing its legs. I thought immediately it would jump down my throat and eat me from the inside out. Then, in yet another twisted image which I truly believed, it *was* inside me, biting and clawing its way through my vital innards. Outside, I heard laughing, then silence.

"Hey—what's going on in there? Do you like your new pet?"

I just stared at the thing. I was too frozen with fear to react. As I watched, the tarantula magnified up into a huge, fantastic alien creature standing tall outside the campsite, over my tent. I was literally paralyzed, a breathless, quivering turd nailed to the ground of being I had studied so much about. I let out a muffled gurgle, all I could manage.

Then, inexplicably, I did something out of sheer self-preservation: I picked the damn thing up and flipped it out of the tent. Sig had told Ferg about my trip, and he profusely apologized, at the same time telling me that tarantulas are mainly very safe, can't bite you without great difficulty. Small comfort.

Hours later, I came off the LSD, still trying to integrate my experiences, my journey, trying to sort it all out. What the LSD did was to help bust up my comfortable set of expectations about reality, trying to control what was on my path. There are great teachings in such experiences, and I think you do not so much learn, but are "learned" by the path taken, and all of the unpredictable events from which meanings must be gleaned.

I had drunk deep from the cup of psychedelic insights. I had been initiated, and I realized that the journey was not simple or easy, but a mysterious blessing given to the heart of an innocent pilgrim in order that he might grow and study and, sometimes, maybe even understand.

Phantasmagoria
Ryan Redfield

The first time I tripped on acid was near the end of my freshman year in college. After my having suffered depression for most of the year, my friend wanted to make me "happy." I had wanted to try acid for quite some time, and it is a rarity for our little college town, being there only once or twice a year and disappearing as soon as it gets there, so I jumped on the chance and bought two hits.

After dropping the first hit, I rode to the park in my friend's convertible, and watched the sunset over the river. A beautiful way to start off a trip if you ever get a chance. I had a camera along, and was snapping pictures the whole time, although the pictures didn't show the entire beauty I had seen that night.

I spent the rest of the night in and around the dorm. I was walking down the hallway and my Resident Advisor came up to me. "Ryan, do you have any milk?"

I said, "No, I don't have any mealk."

"Did you say mealk?"

"Sure," I said, and patted him on the back, laughing to myself.

My friend asked me where I was. So I told him give me an hour. I went to my computer to start typing, and looked through my thesaurus, under hallucination. I came back a few minutes later with a sheet in my hand. He read the single paragraph: "I name this place, Phantasmagoria." With smiles on our faces, we both knew, this name was very fitting. So please, come join me in Phantasmagoria.

Blessing in Disguise
Rico Vaselino

I can't remember how long the tab of acid had been in my wallet, but I'm sure it was long past the expiration date. Normally I'm the kind of person who won't even buy a Twinkie if it's within two years of its "best if consumed before this date" notice, but when it comes to dangerous psychoactive substances that could possibly cause permanent mental discombobulation I naturally throw caution to the wind because when the government tells me not to do something I feel that it's my patriotic duty to immediately go out and do it.

Let's face it, if our founding fathers hadn't had that attitude, then the United States wouldn't have even come into existence. It's like someone once said, "If flags weren't meant to be burned, then they wouldn't be made in China."

My trip started out innocently enough when my roommate, partner, significant other, girlfriend, honey, sweetie-pie, cohabitant, wife-to-be—my whatever—and I decided to stay at home, take it easy and drop that strange little pill that I'd gotten from a previous whatever who swore that it was some of the best acid she'd ever had. So we chopped it in two, happily swallowed it and, sure enough, after a couple of hours had passed, nothing happened. Being good citizens we brushed our teeth and went to bed.

It must have been about two in the morning when I woke up. I sensed there was something amiss when I heard myself say in a voice not unlike Wolfman Jack's during a bout with terminal laryngitis, "Honey, would you put on your high heels and tap-dance on my head for a couple of hours?" My whatever was singularly unimpressed with my strange vocalization and was much too busy sleeping peacefully to indulge in my heartfelt request for some playful romantic contact.

"Can't you wait 'til the morning?" she responded from deep within some sweet dream.

"I'm dying," I croaked.

"Oh, you're just tripping. Take a bath and relax," she whispered as she buried her head under the pillow and went back to sleep.

Leave it to me to get the bad half of the tab.

What the hell. I was alone, abandoned, left to confront my very own demons. So I rolled out of bed, fell on the floor, crawled into the bathroom and climbed into the tub. Now, in those days, before I was working for the Commerce Department, I had the illusion that I was a comedian. I was one of those guys that was desperate to be on the cutting edge, so I was always saying something or other that would anger the audience, and I'd always have to spend the days following a show awash with self-recrimination.

"Oh, why did I have to say those things? What's wrong with me? Why can't I get people to love me so I could be successful and get my own TV show and be a regular person?"

My technique for dealing with these momentary bouts of clinical depression was to get into the bathtub, place a board across it, put a TV on the board along with a book, a magazine and perhaps a newspaper, smoke a controlled substance, drink a couple of beers, have a shot of whiskey and a steady supply of healthy snacks. And then if my anxiety was unabated I would resort to actually filling the tub with water and sit there wondering if after all my self-medication I would have the wherewithall to leap out of the tub before the TV fell in, in case I accidentally bumped it while reaching for a Hostess cupcake—you know, the ones with the cool white squiggle on the chocolate frosting.

However, on this particular morning I was slightly more helpless than usual, and I had to wait until my whatever got up to take care of me. Thank God for relationships! But, alas, my regimen failed to ease my unease and I discovered the true meaning of being "freaked out." I mean I thought that I'd been freaked out in the past but now I felt like a genuine "freak."

I was a freak and I was seriously freaked and it must have been just about that moment when the eggplant came sailing through the bathroom door and into the bathtub, splashing water over the TV and making me fearful to continue channel-surfing and forcing me to watch *The Price Is Right* or risk electrocution. Ignoring the contestants who were busily guessing the price of everything, I picked up the eggplant to throw it back to my whatever when I noticed something strange about it. It wasn't real. It was a plastic eggplant.

My whatever had bought it a few months previously and put it into the refrigerator and was waiting for me to try and cook it. Since it always looked fresh I always ignored it because, let's face it, it takes commitment to cook an eggplant, you've got to do something significant to it to make it palatable, and obviously I had heretofore lacked the culinary courage to address the issue. So finally, on my somewhat less than successful acid trip, I was reminded that the real comedic genius in the house was my whatever and that there were some jokes I just didn't get until they splashed into my tub of troubles.

But then, right at that moment in the midst of what had to be considered one of the world's worst psychedelic experiences, the most wonderful thing happened. Yes, at that very instant when I recognized that I was holding the world's first joke eggplant, I became Joe Carcinogenni, the Purple Poisoner with More Treats and Eats From the Wonderful World of Poison—a radio personality who became an ongoing character on Scoop Nisker's *The Last News Show*.

And Joe said, "Hi, folks, this is Joe Carcinogenni and if you eat this beautiful plastic eggplant it'll stay in your body for at least 100 years, guaranteed! And you'll never have to eat another one as long as you live."

This character was inspired by a radio-and-TV consumer reporter named Joe Carcione, who would wax eloquent about the fruits and vegetables available in the local markets. But Joe Carcinogenni would of course wax eloquent about the toxic treats made available by the oil companies, the chemical firms, the nuclear industry, etc. And if the many broadcasts of Joe Carcinogenni ever increased awareness of environmental issues, then it's for sure that—in this instance, at least—a bad trip did its bit to save the Earth.

Chapter 6

Narrow Escapes

Full Metal Bird
John Fremont

We were at someone's house in the Haight where a dentist was telling a story about declining to massage some addict's hemorrhoids. I can't believe he was actually asked, though I believed it at the time.

We had all dropped acid. It was Halloween and we were thinking about going to Antony LaVey's Satanic Church to see if virgin sacrifices still took place, given the scarcity of virgins and all, but we didn't go. I was glad, because I was kind of scared, but I wouldn't have admitted it at the time.

Anyway, the story I'm thinking of isn't about the dentist or LaVey, but Michael Hollingshead, who brought us there. He was the one who first turned Timothy Leary on, and later wrote a book, *The Man Who Turned On the World*. Hollingshead was a tall, bald, Waspish, whimsical Brit with a manner that bespoke Cambridge. He'd traveled extensively, spreading the gospel according to LSD, and his bearing usually got him through Customs without so much as a second glance.

The FBI hadn't a clue, but Scotland Yard was after him, and Interpol wanted to question him, so when he was busted on a minor drug offense in Sweden, extradition requests were summarily filed. Since he'd recently escaped from their clutches, Scotland Yard was eager to nab him. They sent two agents to Stockholm to fetch Michael, who had just enough time to dip acid beneath his fingernails before he was handcuffed and led aboard a twin-engine craft that seated a dozen or so passengers.

"No need to frighten the other passengers," Michael told the agents. "You can put the cuffs back on me before we land. Besides, I'm sure we can all do with a cup of coffee. You see, it's frightfully difficult to handle a cup without spilling it this way. Wouldn't want to get your new suit stained. Rather decent of Her Majesty not to send bobbies. I can always spot a gentleman. I've a cousin at the Yard, you know."

The talk was pleasant, and Michael was more a gracious host than a prisoner the way he insisted on getting coffee for all of them. "No problem at all, you've had a long day. It's all a dreadful mistake, you know. Not your fault, though. You've shown me every courtesy."

There were no flight attendants, just a pot of coffee on the brewing stand at the back of the plane. The agents didn't notice that Michael carried the cups with his fingers immersed, nor did they mind that he now sat behind them, what with all the pretty pictures they sere seeing.

Just before the plane landed, one agent grabbed hold of the other and said, "B-big b-bird."

"Nice bird," Michael reassured them.

"Nice bird," they echoed, relieved.

Comforted, they kept their seats, though they still clung to one another when Michael debarked.

"You stay now," he said, "and don't look out the window."

"No look."

After breezing through Customs, Michael called Scotland Yard, telling the clerk who answered the phone about the two agents who were enjoying a pleasant trip on board a two-engine plane that had just arrived from Stockholm. He offered suggestions to ease the men back to ordinary reality, and advised that Thorazine be administered to hasten the descent, should the men seem frightened

One of us asked Michael, "Why did you make that call? Why didn't you just get away as quickly as possible?"

"I couldn't do that," he replied. "Those agents were my responsibility."

In my mind's eye, I can still see the agents sitting in their big bird, hugging one another, thinking *Alice in Wonderland* thoughts and wondering if they might find some of that wonderful coffee at a London sidewalk cafe.

Happy Birthday

During the late 1960s I had begun exploring the work of Marcel Duchamp. By 1970 this had evolved into a compelling infatuation, and I developed a great need to see the fabled Arensberg Collection at the Philadelphia Museum of Art, which contains most of Duchamp's best-known work. One of my college classmates hailed from Philadelphia, so during winter vacation I accompanied him on his visit home.

It was a cold, clear morning when we headed off to the museum. In order to enhance what I fully expected to be a momentous experience, I'd dropped acid just prior to our departure, having carefully planned the schedule so that I would be peaking just as we entered the exhibit area.

My friend, considerately, opted to spend the day unwired, in order to look after me. As luck would have it, when we got to the museum we discovered that the Arensberg Collection was closed at certain times—including that one. Fortunately, it would open again in 45 minutes, but meanwhile I was now tripping full throttle.

Rather than pass that time inside, watching the walls shake and shimmy, we decided to go outside to the parking lot, where I could smoke cigarettes. What we didn't know was that the museum had a recent problem with cars being stolen from their lot; hence the local police were keeping an eye on the area, on the lookout for suspicious characters. We fit the bill.

A patrol car came around the corner and pulled up several yards in front of us. The officer barked, "C'mere." We started to move forward, but he said that he wanted to deal with us one at a time, and directed my friend to come up to the car while I waited behind.

As my friend explained our reason for loitering in the parking lot, I stood quite still, trying to convince myself that there was no visible evidence of the illegal substance roiling through my brain.

My friend came back and explained that the guy wanted to see my identification. I gave him my university ID card and waited with outward composure as my friend handed the card to the cop, who subjected it to solemn scrutiny. He knit his brow. Not only did this documentation reveal that I was from out of state; there was also some disparity between the photo on the card and my actual appearance, since I'd recently cut my hair and shaved off my beard.

The policeman, clearly suspecting that the ID wasn't mine, muttered something to my friend, who called out to me, "He wants you to tell him your date of birth."

I thought to myself, "If you get this wrong, you're going to jail."

Forgetting to Declare
Max Entropy

I just took a toke and booted up my PowerPuppy to dump some data that never left the analog realm before. I am paranoid enough to realize it might not be the smartest thing to document doing drugs, but on the other hand, how else am I gonna get a Warhol of fame before I die? (A Warhol is a unit of time named for a pop artist's attention span.) I guess I've always wanted to be a wannabe, and here's my chance.

Suddenly it's the early '70s, before hippies had been mugged by hipsters. I'm an out-of-work twentysomething guy with a useless master's degree, heading back to Boston from visiting the love of my life, who had left town to take a job in Edinburgh, Scotland. It was my first trip to Europe, and I had brought her some pot, double-bagged and rolled up in a pair of socks. It made me a tad nervous, but this was before they were X-raying everything, and I knew the law of averages was on my side. I arrived safely, my lady was glad to see me, and we had a number of groovy adventures.

When it was time for me to head back to my inscrutable future, I forlornly debarked from Edinburgh on Aer Lingus to Boston via

Shannon. As luck would have it, my seatmate was the most delightful Irish lass one could imagine, en route to visit relatives in the Boston area. At our layover in Ireland, I decided to get some duty-free whiskey, and asked her if she wouldn't mind importing one of the two bottles I intended to procure. It was just fine with her, she said, flashing her laughing 18-year-old blue eyes, and I dashed into the terminal to take care of business, barely catching my flight.

At Logan Airport I told her that I'd meet her outside in the arrival area to reclaim my bottle, and we both got lost in the crowd. It was January, and I was wearing a well-padded road-cone-orange parka, a Mao-Tse-Tung-red backpack with a Kelty frame, and carried a Harrod's shopping bag full of little gifts for my family and friends. Nothing even remotely suspicious, just clothing, candy, several skeins of wool for my mom, and various little treats.

After being briefly quizzed at Customs, I proceeded toward the sliding glass doors, thinking about where I'd find the Irish girl and my friend Jay, who was supposed to be picking me up in my van. Five steps from freedom, this young guy puts himself in my way, holding up ID. "I'm a Customs agent. Would you please come with me?" It wasn't a question, I realized, and with nothing to hide, decided not to panic.

So, he led me to a little room without any windows and, for some strange reason, not much light; I had expected an interrogation room with naked bulbs, not a meditation room. There, we were joined by a young woman. "I'm a Customs agent too. Would you mind if we asked you a few questions?" She too was very polite, but so far I'd been asked no actual questions, only rhetorical ones. The first real question brought me about: "Have you forgotten to declare anything?" Mentally racing through my stuff, I realized I had not itemized everything on my Customs form, but my stuff really wasn't worth very much, and as far as I could tell, it was all kosher to import. So I said no, I could not think of anything of value they would be interested in.

Mr. Customs then asked me to take everything out of my pockets, and I plunked down change, Lifesavers, matches and cigs, ticket stubs, my Swiss Army knife, some pocket lint and my wallet. Then he proceeded to check out my shopping-bag items. Extracting my Scottish yarn, he inquired, "How much did this cost?" It was then, as the lady began examining my pocket items, I suddenly realized that, yes indeed, there was something I had forgotten to declare, indeed forgotten for many months, stuck into my wallet. A feeling welled up in me that was like the evil twin of *Eureka*!

Looking back at Mr. Customs, I said, "I don't recall what the yarn cost, but I have a receipt for it," and grabbed my wallet from the table. As I pried open the wallet, Ms. Customs said softly, "Don't worry, if it's in there, we'll find it." But I persisted in thumbing through the little pockets, meanwhile saying, "No, I'm sure it's here with the rest of my receipts." And somehow I managed to stick my index finger into an obscure pocket, and dragged out a little rectangle of tinfoil, wrapped around a piece of blotter paper that I had wrapped up and put in there six months ago, during my Summer of "Like, wow!"

At that time I had this friendly schizophrenic neighbor, Naomi, who had been advised to control her condition with massive doses of niacin and regular supplements of acid. Her guru, a psychiatrist named Humphrey, had connections that resulted in Naomi having a 20 cc supply of Sandoz acid in a fridge in her basement. That's a lot of hits, more than she could ever possibly use, so she shared them with people she liked. I liked Naomi back, but she was kind of a kook even by my loose standards.

She was writing a humongous book which would show that Carl Jung's *Theory of Normal Personality* was all anyone would ever need in order to get along in this world. It seemed sort of contrived, but to this day I can't say she wasn't right about that. And while her acid, a syrupy colorless liquid in an eye-dropper bottle, was exquisite, not all of my four or five trips were completely free of oozing paranoia and oily, existential heebie-jeebies that wouldn't go away for eight or ten hours. But maybe these incidents were due to stuff that the Jungian analyst who Naomi had set me up with was doing to my mind. Learning I might not be in control of my destiny was a heavy trip.

Probably my best chemo-trip happened on a sweet Saturday in June, one of those perfect days when the air smells sweet and there's nothing to do. Late that morning I chewed and swallowed a blotter and let the drug work its way into every cell in my body. Acid is amazing that way; you take two or three hundred millionths of a gram, and somehow those molecules find their way to your pinkies, your butt, your knees, on to organs you never knew were there before. I always wondered how two drops of stuff could completely occupy a space billions of times their size. As this microcosm expanded within me, I felt more and more claustrophobic and restless, and realized it was time to get out of the house. So I strapped on my Walter Dyer sandals and commenced to wander the streets of Harvard Square.

Down by the Charles River, feeling an irresistible urge to connect with the planet, I undid my sandals and hoisted them over my shoulder, reveling in the grass, dirt, and even pavement under my tootsies. I walked for about an hour that giddy way, oblivious to the litter, shards of glass and dogshit I trod over. I explored a tiny park off Mount Auburn Street that featured a statue of Henry W.

Longfellow. Just beyond, across Brattle Street, was the Longfellow Mansion, an imposing, symmetric, Federalist wooden structure smartly painted white with yellow trim. Having seen tourist buses parked out front, I knew it was a museum, and decided now was the time to check it out.

Without any forethought, I ambled up the long front walk, up the stairs, and with my sandals still slung over my shoulder and a strange gleam in my eye, rang the bell. Momentarily the door was opened by a middle-aged Cantabrigian man with thinning, bright orange hair and granny glasses. He said, "Good day, can I help you?" I wasn't sure, as I really didn't know why I had come there. In fact, I felt like a little kid who was trick-or-treating in a strange neighborhood, as if I had a reason, but maybe not permission, to be there. So I asked him, "Can Henry come out and play?" Now this was a long time ago, and my recall isn't what it used to be, but I swear the guy replied, "No, Henry can't come out now. But if you'd like, you can come in and play with his toys." Here I was, barefooted, bearded, and with Jesus hair, acting completely loony, and this guy either felt playful or a sudden need to humor me.

After he let me in, he told me he was the curator, he lived there, and introduced himself. Sad to say, I have long since forgotten the name of this man, who deftly took my arm and escorted me through his sanctum, explicating Henry's stuff, including spectacles, manuscripts, winter clothes, and momentos like Thoreau's inkwell and Louisa May Alcott's recipe for rhubarb chutney. Although I couldn't regard any of these things as toys, they certainly gave me a good, transcendental hit. My host was as cute as a button (in his eccentric, intellectual way), and left me with the impression that he actually enjoyed my sense of curiosity. I said farewell and continued my pilgrimage; playtime lasted several more hours until I crashed into a confused sleep. I never went back to Henry's house, nor did I see the adorable red-headed curator again....

Anyway, I managed to palm the foil packet and handed the wallet back to Ms. Customs, who started tearing into it. But before I could savor the moment, Mr. Customs said, "Now I'm going to pat you down." To suppress panic, I silently chanted my mantra ("I hate when this happens") and, cupping my right palm slightly, turned it downward as I extended both arms. Mr. Customs removed my woolen cap and squeezed it around, then handed it to me. I took it with my right hand and extended my arm again. As he worked his way down, kneading my parka, I maneuvered the tinfoil into the cap's cavity and held it tight. I was glad not to be ticklish.

He reached my boots just as his companion finished examining my little shit, abruptly stood up, and said, "Okay, you can go now."

I carefully reseated my cap, then scooped up my other stuff. As I turned to leave, I said to him, man to man, "This is a major inconvenience. Why me?" He was quite direct: "These down parkas are often used to hide contraband. You fit the profile." Well, I thought, better to be a type than a statistic, so I said, "No problem," and propelled myself back into real life.

Out in the lobby a lot of people were milling around, and it took some time for me to orient myself. Then I spotted my Irish lass with a middle-aged couple who looked a bit peeved, and I ran up to her, apologizing for the delay. She was perfectly fine, and happily gave me my bottle bag while the aunt and uncle scowled. I wished her well on her visit and then cleared out as fast as I could. Soon I found Jay, was escorted to the van and driven home into the wintry twilight, toward a future dim with possibilities. Even though it seemed that hours had elapsed in that room, in fact it had been less than a Warhol, and maybe it was even an anti-Warhol. Now I remember what I forgot to declare: It was this story.

Chapter 7

Prisoners

Jail Trip
Dead Joe Jones

There were several of us from the *Third Paper* hangin' at Uncle W.'s place in Red Chute. Plannin' the next issue and burnin' a lot of herb. Me, I was there to test-drive the honey-packed silly-sign-ben 'shrooms. I was swallowing the last of a dozen when the door behind me burst open and an officer placed the barrel of his riot pump at the base of my skull and shouted, "This is a bust! Don't anybody move!"

We didn't. We sat at the table and cracked jokes and trembled while they proceeded to search the place. Well, they found the pot and a box of baggies and also noticed (but did not take) the jars of 'shrooms. In searching the refrigerator, they missed the 50 hits of acid nestled in an ice tray.

Thinking quickly, Mikey asked the officers if it would be okay to get some ice so that we might have some chilled cola before they carted us off to jail. Having already searched it, they figured this would be okay. So Mikey goes to the fridge and gets out the ice tray and proceeds to dole out ice cubes to everyone's glass.

When he gets to me, he whispers, "Oops, out of ice, drink these quick," and dropped half of the acid into my glass, quickly followed by a shot of Cola. I sucked it down and went on with getting busted.

Thirty minutes later, we were in the process of getting booked into the parish jail when the acid hit us with the cosmic giggles. I mean we couldn't stop and it was infecting the others and infuriating the cops. So much so that they said, "Keep those two away from the rest and away from each other."

When they were through with us in booking, they sent us off to cells, placing me in one of my own. Within minutes, I was peaking and sitting cross-legged on the bunk. I left. Oh, the meat was still there but I was gone.

The next morning, they came to let me know that someone had posted bail, and it took them 30 minutes to get my attention. They thought I had gone into a coma and were fixing to call the medics.

Needless to say, I was still buzzed and, rather than hang out in a cell, I had spent the last 10 hours in Xanadu.

Invisible Tattoos

I had a change of venue so my trial was in Phoenix, Arizona. I was in the Maricopa Jail. There was a little hall between the control room and outside visitors area. In the hall was a door with one of those slots/traps that open.

A "trusty" (of course he was a trusty; I trusted him with my dope!) would act like he was cleaning the window, looking into the visiting area by the trap, and a visitor would have drugs in straws so they could be passed through the crack in the slot of the door. The trusty would then hide the straws in the cleaning rag and head down a tier to hide the stash.

I had a person pass a sheet of acid in this manner during the trial. At this stage in my life, I was not very good at rationing dope—man, 50 hits of acid didn't last long. Only drawback was having to maintain in court where I tripped on the 12 people who were going to decide if I lived or died. Yep, a handful of acid in court and trippin' on the jury.

One witness, who claimed she saw me driving in Tucson, seemed as if she was right out of a Harlequin romance novel. The sweater, hair and movements. What a trip. I was maintaining by taking notes or drawing. So, in listening to this witness, I heard her claim that she looked out her window and saw me parked in the street sitting in my car.

My attorney asked her if she saw various parts of me, including my arms. She was answering in the affirmative. Suddenly, I recalled the strategy sessions with my attorney. Shit, this was the part where we were to lead her into saying she saw my arms but there were no tattoos and then I would be asked to stand up, remove my coat and display my heavily tattooed arms. Oh, no, I thought, not now, I'm *way* too stoned for this.

Yes, now.

My attorney asked her about arms, then tattoos. She said she saw my forearms, one rested on the driver's window, so she had a clear view. My attorney, with much splendor, had me stand up to remove my coat. I roll up my sleeves—the courtroom was packed, media were there, gavel-to-gavel TV coverage was there, and I'm blown out of my mind trying to stand up—and display my tattooed arms.

The witness got all red in the face, I gladly sat down, and my attorney asked if those were the arms she saw that day. She said no, but I was the man she saw. My attorney then asked if she thought I had detachable arms. I started cracking up. Fuck maintaining, this shit was simply too funny. Thankfully, everyone was laughing, so I was unobtrusive in my momentary lapse of reason.

Courtroom Daze
Frank J. Atwood

I had just dropped four hits of acid (about 125 mcg each, 500 mcg of clean LSD) and began to feel those familiar body tremors as

I started to come on. Of course, that would generally be a rather intense dose. However, sitting in that courtroom, on trial for my life, caused me to wonder if I had taken an insane dose.

See, I had been in jail for nearly two and a half years while waiting for trial on first-degree murder and kidnap charges. I was now halfway through the jury trial—I had already been convicted in the press, so the "trial" seemed to be a mere formality with a foregone conclusion of guilt—and the government was seeking the death penalty. Moreover, intense media coverage caused a circus atmosphere, adding to the surreal scene of the judicial system of injustice.

So there I sat, coming on to 500 mcg of kick-ass LSD, while cameras televised my "trip" statewide. My "lifeline" was writing; no way was I going to deal with the Establishment System of Death in such a condition. What follows are my notes from that fateful day:

Whew, writing is so bizarre. Words, or at least letters, are living in my pen and by moving the pen words are formed and then released from the pen. Oh wow, the words have become imprisoned by paper and these lines, destined to the order in which I've chosen. Whether in prison (jail/pen) or out (free world/paper) there seems to be no liberation.

I've tried to completely absorb myself in writing, yet, as I write, parts of my brain watch the courtroom. Then there is the "ego" observer that watches my every move to ensure its propriety. Fuckin' cop in my head and cops in the room, they're everywhere.

Ah, I see, it's all about being able to keep my head on several levels at the same time. Writing, the trial, and so much more... all simultaneously. I wonder if there is always this much going on at the same time? The thoughts, impressions, are so clear and on so many simultaneous levels. Yet, there's always the "watcher" who makes sure that everything I do is okay (I try to trip up the "observer" by writing a few letters backwards, it simply watches and keeps a note of it).

Oh man, I am so very aware of what's on the surface... and what's below.

I momentarily cease writing and look around the courtroom. Amazing, it's as if I can see the thoughts of others and everything appears so crisp and clear. Patterns, mostly checkerboard, cover the walls and dance in midair, all seeming to possess a life of their own.

My lawyer touches me and, as I turn to look at him, I realize he's "talking" to me—I hear no sound but words seem to exit his mouth, I can almost see them yet am unable to understand. Forgetting I am wearing a watch, and wanting to say something, anything, I ask my lawyer what time it is. He mumbles some numbers, they are meaningless, but I nod anyway.

* * *

I felt the need to look busy, tried to write again but lines fell out of my pen, onto the paper and then seemed to tumble through the table. I leaned down to look for these lines on the floor but almost immediately forgot what I was looking for. I did remember that the ink had escaped its prison.

Suddenly, I lost track of things and could see the world left behind. I waited for time to pass, it never did and I was locked in this moment forever. Then, just as suddenly, this phase faded and I felt as if I had been somewhere far, far away; perhaps on another side of the galaxy. Finally things became crystal clear again and everything was connected. I was awakening back into reality and experienced a sense of calm, flowing, euphoric well-being.

"I'm all better now," I thought.

The Death Row to Neptune Express
Joseph A. Morse

San Quentin Prison's Death Row, 1972.

After nearly a decade of subsisting on valium, secanol, prison-made wine and a little heroin, I was introduced to LSD. My fellow condemned prisoners were a little reluctant to try the new chemical because of the gloomy environment, but I had practically been raised on death row.

I had arrived there at age 19, and after nearly a decade I was still about 19 mentally and emotionally. So, what the fuck? Bring on a bad trip. How could it be any worse than reality?

I'll leave out some of the particulars, saying only that we had access to a considerable amount of acid, of pretty decent quality. Not quite the caliber of Owsley's but several notches above windowpane.

I had taken a couple of preliminary launches early in the year to get my confidence. Then boredom and youth allowed me to decide: "Let's see just what this shit can do. Look out, Neptune, here I come."

It was about 4 p.m. when I swallowed several hits. I lay back on the bunk in my 4-1/2' x 12' cell and put the institutional earphones on. I heard America singing something about a "horse with no name" when my neck and shoulders turned into solid rock.

"Uh-oh," I thought. "I think ya might have fucked up, pal." This was nothing like I had felt at the start of my earlier launches. I had never felt terror like this in my entire stay on death row, and they were executing people pretty regularly when I first arrived there.

About a tenth of me was arguing that I yell for help. The rest of me responded, "Naw, fuck that. You got yourself into this. Shut the fuck up and ride it out." It was probably lucky that I started with that frame of mind. I immediately headed toward the things I feared most.

A heavy steel door slammed shut. I was in a dark cell. Voices outside were saying, "He has gone insane. Nothing we can do."

"I don't wanna be no fucking looney tune," I thought. "Can't you motherfuckers do *something*?" Several long minutes were spent bemoaning my status as a blithering psychotic. "Man, what's my girlfriend gonna think now? Bad enough her boyfriend is on death row. Now he's a fucking Fruit Loop."

It was my internal dialogue that made me finally realize that I could still think coherent thoughts. There was no pain. The confusion subsided. "Hey, insanity ain't so bad," I decided.

I started feeling half-ass cocky. "LSD ain't shit. Drove me all the way nuts and I still have control. Maybe I shoulda taken more."

Whoever scripted that trip wasn't done with me yet. Since insanity hadn't frightened me enough to say "Never again," I was given a taste of death.

A thundering explosion. I was instantly buried alive under a pile of steel I-beams, concrete, automobiles and people. Los Angeles had collapsed, and I was buried alive under it. I was going to die. "Man, I'm too fucking young to die! Not like this!"

Minutes of silence. Then a beam of light. "Hey, I can see out. Being dead ain't shit either!"

I found myself inside a cavern, complete with a seven-foot Grim Reaper standing there. He was going to introduce me to some people. "People? I don't wanna meet no stinking people." I knew this had to be a trick. A large wooden door opened. Inside there were several infants.

"Where's the people?" I asked.

"These *are* people," the Grim Reaper replied.

I began muttering, "These ain't no stinking people," when I heard my name being called.

"Morse!"

My eyes opened. At my cell door stood a prison guard, normal from the waist up. From the waist down he was a skeleton.

"How ya doing?" the guard asked.

"Huh?"

"What do you think about the news?"

I said nothing, thinking to myself, "You ain't tricking me, you motherfucker."

The guard remained there until he concluded that I had nothing to say. He walked off and the man in the next cell yelled, "Hey, Joe, here it is again." I was told to put the earphones on and listen to a news broadcast coming over the television that was bolted outside our cells.

I apprehensively plugged in the earphones and heard a news-caster saying, "A radio station in Los Angeles is announcing that the California Supreme Court has abolished capital punishment. Details to follow."

"Right," I chuckled. "As if I'm so fucking stupid I don't know this is part of the trip." I had peaked enough to plug back into the radio and lay back on the bed. The music in that era was rather soothing, so I listened and relaxed as someone sang about "Me and you and a dog named Boo..." I drifted off down a highway with a hippie broad, paying no attention to the growing talk back and forth between the death row cells.

At 10 a.m. the following morning it was our exercise time on the tier. My fellow convicts were still talking about the court rul-ing. "What the fuck's wrong with these guys," I wondered. I would walk up to two or three men discussing it and listen. Then I'd walk to another group. Same chatter.

"Man, *all* these motherfuckers are trying to psych me out."

At noon I listened with everyone else to the news broadcast. It had not been a trip. A friend said, "Hey, fuck it. We're outta here. Let's celebrate. Got any acid left?"

I had quite a bit left. I gave him some, but didn't go into orbit with him. I hadn't taken my last acid trip, but several weeks passed before I had the balls to try it again.

Chapter 8

Various Acid Trips

Flashback
Steve Bloom

I was 16, never did anything worse than smoke a joint. I was a senior in high school, 1971, De Witt Clinton, Bronx, NY. We had a day off, or half-day. The New Riders of the Purple Sage were playing a free show in Central Park at the Bandshell. I took the subway downtown with my older brother Barry and my friend Matt. Matt had his arm in a sling; he'd cut his hand in a lawn-mower accident a week or so ago.

We settled in on the grass, smoked a few joints and waited for the New Riders. Then a clear glass jug containing an orange-looking drink was passed to me and Matt. We looked at each other like, "You know what this is?"—and then proceeded to take several gulps. A half-hour later we were full-blown tripping. I don't remember leaving our little patch of grass.

The New Riders played as the clouds zoomed at super speed across the sky. My brother came by and asked how we were doing. We looked a little spaced. I told him we drank something. Unworried, he split again. When the show was over, we all left the park and took the train back uptown, home.

Matt seemed disoriented. He didn't know where we were, what day or time it was. He was suddenly "out of it." He kept "flashing back" to his recent hospital stay and perhaps the morphine they gave him. We had to keep telling Matt what day it was, where he was and so on.

For some weird reason, we went straight home. It was about 6 p.m. We lived on the first floor of an apartment building. Matt lived on the sixth floor. My parents were home from their respective jobs. They didn't notice anything "wrong" with me at first. Then Matt's mother called asking what was "wrong" with him.

I took the elevator upstairs and entered Matt's room to find him sweating under the glare of a hot desk lamp. Matt's mom was hysterical. "What did you do to him?" she shrieked. I hung out with Matt for a while, then headed back downstairs. That walk down five flights was one of the longest, strangest trips down the stairwell I'd ever taken.

It was dinnertime at the Blooms. We took our respective seats, me across from my brother, my parents across from each other. With my eyes bugging out, hallucinating on the wallpaper, they both asked what was "wrong with Steven." Barry said I took something at the concert. What? "Something," he dodged.

But as mom's hair turned into a beehive and dad's head sported Viking horns and I barely touched my meat-and-potatoes dinner,

Barry revealed that I had accidentally taken LSD. That sent off shock waves, which included the comment, "What's next, heroin?" After some moralizing, my father decided to just shrug the whole thing off and started laughing at my obviously fucked-up but peaceful condition. They excused me to our room (Barry and I shared). I turned on the Mets game and enjoyed the trails of the baseball flying all over the field. Baseball on acid, what a concept! Periodically, I walked into the dining room and stared at the wallpaper. The pattern was still moving psychedelically. Finally, by midnight the walls stopped moving. My first acid trip had come to an end.

Like Geometry
April Avery

I was a freshman in high school in 1992. I was taking all the "smart" classes, and advanced geometry was by far the hardest. I'm not real great in math anyway, so how I ended up in that class is way beyond me.

Exam time was coming up and of course I had to take it. I never studied for any test and even though I knew I would fail it, I was not about to study for geometry. I got to school the next morning and I ran into this guy I knew. I was telling him how bad I was dreading this test, and he told me that he had something that would change my whole view on shapes and numbers and graphs. I took two and a half hits of acid.

This was my very first acid trip. I had to go to homeroom before the exam, so by the time I got to math class, I was tripping pretty hard. I'm not sure if I hid that fact well or not, but I swear I do not remember taking that exam. I do not recall anything until I was picked up by my dad later. I was still tripping then and starting to see bubbles everywhere (it was cool), but at least I remember that.

I got my grade for the exam two days later. Knowing I had completely flunked, I prepared myself for the worst. The teacher announced that one score was the best in the whole school and guess who that was? Me! I scored a 98! I'm not sure how I did that but I was so excited. Maybe research should be done on the positive effects acid has on things people don't know. Like geometry.

Trembling
Mike Serena

One wintry weekend evening, my wife, a friend and I gathered at our apartment to drop acid. Since none of us had a car, we had made sure that we had all of the toys and munchies that we thought we would need. After the normal rituals involved had been observed (candles, music, coloring books, etc.), we dropped the acid. There had been rumors of bad acid circulating, but we were confident of our source, so did not worry.

All was going along nicely for the first couple of hours, but then first my wife and then our friend and then I began to feel a slight trembling. We discussed it and deemed it unimportant, but it kept on. As time wore on, the trembling was getting worse and after a while it had become full-fledged shakes.

We became very nervous, trying to figure out what to do; at last the shaking had become so bad in all of us that we concluded that the only sensible thing to do was to call a cab and have it take us to the hospital. The consequences of being admitted to the drug ward or even to jail seemed a lot better than being admitted to the morgue.

I was elected to go out to the kitchen where the phone was. On the way out, I glanced at a thermometer. The temperature in our apartment was 38°! At some point in the evening, the heater had gone out and the three of us were sitting there shivering from the cold, thinking that we had consumed poisonous LSD and were about to die.

I returned to the living room with some blankets and sweaters and explained to my wife and friend what was really going on. They both had to go look at the thermometer for themselves, to be sure that I wasn't too paranoid to call the cab. When they saw that it was indeed 38°, we all bundled up in the blankets and had as good a time as possible while being that cold.

Pelicans
Hank Rosenfeld

I went in a van with a bunch of friends up the coast to Gualala on the Mendocino-Humboldt County border to camp out and take acid—one of those group LSD trips where you all end up around the campfire on a bummer because nobody knows the same show tunes to sing.

I spent three hours on the Gualala beach that day staring at pelicans. Staring with reverence and admiration, love and yearning, until I finally realized: I *know what I want to do next in my life. I want to be a pelican.*

It's amazing to me how pelicans always seem to fly *together*, and I wished and wished, and then noticed my feet starting to hurt. I'd been walking along a bluff there above the Pacific that was covered with dune grass and burr reeds, and the burrs were all sticking to my feet.

Only, my mind being so *out there*, it had taken this long *up here* to register that I was now in great pain *down there*. So I sat down in a dune, and as I started picking the burrs out of my feet, each prickly, pincer-like burr I plucked resembled exactly a tiny yellowish-white *pelican's beak*.

When I told my brother-in-law about my latest trip, he said, "A pelican? Ugliest bird in the world. But so beautiful in flight."

A Real Pisser
St. Alice

I was tripping on acid. My husband Jerry was driving me around the city, and I was admiring the trees. He told me he wanted to stop at Kathy's house for just a minute, and that was fine with me. Everything was fine with me at that point. We pulled up in front of her house, which was across the street from a park. He said, "Why don't you just wait in the car, I'll only be a minute." Of course, that was fine with me, too.

I was sitting in the car tripping my brains out, peaking, watching the trees in the park wave at me. Some guy with kind of creepy vibes came walking by, and suddenly I felt very vulnerable and decided I didn't want to sit there alone in the car tripping. I managed to cross the street safely by myself and knocked on the door. Jerry was surprised to see me. I said I had to go to the bathroom, which I then realized was true.

I had met Kathy before. She worked at the state mental hospital. I had never met her roommate Steve before. She introduced me and then pointed the way to the bathroom.

I got into the bathroom and closed the door, and then I couldn't remember what to do next. I stood there thinking real hard. I was standing there; I could see the toilet. I knew I wanted to sit on the toilet and empty my bladder, but if I just sat down and did it, I'd pee all over my pants. I knew I didn't want to do that; but I couldn't remember the procedure. I stood there for what seemed like forever and thought real hard, but I just couldn't remember what to do. I finally decided the only thing to do was to get help from Jerry. Surely he'd know what to do.

I went back out to the living room where the others were standing around talking. Jerry asked me, "Well, did you go?" Normally he doesn't ask me for a report when I return from the bathroom, but I guess he knew what kind of shape I was in at the moment.

"No. I got in there and I couldn't remember what to do. Would you come in and help me?"

Steve and Kathy looked at me like I was psychotic. Steve was probably thinking I was a state hospital patient out on leave for the day.

"She's tripping," Jerry explained to them.

"Oh." They understood.

"Alice," Jerry reminded me, "you know how to go to the bathroom, you don't need any help."

"Oh, yeah, right." It was all coming back to me now.

I went back, and the second time around everything turned out okay. What a relief. That's all.

Saying No to Owsley
Jerry Hopkins

I may be the only person on the planet who's said no to both Owsley and Tim Leary when they said, "Open your mouth and say, 'Ah!'" Once, Paul Krassner said on stage about me that I represented the new breed of head-shop owner, the ones who never dropped. But I had good reason.

You see, I had the first head shop in Los Angeles, the third in the country (after San Francisco and New York) and I was, for 15 minutes, one of the acid spokespersons of my generation. I was even interviewed by Art Linkletter on his TV show, wearing a bright red Sgt. Pepper jacket and insisting that "psychedelic" could mean a mind-expanding walk on the beach. I swear Linkletter didn't even argue with me. This was before his daughter took her famous dive out a window.

Anyway, I was standing behind the counter in my shop—called Headquarters and located in Westwood, near the UCLA campus, for those of you who are "graduates"—when a shaggy-looking guy walked in and noticed a display of silver roach clips. These were my top-of-the-line clips, created by a superb jeweler, the handles taking astrological and other animal forms, and costing about $50 apiece, which was a lot of money in 1966.

He asked to look at a clip with a bear on the handle and I gave it to him. After a moment, he said he liked it, but was a little short of cash, so could I put it aside for him if he'd send someone in later in the week with the bread. I said yes and he asked if there was a place where we could talk privately.

My store wasn't big. Besides the front room, there was a toilet which doubled as a storeroom and office, and a tiny alcove where I had several "light shows" set up for tripping. The displays were for sale, of course, but I don't think anyone ever bought one. Once inside the room with the blinking lights, my customer produced a silver pillbox and offered it to me.

"I like your store," he said, "and I want you to have this as a token of my appreciation." He opened the box, revealing about 50 small white pills. That's when it hit me. This was Augustus Owsley Stanley III, the infamous LSD king, the Bay Area chemist who fueled and fired the Trips Festivals and hung out with Kesey and the Grateful Dead... also known as The Bear. That's why he wanted the roach clip with the bear on it. Far out!

Or was it? Was it really Owsley, or was it a cop? By the time this guy walked into my store, the young Ms. Linkletter had taken her last flight and running a head shop was like painting a bull's-eye on your American-flag T-shirt. So, deciding that caution was the better path, I thanked my customer and said I appreciated his kind offer, but I knew he'd understand why I had to say no. He smiled and said he did and left.

A few days later someone showed up with $50 to pick up the roach clip.

Confetti and Drums
Gay Vickers

I was 38 years old, the mother of a 19-year-old stepdaughter that I had had in my cache since she was pre-pubescent when we had one wild-ass New Year's Eve party. Old friends, new friends, almost grown children. You get the drift.

So... much earlier on, one of my finest friends had given me about 50 confetti-filled eggshells. Obviously a tradition in Victoria, Texas. Man, that was fun. Busting those eggs on everyone's heads. Confetti fuckin' everywhere. And especially on the deck of the backyard saloon my then-husband and I had built.

Well, whaddaya think happens but someone shows up with some acid. One big dude took a half, leaving a half to my then-husband. Being gentlemanly, he thirded that half with my big friend's wife and me. *But*, being the total hostess and in-the-dark chick, I thought my old man was trying to feed me egg confetti so I didn't try all that hard to catch it on my tongue.

When I finally realized it was for real I was kinda quasi-cool-desperate trying to find it among all the confetti from the cool-as-shit eggs I had busted on people's heads earlier. Go figure. Well, my ex came out and saw my consternation, called me a mo-roon, and proceeded to pick the 1/3 of 1/2 out of the one million pieces of confetti and fed it to me. You know, I didn't have much faith in trippin' at that point.

So I did what any red-blooded middle-aged stoner American would do at that point. I went and sat down behind my trap set and commenced to play. It was going great. Right up until the time my toms started looking like Oklahoma, Arkansas and Tennessee.

In the exact appropriate proportions. It's hard drummin' across state lines.

The next thing I noticed was that I was tired of drumming and my legs seemed to be locked in some polio leg-brace. This would be the chrome on the settings of my Tamas. Wildass, man. It took a nice pair of 38-E breasts dangling in front of my tom to (thank you Gina-Sheena) convince me that I could escape my steel prison and I got out alive.

Damn good thing, too. Cause my step-angelchild's girlfriend started doing the side-stepping frog dance and enacting the "Hello My Honey, Hello My Baby, Hello My Ragtime Gal" song across the deck of my saloon and I got it. Totally unbelievable. Except for seeing my newborn kittens stretching like Gumby and Pokey on a previous trip, that was probably my most memorable. One of only three acid-induced trips. Perhaps I'm just not cut out for this.

How I Passed the Acid Test
Michael Simmons

One night 26 years ago I lost all touch with reality only to regain it during a bout with lysergic insanity.

Chronologically it was January 1974, but it was still the '60s. I was 18 and had long flowing hair which, to paraphrase Frank Zappa, I could style so that it looked *really good in the back, maaaaaaaaan*, and for which I could still get my ass kicked a la *Easy Rider* by the redneck townies of upstate New York. I was a student—or rather I was enrolled—at Bard College, one of the most notorious freak colleges in Amerika which right-wing columnist Walter Winchell had once dubbed "The Little Whorehouse On the Hudson" after his daughter had allegedly gotten knocked up there during a weekend visit.

Oh, yeah, and the Liar-In-Chief *du jour* was being threatened with impeachment while a future prevaricating President was a budding political hack from Arkansas who wasn't inhaling the joint he was holding.

We'd just returned from Christmas break and the grounds were covered with pristine snow. Bare trees, white snow and very young adults who had no rents to meet, who insisted that we would not become our parents and who had grown lots and lots of hair. The drinking age was still 18 and our favorite trough was a joint called Adolph's which had a broken water pump outside that was, according to yet another legend, the pump that didn't work cuz the vandals took the handles, as Dylan had sung in "Subterranean Homesick Blues."

After an evening of indulging in my newfound libation of Jack Daniel's sour mash whiskey at Adolph's, I found myself at Tewkesbury,

the newest dorm on campus which resembled a Holiday Inn, looking for female companionship from any female that was in the
mood to provide it. Around 2:15 a.m. I ran into Mark Groubert and
Chuck Goldberg in the hallway and, even in my alcoholic haze, I
ascertained by that very specific rocket's-red-glared, pinned-look in
their orbs that they were peaking on Dr. Hoffman's Bicycle Bis-
cuits—LSD. Grobes instructed me to stick my tongue out, onto
which he dropped a tab of windowpane. The deranged duo disappeared into the night and I strolled through the snow back to my
dorm, thrilled with the brisk winter air and the knowledge that I
would soon be in a headspace that I dearly loved.

I'd tripped dozens of times before. All my trips were fantastic
but they were also all group excursions. I'd heard that flying solo
was risky but, hell, I was 18. I was going to visit uncharted regions
of my consciousness and make notes. Perhaps my notes would
prove to be maps of New Worlds. I was really fucking excited.

Frank, my roommate, was slumbering but I could've blasted
Hound Dog Taylor and he wouldn't have budged, so deep was his
ability to sleep. I slammed the door to our room, turned on all the
lights, stripped down to my underwear and prepared my notebook
and multi-colored magic markers for observational notation and
psychedelic illustration. The acid started to kick in and I entered
the initial giggle stage—one of the most exhilarating parts of good
ol' Lucy in the Sky is take-off. I sat on my bed laughing to the
stand-up comic in my cells who was riffing on the silly absurdity of
sober reality. Grabbing my notebook, I duly noted.

The visual distortion began. All inanimate objects were breathing. The entire room became anthropomorphized. The window
shades held more life than my sleeping roommate. This hallucination grew in intensity until even the wind outside took on a low
human roar. Then I realized that the entire universe was breathing
as one infinite solitary being. I began to write this observation in
my notebook but the tip of the marker was dissolving through the
paper as if solidity of any kind was an outmoded concept. What I
was able to transfer from pen to page had taken a liquid form; my
words flowed in random, meandering patterns all over the page
and it was absolutely unreadable.

I put the notebook down and lay back on the bed and closed
my eyes. I was moving through space, surrounded by millions of
glowing stars, a wild distortion of my childhood spent at the Hayden Planetarium near Central Park. My movement accelerated until
the stars became streaks of light and my whole field of vision was
flooded with a great blinding all-whiteness. I could feel and hear
my heartbeat become slower and slower and faster and slower and
faster and faster and slower until it had no regularity at all.

Better concentrate on my breath.

I tried slow, deep breathing exercises but my breath, like my heartbeat, soon lost any semblance of rhythm. I couldn't find my breath. I couldn't find my heartbeat. The universe had become a totally rule-free zone where nothing could be counted on. There was no center, no balance, no ground to stand on, no shoulder to cry on. I was a free-floating astronaut receiving an advanced seminar in chaos theory, only it was no longer merely theoretical.I'd broken through to the other side and I was scared shitless.

Should I wake Frank up? Nah, don't wanna bother him. What could he do anyway? And even in my egoless state, a little macho posturing found its way into my decision-making process: "I'm tough. I've got to figure out how to make it through this one on my own...."

I opened up my eyes and walked out into the hall. It reassuringly bore some resemblance to the hallway of my dorm that I'd been a resident of a couple of hours before. I had an urge to run screaming through the dorm: "*I've broken through! I've broken through! Help me!*" Once again, a vestige of my ego appeared and reminded me not to act like some embarrassing, stereotypical, bum-tripped acid casualty. The kind of uncool jerk who'd writhe on the floor at a Grateful Dead concert, claiming to be telepathically communicating with Jerry Garcia. I went into the bathroom, splashed water on my face and looked in the mirror. There was energy pouring out of my forehead or third eye or whatever. My mirror image morphed into that faux-Hindu imagery that graced Jimi Hendrix's *Axis: Bold As Love* album cover. I'm sure there are Jungian, shared genetic-consciousness explanations for that shit.

I went back to bed, determined to beat madness. I realized the two primary elements that I was lacking were Time and Space. I turned to my right where my night table was and for the next six hours I held on to the table leg (Space) and watched the hands of the alarm clock go around (Time). Why the table leg or alarm clock didn't dissolve along with the rest of reality says something about the power of human will. It's an extraordinary exercise to do absolutely nothing for six freaked-out hours and watch the hands of a clock go from 3:32 to 3:33 to 3:34 to 3:35 to 3:36 to 3:37 to 3:38 to 3:39 to 3:40 to 3:41 to 3:41 and 1\2 to 3:41 and 3/4, etc.

By 9:34 a.m., I felt secure enough to let go of the table leg and was able to look at something other than the clock. Bug-eyed, wild-haired, underweared, and chortling in bravado over my victory over self-induced schizophrenia, I rolled about 10 joints and, sitting cross-legged on my bed, proceeded to chain-toke them. Frank woke up and looked at the madman in the bed across from him.

"What the fuck have you been doing?" he asked.

"I've been tripping," I chortled.

"How was it?"

"It was the worst trip I ever had and it was the best trip I ever had," I answered truthfully.

I learned more in that one night than I've learned in the last 25 years. When you realize that reality is nothing more than a table leg and an alarm clock, what else do you need to know?

Infused with Love
Cat Simril Ishikawa

In my 17 years in Japan, I encountered acid only once. Synchronistically, it happened when the movie *Blade Runner* came to Tokyo. Based on one of my favorite novels by Philip K. Dick, I leapt at the chance to see the flick under the influence of a drug that had influenced the author, and would surely enhance the film. It was worth the two-hour train trip to the Shinjuku theater district where I split the tab with a fellow Dick-loving friend and went into the matinee.

Although the film said so, this sure didn't look like my old hometown Los Angeles. Instead, the movie seemed to be set in Shinjuku, one of the sleaziest and most crowded sections of Tokyo, but with the film's sky full of L.A. cars instead of Tokyo's elevated trains, and I too felt a rush when the blade runner Deckard's magic machine showed what was around the corner in the photographs he was viewing. This must be the acid, said my head. I soared to new heights, higher than the police helicopters that colonize the real L.A. sky in search of criminality.

All that violence was hard to take, and the film bore only a faint resemblance to Dick's classic, but when the dying android Roy Batty said, "I've seen things you people wouldn't believe," it seemed that Dick was speaking from his grave. When the lights went on, we went out into the sunset sky with electric billboards selling *Blade Runner*-like ads in the saturated Shinjuku smog. We took refuge in a little bar to watch sumo and feast on great Japanese bar food. The sumo wrestlers looked like clouds in combat, and my favorite won. Outside, the sky was medium rare. Inside, we were full of sake and enthusiasm well done.

I caught the 6:10 back to my house in the countryside and got back just as my four-year-old daughter Monique was coming out of the bath. "Welcome home," she shouted. The slick wood hallway filled with happy bathwater. I have never been more infused with love than at that moment.

They say acid gives you hallucinations and fills you with love. The five times I tried it (four times in the early '70s, the last time on this occasion in 1982), I never hallucinated anything. It made the visual world perhaps a bit more interesting, but no more so than grass. I would have said it was a useless drug except for that profound feeling of love I felt for my daughter on that day.

I don't think it was the impotency of the acid, as others who took it with me on those five occasions reported profound hallucinations from the tabs we shared. Perhaps my brain just isn't wired that way. Other "hallucinogens" I tried had an equal lack of results. As such, I don't think anyone should generalize the "drug" experience as there is no generalized human brain. For me at least, they were right about the love.

Taxi Dreams
Stewart Gilbert

I met Bob over a small bottle of LSD, a half-ounce of liquid pixie dust in translucent polyethylene, with a sticker on the side that read, "For Pharmaceutical Use Only." Bob did the Dylan look well: curly brown hair, pale skin, leather jacket, beat-up guitar. He was older, and got laid a lot, so I granted him what wisdom and authority I could.

But I was the one who had the bright idea of dressing the stuff up in its historical costume: one drop on a sugar cube, with a drop of red green yellow blue food dye on each side. Bob and I took our job seriously, so we usually ate up all the profits. And we even tried diluted drops in our eyeballs once, in case there were any ocular connections we'd overlooked.

My roommate at the time was a black musician from Bump City. He and his musician friends wouldn't touch my crazy honky drugs, but they laughed pretty hard one night when my teeth glowed psychedelic under a black light. (Everyone's teeth do.)

Humboldt County was a foggy oasis back then, a place where clocks ran slow and shaggy people dressed like elves. We looked out upon the rest of California as if it were another world. And when you left town, you did so as an astronaut, prepared for entry into another world.

One day we blasted off for San Francisco, screwed down into our seats with a handful of sugar cubes. Bob flew his Pontiac south down the highway, down the back of that asphalt snake, through redwood groves so dark you needed headlights and plenty of pixie dust in your eyes. Buried there under the ancient ferns and moss and millennium-old trees, we found the landmarks that define culture in Northern California: the Drive-Thru Trees, the World Famous Tree House, Confusion Hill.

At Laytonville, we passed a knockdown commune with a couch full of freaks sitting out front. They were waving at the passing cars like a clump of merry fools so we drove back to take a look. They scattered, quickly—no one wanted to be eye-level with that Pontiac's grill when Bob came tearing up the emergency lane.

After introductions, a man and woman led us on a tour. There was a shack perched near the road, and inside, three women were baking bread in a tiny kitchen. "Ten thousand people tonight," they shouted out between slams of the oven door. "We'll feed 'em all."

A fuse box on the side of the shack had a dozen extension cords grafted into its innards, with pennies and wads of aluminum foil in the sockets where the fuses should be. We followed the cords downhill toward a rude stage, and there a peaked roof was going up, made from tree limbs and wire. Our guide told us that their leader, Lone Dog, was leaving them that night.

Pyramids were popular back then, and the pyramid over the stage would call down aliens to carry Lone Dog safely out of reach of the law and its evil warrants. The members of the crew on the stage were sporting pyramids of small sticks on their heads as they worked, so I reasoned if there were one place on the planet that aliens would not be visiting, this was it.

Bob disappeared into the woods to look for camping sites. And I got into a staring match with Lone Dog himself. I was sitting on a little dry hummock in the mud, watching this small group of human ants preparing for the supposed onslaught of thousands. Then I noticed him sitting about 30 feet away, watching me.

He looked like Charlie Manson's brother: beady eyes, long black mane, rough beard. He was sitting perfectly still, staring, but such was his mistake. I could have outstared a corpse that day, if I had to. And so as I stared back, his face turned green, then purple and yellow, until it blended with the countryside behind him and disappeared.

My unfulfilled mantra back then was *Coito Ergo Sum*—"I fuck, therefore I am." And this insipid contest of wills reminded me that in San Francisco, there was a young woman waiting, who had already expressed a desire to fulfill this mantra with me in the bathtub of her father's vacant apartment. Somehow I'd forgotten that. Lone Dog winked out of my awareness. I rustled up Bob, and we were on the road in five minutes flat.

It was dark when he dropped me somewhere off Clay Street. The fog was rolling in off the Bay and lay wet against the gray buildings of the Tenderloin. I found the right door, and little brass plates with bits of tape laid over where someone had written names of the current tenants. I pushed the button. No answer.

An hour after the laundromat across the street closed up, a guy came by and asked if I'd watch for cops while he climbed in through the transom window to get his clothes. When the cops did come by, their cruiser just materialized out of the fog, quiet, with no lights. But they never saw the guy in the laundromat, and mistook me for a piece of trash, and so just rolled on by. The last thing I remember was curling up on the stoop like a bum, shivering, chanting my mantra through clenched teeth.

I found Daphne the next morning over at Ghirardelli Square. It was a brilliant San Francisco day, the air full of sunshine and kites. Daffey had a dimpled smile and a set of those curves that greatly impressed a lad such as I. She was younger, and got laid a lot too, though I was pretty sure she'd never met Bob.

We worked on my mantra that night, back at the tub in her father's flat. And we were working on it in the worn-out Murphy bed in the middle of the living room when her father stumbled in the front door. Drunk, he was raving about miseries only a cabbie would know. Daffey and I cowered, naked—but those were the days when you could be interrupted by the father of the young woman underneath you and not worry particularly for your safety.

Then he started eating sugar cubes. These were Bob's astronaut cubes, plain, no wrapping, still in their pink from-Hawaii box. They were sitting on a table, and he went at them one cube at a time, yelling something about potholes and wet cable-car tracks. By the time he got to the mayor and what a shame it was he ever got elected, he'd popped enough cubes to sprout another head.

In the middle of a good rant about bum fares, he suddenly shouted, "I woosh neder consiber dribbling a goddab cab with a hagerover!" Then he fell face-down on a couch at the foot of the bed and passed out. I looked at a clock: 1:40 in the morning, and thirty minutes to go—a smooth crescendo of disorientation, then several hours of howling madness, perhaps sedation under leather straps in a hospital bed, followed by hours of psychotic meltdown.

We waited in horror as he snorted and snored in his sleep. As the half-hour passed, his wrinkles softened and a smile grew across his face, wider and wider, until each tooth practically shone through his lips. His breathing fell into time with the foghorns blowing across the bay, and he just lay there, like a drunken cherub in wrinkled gray clothes.

I didn't sleep a wink that night, watching, gauging the distance to the fire escape. But at dawn, he was still snoring, and that toothy smile had settled down some. So we left him right where he was, left him to his dreams of big fares and bigger tips.

Daffey and I drifted apart and never saw each other again. And for all I know, her dad still drives a cab in San Francisco, still sleeps off his drinks in a flat in the Tenderloin—but I would have given anything to be his first fare after that night he got into the sugar cubes. I would have tipped him big, I'm sure of that.

Shirt Inspector
T. Dub

My lady and I were living in an ancient farmhouse in the middle of 400 acres in southern Indiana. We dropped some windowpane and started to decorate the Christmas tree. I was untangling the lines of tree lights by looping them over my neck. The lights hung down over my chest nearly to the floor. I plugged them in, and all of them began flashing colors, just as I started to get off on the acid.

Then the phone rang. We rarely received calls, and the rule of the house was to never answer calls while tripping. But I knew that Santa Claus was calling me to check on something I had written on my Christmas list, so I picked up the phone and said, "Ho, ho, ho. Merry Christmas!"

My mother was on the phone, and she asked me what shirt size I wore because she was going shopping the next day for a gift for me. I of course had to check the label on the neck band of the flannel shirt I had on, but I couldn't reach behind me or take off my shirt because I had the tree lights strung around me.

I told my mother to hold on, and I went to my closet to check the size on another shirt. When I got to the closet, I found a favorite shirt I hadn't worn for a while, so I took off the lights and changed into the shirt, forgetting, of course, about my mission to find my size. I tried on a dozen shirts before I found one that was just exactly right.

Beaming with my new attire, I returned to the living room and noticed that someone had left the phone off the hook. I was going to hang up the phone, but I thought I'd say hello into the mouthpiece to check out my voice buzz over the airwaves.

"Hello," said my mother.

"Hi, mom, how are you?"

"What's your shirt size?" she asked.

Holy shit, I thought, and our previous conversation came back to me.

"Hold on, I'll check," I said. I ripped off my shirt and told her, "It's 100% cotton. Gotta go, goodbye."

I hung up the phone and it flashed on me that "Large" was the information she wanted. I spent the next hour in a panic, convinced that my mother was en route for the four-hour drive to my farm to find out what lunacy had descended upon her son.

Driving to Distraction
Terri Scott

We drove the long and winding road to a party. While at the party, we took LSD. I don't know why we were driving back in the middle of the night. My then-boyfriend was driving the VW bus, and I was copiloting. The van was loaded with people in the back.

Suddenly the driver took his hands off the wheel and said, "Look! The car is driving itself!" He crossed his arms over his chest and let the car drive. As copilot, I checked it out. Sure enough, the car was driving itself. It was following the road.

A passenger leaned over the seat and said, "Okay, the car is driving itself, but let's put our hands back on the wheel now, okay?" But the driver insisted for some time on encapsulating us all in this brief moment of LSD history. We had a discussion about whether or not this was truly happening. I remember looking at the passenger and laughing. What little faith he has! But we might as well keep him calm and drive the car by hands, not by minds. I convinced our pilot to put his hands back on the wheel, and the high was over in that black night.

* * *

One time my boyfriend and I drove to Issaquah, WA to visit friends. (This is the same boyfriend who could drive his car by mental powers alone.) The next day the consensus was that we would all take LSD. I was feeling particularly cautious that day, and decided not to. Everyone else did.

They started the day by snowboarding down this steep hill. They were so stoned. Then they remembered they had made an appointment with a real estate agent to go driving around to look at properties. We all climbed into the realtor's car. I was sitting in the front, in the middle between the realtor and a girlfriend.

As we were driving, her smile kept getting bigger and wider. She was glowing. I was smiling politely, answering the realtor's questions. Looking in the rear-view mirror, I could see my boyfriend glued to the seat, petrified in some sort of post-snowboard doom.

The girlfriend at my side said, "Stop here! Stop here!" And she leaped from the car. She began twirling and spinning and throwing her arms in the air, in celebration of a beautiful spot and life. Finally she got back in. We then went to look at an empty house. Everyone fell out of the car and went in every direction but to the house. By then I was laughing, and the realtor was baffled as hell. I just kept thinking, I sure am glad I didn't drop today.

Physical Education
Mark Neistat

"Jacobson, you're beating the system," yelled Don Browning, the thick-necked, flat-topped, wrestling coach.

Coach Browning, teaching his regular gym class, caught my high-school friend, Jay Jacobson, hiding behind the Universal weight machine, to avoid doing wind sprints. The coach, who went to military school, hated people who tried to beat the system, and Jay was always trying to beat the system, especially when it came to physical activity.

In gym, during push-ups, Jay would lay prone watching the coach, only moving when their eyes met. After standing on a chair to reach it, he would just hang on the wood pull-up bar, which was seven feet above the floor, only making halfhearted attempts to hoist his pear-shaped frame when the coach yelled at him. He would walk around hurdles, run under the high jump bar and roll weights across the floor rather than lift them.

Jay and I met in grade school and became friends immediately. He was a pudgy redhead and was into sports as a spectator, not a player. But he was a player with all the drugs that seemed to float around high school in the early '70s. We started and finished our drug experimentation together and went through high school more or less stoned the whole time. Jay also loved hallucinogenic drugs, especially windowpane acid, which he would use regularly on the weekends but never take it in school.

However, things were desperate at school as Jay needed to pass gym to graduate, and Coach Browning was not sympathetic to his plight. To pass his class, all students had to complete an indoor obstacle course in under one-and-a-half minutes. The coach took special delight in failing students who he felt were beating the system.

The obstacle course started with a series of yellow traffic cones that you had to zigzag around. This was followed by quick stutter-steps through a row of 10 pairs of car tires, followed by a climb over a 12-foot rope fence, through a cloth tunnel, over five hurdles, a leap over two barrels and then a short dash to the finish line. Usually, all of these activities were performed with the sun in your eyes, as the gym was on the first floor with glass windows and doors facing east. Jay never made it once under three minutes. He decided he had nothing to lose so he took a hit of windowpane acid.

As he waited in line to begin the course, under the coach's dagger-like gaze, Jay later told me he found himself surrounded by long-haired, pointy-eared, samurai demons. He was sweating profusely and the gym looked like a Yes album cover. The demons were touching him and when anyone moved a limb he saw tracers. Although there was one person ahead of him in line, when he heard the coach yell "Go," he took off around the first person and started running the course.

Jay zigzagged like a downhill skier through the traffic cones, worked his legs like pistons through the tires, was at the top of the rope fence in two moves, then flipped himself over the top rope with his legs pointed straight at the ceiling, landing in crouched cat-like position. Jay dived into the cloth tunnel and exited it with a front somersault. He flew over the hurdles, cleared the barrels with two feet to spare, and dashed toward the finish line in—according to the coach's stopwatch—under one minute.

Then, instead of stopping to the sound of the coach's jaw hitting the floor, Jay leaped onto the wood pull-up bar and whipped off 15 military style chin-ups without showing any strain.

"Jacobson, what's got into you?" the shocked coach screamed.

"I ate my Wheaties," Jay yelled back, then promptly ran out the glass doors, across the school's front lawn and into the parking lot of the shopping mall across the way. Still in his gym clothes, Jay shrank into the morning sunlight and vanished into the stores.

That was the last the coach saw of Jay Jacobson. He passed gym.

Fair Exchange
John McCleary

Jim and I are artists. He's a painter and I take photographs. We often found each other watching the same sunset. We ate *hors d'oeuvres* together at art openings and drank their cheap wine. We passed a joint to one another at parties. And we liked the same sort of women.

There was this one girl, Jan, waiting tables at our favorite coffeehouse. I was on the prowl for some time. Jim noticed her too.

I flirted with her as she brought my cappuccino and bagel with ham. I stopped by her house from time to time to see if any chemistry was developing. I didn't drop in just before bedtime or in the middle of a drunk night. I wanted it to progress naturally.

One morning I arrived after breakfast and Jan offered tea. She was in the kitchen talking to me as I sat on the floor of the living room in front of a warming fireplace. I was staring down at the shag rug wondering if this would ever develop into anything.

"Jim was here last night," she said with nonchalance. "He just left. We were going to split some windowpane, but he dropped it on the shag rug and we couldn't find it."

At that very moment I saw a tiny, shiny square nestled in the fibers of the rug. I was already licking the end of my finger. I reached down, snagged it, and placed it on my tongue.

I left after the tea. Went down on the rocks by the sea.

Jim got the girl. I got his acid. I hope his trip was as good as mine.

Foreplay
Susie Bright

When I was 16, and my best friend Nicole was 15, we ran a baby-sitting and housecleaning service for every hippie with disposable income in the West L.A. canyon we lived in. One guy we cleaned for, Jimmy, was a 35-year-old UCLA film-school dropout who had a very messy apartment and a lot of drugs. He paid us in cash and pot.

One day we were cleaning at Jimmy's and, while I was running his dishwasher, he got off the phone and said he had tickets to the Cal Jam, a massive rock fest at the Ontario Speedway that was supposed to turn into a mini-city of heavy metal fans.

"I like Deep Purple; I don't care about the rest," I said, but Nicole, who was folding socks, lobbed a pair into the sink.

"I think it sounds cool." Nicole often said yes for both of us.

Jimmy drove us in his Impala, with us in the back, and some woman his age in the front, his proper girlfriend of the moment. I looked at the back of her head and thought about his favorite thing to do with me: have me sit on top of him, straddling his cock, and feed him little spoons of cocaine while I rocked on top of him.

She looked too old-fashioned to do that, in her Renaissance Fair outfit and a million pins in her bun. But she was nice, she didn't seem to mind at all that we were coming along. In fact, she was the one who turned around to face us in the back seat, our bare legs in cut-offs getting sweaty on the Naugahyde, and ask us if we wanted a hit of acid.

Her pretty pink finger, a finger that looked like it had never washed so much as a teacup, had some little windowpane tabs on it, with Mr. Natural perfectly printed on each one. "Oh my god, those are so *cute*," I said, and wet my own finger to pick up the little bits of animation. Jimmy's lady turned back to fiddle with the radio, Nicole and I just sat there looking at the little cartoons on my palm. That was our very first pause—you know, that strung-out second when you wonder if you're really going to do something.

I don't remember having that moment before we fucked a guy together for the first time. I don't remember hesitating when kids next door dared the two of us to jump off the Santa Monica Pier, or the first time we hitchhiked all the way to Topanga and back.

I guess we'd both heard the same story about acid: that you'd go crazy and never come back. Art Linkletter's daughter flying into the deep blue sea and all that shit. But man, everything else Art

Linkletter said was bogus, so why should we believe this? He thought marijuana was bad too.

I just hated the thought of being out of control, that's what bugged me. I'd rather watch someone else take acid and ask them every five minutes what they were thinking.

Nicole looked at me and did that "C'mon!" squint of hers, where her brown eyes got all crinkly and her mouth pursed up like a duck. She slipped the windowpane off my hand and onto her tongue, closed her thin lips real tight, and then smiled like a Cheshire cat. Like I was a total pussy to miss this. Okay, fine. I stared back at her and licked Mr. Natural off my finger like turning a page....

Those Manson Girls
Paul Krassner

Charles Manson was on Death Row—this was before capital punishment was repealed (and later reinstated) in California—but I was unable to meet with him. Reporters had to settle for an interview with *any* prisoner awaiting the gas chamber, and it wasn't very likely that Charlie would be selected at random for me.

In the course of our correspondence, one letter consisted of a few pages of handwritten gibberish about Christ and Satan, but at one point, right in the middle, he wrote in tiny letters, "Call Squeaky," with her phone number. I called, and we arranged to meet at her apartment in Los Angeles. On an impulse, I brought several tabs of LSD with me on the flight from San Francisco.

Squeaky Fromme resembled a typical redheaded, freckle-faced waitress who sneaks a few tokes in the lavatory, a regular girl-next-door except perhaps for the unusually challenging nature of her personality plus the scar of an X that she had gouged and burned into her forehead as a visual reminder of her commitment to Charlie.

That same symbol also covered the third eyes of her roommates, Sandra Good and Brenda McCann. "We've crossed ourselves out of this entire system," Sandra said. They all had short hairstyles growing in now, after having completely shaved their heads. They continued to sit on the sidewalk near the Hall of Justice every day, like a coven of faithful nuns bearing witness to Manson's martyrdom.

Sandy Good had seen me perform at The Committee in San Francisco a few years previously. Now she told me that when she first met Charlie, and people asked her what he was like, she had compared him to Lenny Bruce and me. It was the weirdest compliment I'd ever received, but I began to learn about Manson's peculiar charisma.

With his sardonic rap mixed with psychedelic drugs and real-life theater games such as "creepy-crawling" and stealing, he had deprogrammed his family from the inhumane values of mainstream society, but *re*programmed them with his *own* inhumane philosophy, a cosmic version of racism perpetuated by the prison system that had served as *his* family.

Manson had stepped on Sandy's eyeglasses, thrown away her birth control pills, and inculcated her with racist sensibility. Although she had once been a civil rights activist, she was now asking me to tell John Lennon that he should get rid of Yoko Ono and stay with "his own kind." Later, she refined her position: "If Yoko really loved the Japanese people, she would not want to mix their blood."

The four of us ingested my little white tablets containing 300 micrograms of acid, then took a walk to the office of Laurence Merrick, who had been associated with schlock biker-exploitation movies as a prerequisite to directing the sensationalist documentary, *Manson*.

Squeaky's basic vulnerability emerged as she kept pacing around and telling Merrick that she was afraid of him. He didn't know we were tripping, but he must have sensed the vibes. I engaged him in conversation. We discussed the fascistic implications of a film, *The French Connection*, and he remarked, "You're pretty articulate—"

"For a bum," I concluded his sentence, and we laughed. He may have had a touch of contact high.

Next we went to the home of some friends of the family, smoked a few joints of soothing grass and listened to music. The Manson girls sang along with the lyrics of "A Horse With No Name": "In the desert you can remember your name/'cause there ain't no one there to give you no pain."

I was basking in the afterglow of the Moody Blues' *Om* song when Sandy began to speak of "the gray people"—regular citizens going about their daily business—whom she had been observing from her vantage point on the corner near the Hall of Justice.

"We were just sitting there," she said, "and they were walking along, kind of avoiding us. It's like watching a live movie in front of you. Sometimes I just wanted to kill the gray people, because that was the only way they would be able to experience the total Now."

This was an expression Charlie had borrowed from Scientology. When ranchhand Shorty Shea was killed, he was first tied up, a few of the girls performed fellatio on him, and when he climaxed, they chopped his head off because he had reached the total Now.

Later, Sandy explained to me that she didn't mean it literally about killing the gray people, that she had been speaking from another dimension. She told me that prosecutor Vincent Bugliosi had once snarled at her as she kept her vigil outside the courthouse:

"We're gonna get you because you sucked Charlie Manson's dick."

Bugliosi had also accused Squeaky of threatening him during the trial, although reporters who witnessed a confrontation between them on that street corner heard *him* threaten to send *her* to the gas chamber. The girls just sat there on the sidewalk and laughed. They knew that oral-genital relations did not constitute a capital offense.

When we returned to their apartment, Sandy asked if I wanted to take a hot bath. I felt ambivalent.

I knew that one of the attorneys in the case had participated in a memorable *menage a trois* with Squeaky and Sandy, but I had also been told by a reporter, "It certainly levels the high to worry about getting stabbed while fucking the Manson ladies in the bunkhouse at the Spahn Ranch—I've found that the only satisfactory position is sitting up, back to the wall, facing the door."

Visions of the famous shower scene in *Psycho* flashed through my mind, but despite the shrill self-righteousness that infected their true believer syndrome, these women had charmed me with their honesty, humor, and distorted sense of compassion. They sensed my hesitation, and Squeaky confronted me.

"You're afraid of me, aren't you?"

"Not really. Should I be?"

Sandy tried to reassure me: "She's *beautiful*, Paul. Just look into her eyes. Isn't she beautiful?"

Squeaky and I stared silently at each other for a while, and my eyes began to tear as I recalled that Manson had written, "I never picked up anyone who had not already been discarded by society." There were tears in Squeaky's eyes too.

She asked me to try on Charlie's vest. It felt like a bizarre honor to participate in this family ceremony. The corduroy vest was a solid inch thick with embroidery—snakes and dragons and devilish designs, including human hair that had been woven into the multi-colored patterns.

Sandy took her hot bath, but instead of my getting into the tub *with* her—assuming she had invited me—I sat fully dressed on the toilet, a slightly less presumptuous posture, and we talked. I was thinking, "You have pert nipples," but I said, "What's that scar on your back?"

"It's from a lung operation."

Brenda asked for another tab of acid to send Manson in prison. She ground it into powder which she glued to the paper with vegetable dye and the notation, "Words fly fast," explaining that Charlie would know what it meant. She stayed up late that night, writing letters to several prisoners with the dedication of a polygamous war wife.

Squeaky visited me a few times in San Francisco. On our way to lunch one day, she lit a cigarette, and I told her about the series of advertisements by which women were originally conditioned into smoking: a woman standing next to a man who was smoking; next a woman saying to the man, "Blow some my way"; and finally a woman smoking her *own* cigarette. Squeaky simply smiled, said "Okay," and dropped her cigarette on the sidewalk, crushing it out with her shoe.

Another time, when I attempted to point out a certain fallacy in her logic, she responded, "Well, what do you expect from me? I'm crazy!"

Once she told me she had been beaten up by members of the Mel Lyman family from Boston because she wouldn't switch her allegiance to them, even though they'd had plans to break Manson out of jail while his trial was taking place, by means of a helicopter. She said they were "well organized."

Squeaky mailed me her drawing in red ink of a woman's face with a pair of hands coming out of her mouth. Written in script was the song lyric, "Makes me wanna holler, throw up both my hands..."

Originally published in Rolling Stone.

Dorothy Horsefeathers

I lived for about three months in the Straight Theater in Haight-Ashbury, summer of 1967. Summer of Love, 30,000 young people descending on San Francisco seeking the Revolution, determined to deny and abandon the mindless gray-flannel Great Society of the mainstream culture and to found the truly New Society right there and then. It was Utopia, it was Hell. It was joy and delight and free love, it was hunger and abandonment and total paranoia. It was psychedelic-expanded-consciousness-bliss, it was hysterical-frightened-compulsive-freak-out. It was panhandling for dimes and nickels, it was raising $25,000 in half an hour for a deal.

The very intensity of the positive, spiritual, awakening forces that were exploding there in a flowering frenzy created a cloud of equally intense negative, paranoid, exploitative forces to create a balance, much as an electron is an infinite negative charge which creates a positive cloud around it to almost, but not quite, mask it out. Or so we theorized at the time....

It was the Autumnal Equinox, and the Straight was having another benefit for the Free Food people, and Kenneth Anger was going to put on a show and film it (later released as *Lucifer Rising*). Before the show, Stanley Owsley, the counterculture hero LSD maker, came by and passed out four-hit Purple Barrels, which, once the show had started, the whole crew took. Which was unfortunate, because things got a little out of hand. Kenneth Anger was running all over, destroying curtains and other property, instruments were stolen, and chaos generally ensued. By the time everyone had gone, I was left alone, and really peaking, to shut down the theater.

I made a round of the ground floor, checking all the doors, and continued upstairs, through the mezzanine, and up to the projection booth, where I lived, tracing an ascending spiral as I ritualistically sealed my environment, and came to rest seated in a lotus position, nestled in the old theater curtain which was my bed. I sat there and felt a power flow through me, and I had the image of being a giant radio antenna, high on the point of a pyramid, beaming all this energy out into space, There was nothing else I could do. I had no idea where the energy came from or where it was going, but all my being at that moment was acting as a transmitter for it. As I sat entranced, a voice kept repeating a mantra in my mind. Over and over again it chanted the name: "Dorothy Horsefeathers, Dorothy Horsefeathers. Dorothy Horsefeathers."

Flopsy, Mopsy and Cottonmouth
Emily Brown

Matt wants someone to trip on acid with him. It's the night before Valentine's Day, and I'm camping with some friends who are back from college for the weekend. The urge to try it is just too much, so I hold a blue gel tab on my tongue, and in 45 minutes I'm thinking, "Okay, the sky is dripping on me, and I can handle that, but Matt's voice is not supposed to be echoing...."

The gnarled pine trees around us look like the zigzags on Charlie Brown's shirt, or maybe sharp teeth in a huge, sinister mouth. Our faces shimmer with firelight, smoke rising into the cold Georgia air like a gray serpent. "Bread products!" Joel yells, and tosses his crumpled beer can into the fire. I watch him shove piece after piece of stale white bread into his mouth, laughing hysterically. His glasses slide down his nose, and for a second he reminds me of an insanely demented White Rabbit from *Alice in Wonderland*.

I stare at the fire, trying to ignore the trees melting into pools at my feet. Pinwheels of color spin crazily around me, congregating in the depths of the fire and then shooting back into the sky. Suddenly the flames and charred branches develop tiny puncture holes and start gushing blood. My eyes widen and I quickly look away as wildflowers sprout out of the fire's wounds and twine around each other.

Hayden, Liam and Jennifer are out in the woods searching for firewood, and I can hear them laughing and stumbling around in the darkness. Matt's thickly shadowed face appears in front of mine, making me think of a leering Jack-O-Lantern.

"Hey, is it working yet?" he asks, although to me it sounds like he's yelling the words underwater.

He wiggles his eyebrows, and I shake my head no and look up at the sky. It looks like an incredibly vivid Van Gogh painting, but I don't think I can handle looking into the fire right now. Jennifer comes up behind me, laughing like an evil stepmother out of a Disney movie, and Liam and Hayden follow her, carrying armloads of branches.

Everyone settles down in a circle around the fire, shivering and eating food taken from Matt's parents. A shrill scream pierces the night as Liam accidentally sets his curly hair on fire, lighting a bowl. Everyone laughs as the wind changes direction and he gets smoke in his face and chants, "I hate white rabbits, I hate white rabbits," like some sort of strange mantra.

Matt gets everyone's attention and begins dancing a jig on top of the loaf of bread. In his flannel shirt and gray ski cap, he looks like a scrawny, disfigured lumberjack gone mad. Joel lets out a cry of indignation and leaps over the fire to save his "bread products."

Eva asks me repeatedly if I'm okay, and I nod, trying to block out Joel mumbling, "Flopsy, Mopsy and Cottonmouth" to Hayden and Jennifer. They laugh loudly, sounding like a chorus of hyenas who have been huffing helium.

I look for my pen in the dirt for almost five minutes before I realize it's in my pocket, and I glance around at everyone, wondering how stupid I look. Matt and Jennifer keep trying to get me to talk, but I feel like my lips and tongue and teeth aren't my own, so I just take in everything with my eyes, my senses on overload.

George skirts the outside of the circle, looking like a technicolor Grim Reaper in his black hoodie, and I smile as the sky drips its blinking stars on me. One by one, people go into the tent until only Jennifer, Matt, Liam, Hayden and I are left. Colored lightning bolts whiz in front of my eyes like tiny missiles as we move the logs we were sitting on to make room for the sleeping bags.

It's freezing out, the middle of February, and we only have three sleeping bags. Everyone settles down, and everything's quiet except for the crackling logs and my tossing and turning. I can't control my mind, and my thoughts keep shooting off in different directions.

Somewhere around four in the morning, Matt and I crawl out of our sleeping bag, get into his truck and turn the heater on. Vines twist out of the radio and spill glittering shapes off of their leaves. Stretching out in the reclined seat, I watch the sky blink on and off through the sunroof.

In the middle of the night, I slide out of the truck, about to pee in my pants and wishing I had someone to talk to. I manage to find the toilet paper in the pitch-black darkness, although after I piss on my hand I forget to use it.

Jennifer and Hayden's laughter wakes me up, and the morning sky blurs in front of my eyes as I stumble out of the truck and almost fall face-first into a frozen puddle. We load everything into the trucks, burn the remaining products, and end our strange pioneering experience by picking daffodils and singing along with the radio so loud it makes my throat hurt. Happy Valentine's Day!

The Day We Destroyed the World

In October of 1993, I had just established the relationship of my dreams with a beautiful, dark-haired, semi-anarchic artist. It was kind of like dating Winona Ryder with the brains of a James-Joyce-soaked freelance terrorist, only she was much smarter and cuter. Her name was Sandi, and this seemed to be what I had always hoped for.

She (like me) was a television producer. We were going to set *The Simpsons* and *60 Minutes* on their ass with the shit we could come up with. Ours was a relationship destined for Great Creations.

My best friend, Graham, saw that this was indeed one of The Most Amazing Relationships of All Time and in an unparalleled act of generosity, laid upon us The Ultimate Gift—eight hits of actual, real, given to him by *the guy himself*, Owsley acid from the 1960s, scientifically preserved in a hermetically sealed container and kept continually frozen since that heady era.

There was one condition: We had to go away and take it at my family's secluded house in Martha's Vineyard (rather than at home) and Create a Great Work of Art as a result.

By what I thought at the time was a fortunate coincidence, a major network had given me the green light to "go crazy" and come up with a "wacky" premise for a comedy series with a "bold new direction," which they would let me control completely, no questions asked. All the ducks were lined up. Sandi and I were all set to Brew Some Modern Alchemy that would turn the world on its ear.

I knew all about acid. I'd taken a good dozen or so trips in my 35 years on this planet; set and setting were the key. With the dog packed in with plenty of candles, incense, tapes of Marx Brothers movies, books of surrealist art, Persian tapestries and fresh flowers, we set off to the Vineyard to set the world on fire. Little did I know how prophetic that phrase would become.

Even though it was almost Halloween, the Vineyard weather was mellow and beautiful. We arrived late in the night Friday, and immediately set about preparing the place for our excursion into the inner realms. With a breathtaking sunrise the next morning, we had a light breakfast of fresh fruit and coffee, and ceremoniously dropped a tab each. Fifteen minutes passed. Nothing. Another 15. Zip. Then an hour. Not even a tingle. Despite his careful attempts at preservation, it appeared that Graham's Owsley acid had gone the way of a Fillmore poster kept in direct sunlight.

I called Graham at home in New York.

"That's weird, man," he said. "I took three and it was really great. Mellow but intense. Yeah, that's it. You gotta do, like, three each."

I thanked him, and Sandi and I dutifully, doubting the results, dropped two more hits apiece. We were beginning to feel like kids who'd been promised a trip to Disney World, but had to make do with the playground at the local McDonalds.

Nearly another hour passed, and our mission was beginning to look like a total dud. We each dropped one more—the remaining two hits—just in case they were actually the "good ones."

Just then, the phone rang. It was Graham.

"Oh, yeah," he said, "I forgot to mention. I don't know why, but it took, like, over two hours for it to take effect the last time. So don't worry. It really should work, just be patient."

I thanked him again, and just as I hung up the phone... it was like one of those shots in a film where the camera pulls back but zooms in, in perfect increments, warping the background but leaving the subject unchanged. "Oh, shit," I said, looking over at Sandi.

She was feeling it, too. For there was one major difference between us and Graham. At six-foot-four, Graham tipped the scales at a healthy 275 or so. Sandi and I matched each other at around five-foot-six, and more or less exactly half the weight. Can you say "body mass?" Anything *he* experienced, *we* were going to experience *twice as hard*—and we had taken an *extra hit*. Standing in the kitchen, the sensation was like suddenly standing vertical in a roller-coaster car on the Coney Island Cyclone... but we were going three times faster.

"Fuck!" said Sandi. I wondered if the terror in my eyes was as visible as it was in hers, but this was *no time to panic*, I told myself, furiously attempting to summon my inner Good Trips Guru. We headed into the living room, which we had bedecked with the candles and pretty-things-to-look-at accouterments. I looked at the clock: 10:30 a.m. A trip lasts four hours, right? Whatever was going to transpire, it would all be over in four hours. Right?

I fumblingly inserted a Peter Gabriel CD into the boom box. Music. Yes, yes, music. Music will make it All Good, especially a Good Man like Peter Gabriel's music. It sounded horrible, tinny, shrill and pathetic, like a warbling hamster trying to dance on ice cubes. Brrrr! It was cold in here! Sandi lay shivering on the couch. I spoke to her in soothing tones, laying a knit caftan over her. I was going to make it all right, I told myself. I Love Her! If she's having a bad trip, I'll make it good! I could handle this. I had experience. Fire. Yes! A cozy, warm fire in the fireplace. I ran outside to gather wood. The trip was coming on me stronger every second.

Looking down, approaching the woodpile, I realized I was naked. Somehow, I had shed my clothes after putting on the CD. My bare feet looked all white against the cold ground, with pulsing red and blue veins. My penis was shortened and shrivelled to the size of a French dime. Luckily, that side of the house was out of sight of the neighbors. I somehow soberly gathered a generous number of logs and went back inside. Summoning the Spirit of my Yeti Firemaking Ancestors, I built a lovely, crackling, successful fire. Ahh. Yes. It was going to be All Right.

I looked at the clock. It was 10:36. Six minutes had passed since our trip had begun in earnest. Hoo boy. Just three hours and fifty-four minutes to go.

At this point, I realized I was no longer wearing my glasses. But what were "glasses?" I remembered, of course! "Glasses" were the strips of gold-colored wire that were fastened, from one wall to another, at around eye-height in any room. A ribbon of glass hung along the bottom of the wire—all you had to do was find the part of that glass ribbon that you could focus through, and that was the part of the room that was in your "prescription." Quite simple, really. Just stand there, and you'd be able to see just fine.

I spent the better part of what seemed like two hours looking for my "glasses" in the various rooms of the house, to no avail. I calmed myself down by remembering that if one was tripping, finding one's "prescription" could be difficult. It would all be over soon. I walked up to the kitchen clock: 10:47. Well, so, time was just going a little slower. Something really fun and interesting would no doubt happen soon, I thought, making the rest of the trip just as groovy as I hoped it would be.

I returned to the living room and somehow managed to replace the Gabriel caterwauling with some late '30s Billie Holiday, the good stuff, which sounded infinitely better. The coffee table was laden with a basket of fruit, a ream of paper, colored markers, pens, and my notebook computer, which I had purposefully set going on a new, blank document, so that we could just casually squirt the essence of our Masterpiece onto it when the Moment came upon us. Something told me it wasn't going to be as neat and easy as I thought.

Sandi was still on the couch, but hugging her knees now, fetus-like. I sat down next to her. "How ya doing, kid?" I said, trying my best to feel like Jimmy Stewart. A short, hairy, naked, essentially blind, tripping Jimmy Stewart.

"Bluh!" she said. "... hubble... my *mom! Language!* I'll *never* see my mom *again!*"

She began to cry; huge, wracking sobs, and I held her. Good. I was doing Good. Comforting the poor, tripping girl. It was at this point... that we *merged*. And the acid really started to kick in. Her trip... became my trip.

"Of course you will," I offered. "Your mom is alive and well at her house in Greenfield. She's fine! We'll go see her first thing when this is over, honey. I promise."

"*Nooooooo!*" screamed Sandi, terror-stricken. "It'll never be over! We're destroying l*anguage!* We're destroying *everything*! Look at the *dog*! Look at his *eyes*!"

My dog, a fairly simple-minded beagle, was staring at us. For some reason, his eyes were glowing red, a deep crimson. I laughed, scoffing at this cliche hallucination.

"Oh, honey," I said, chasing away the demonic atmosphere for a moment, "that's just a laughably typical LSD illusion! The dog isn't really the *Devil*. You and I don't believe in the *Devil*."

"*No*," she said, "it's *worse* than that! It's all *our* fault! *You* and *me*! What is *language*? *See*!?!? You don't remember what language *is*!" She was right. It made perfect sense. She continued: "It's *all coming apart at the seams*! By the time we're done, there won't be any *words*, there won't be any *people*, there won't be any more *world*! It's *already happened and there's nothing we can do!!!*"

I looked around. We were no longer in the living room. The couch was sitting in a hellish, Precambrian, steaming crater. All around us little fires consumed remnants of anything that Had Once Been. The dog glared at us: *Guilty!*...

The next 11 hours or so are hard to remember. I recall the phenomenon of sound echoing endlessly, of Sandi and me talking, comforting each other in the prehistoric, devoid-of-life world. We had somehow hurtled backwards in time, we had destroyed the beautiful house my parents had built with love and respect, life had never existed at all—*because we took too much*.

And that's when the Good Part happened. The part that made it all worthwhile. The Earth was empty. Dead. Life had simply Never Been. But... here we were. And we were real. We were alive. The Secret was Simple. It had been in front of us all along: To bring back everything, all we had to do was make love. And here we are. So it must have worked. We never did get that pilot written.

Joel on Adams Street, 1968
Lenny Lipton

Joel the carpenter,
the philosopher of wood,
seeking patrons,
not customers,
drinking whiskey,
smoking dope and dropping acid,
the two of us snarling at the war,
laughing at the hippies
the two of us laughing at
the melting ball of wax.

The harmonica and I,
Pursuing Red River Valley,
somewhere between the chicken coop
and the fence by the creek,
in Joel's hard-packed yard.

Joel smiling faintly,
hiding behind a mane of brown hair,
sentences like fading fugitives,
hands making circles in the air,
tracing out the ineffable,
or is he conducting Wagner?

Maybe he smoked too much dope,
maybe he drank too much whiskey,
maybe he just forgot to breathe.

If I could visit him one last time,
I'd push open the gate,
and walk down the jumbled path
to the hundred-year-old house
on a dead-end street in Berkeley,
I'd hear the hi-fi playing;
they're playing rock 'n' roll in the park,
freaks high on life and Owsley's best
dance naked in the sun on Hippie Hill;
tribal pennants ripple in the breeze;
people swear the new age has begun.
I'd knock on his door,
and there he'd be, smiling faintly
his face haloed by a shock of brown hair,
my faded friend, Joel.

Hail and Farewell
Lane Sarasohn

I started taking LSD when Timothy Leary was still a professor at Harvard. At first our acid arrived in the form of sugar cubes wrapped in aluminum foil. Our Cambridge-based connection assured us it was the same pharmaceutically pure acid enjoyed by Leary, Alpert and Metzner, manufactured by Sandoz Laboratories in Switzerland where LSD-25 was born.

The first few trips were revelations, as meaningless distinctions such as Good and Bad, Here and There, and Me and Not Me dissolved in the palpable, overwhelming and exquisite experience of being at one with the Oneness of All Things.

For the next three years I took acid religiously, every Friday, after work, sometimes alone, sometimes with friends, sometimes for fun, but usually as part of a spiritual quest. Like many others of my generation, I thought I'd found a shortcut to Enlightenment and "How ya gonna keep 'em down on the farm after they've seen Nirvana?"

In the Summer of '65, I was working in Washington, DC for a little New York publishing company that had contracted to publish in 68 large, hardbound volumes the entire card catalog of the US Department of Agriculture Library.

My job was to make a little mark on each and every three-by-five file card to separate the file card information that was pertinent from the file card information that was extraneous. Subsequently, the cards would be photocopied and a team of paste-up artists would use my little mark as a guide so that the finished product would amount to 68 volumes and not 168 volumes.

The tedium of the job was only relieved by an occasional bizarre book title or unusual author's name. (Two of the names I came across still amuse me: Jesus H. Christ and John L. Senior, Jr.) Needless to say, my Friday acid trips were consistently the highpoint of my week.

Though I was in DC for six or seven months, 30 years later I can only remember two of my trips there. One took place during a day off, when I dropped acid and rented a paddle boat at the Tidal Basin near the Jefferson Memorial.

Paddling out to the middle of the basin with my Modern Library edition of Laotse's *Tao Te Ching* on the seat beside me, I experienced a rush of acid intoxication, no doubt accelerated by the physical exertion required to propel the ponderous paddle boat across the little lake. Weary, I stopped paddling, only to begin drifting in a slow circle, sitting like a zombie, alone in a paddle boat as Washington's famous monuments spun, shimmered, danced, and dissolved around me. Vaguely, I wondered why in the world I had ever thought taking acid in a paddle boat would be either enjoyable or enlightening. And that's when the wind came up, followed by a downpour of rain *and hail!*

Never having been outside in a hailstorm before, I thought that someone behind me was bombarding me with mothballs. My rational mind, faint, but still perceptible, piped up that it was probably hail and not mothballs. Frightened and upset, but also amused at such an unlikely predicament, my ego returned in a hurry as I paddled back toward the dock, cold, high and wet, protecting my head from the icy pellets with Laotse's enduring classic.

The other memorable DC trip went awry in a totally different fashion. As was my custom, I dropped acid in the early evening and spent the First Bardo contemplating the Great Void in the comfort and security of my modest furnished apartment on 16th street about a mile up the road from the White House. When the Second Bardo arrived I ventured out to my car and drove several blocks to a fashionable area where I thought it would be safe and pleasant to stroll.

Because of one's heightened sensitivity, the world as seen on acid is intensely detailed, color-saturated and surreal. Washington's broad tree-lined boulevards, among the world's most elegant, took on added interest, grandeur and charm when viewed through crystal spectacles.

Focusing my expanded consciousness on the mundane requirements of parallel parking, I backed into a space and edged up to the curb, mindful not to make contact with the car parked in front or the car parked behind. As I got out of my car a nice-looking young man from India who had watched me park commented with a thick but melodious accent, "That is a very nice car."

"Thank you," I said, thinking that would be the end of our conversation.

"What kind of car is that? A Buick?"

"Yes, it is. A Special." And then, not to be curt, I asked him, "Where are you from?"

"I am from India. But I live here in Washington—I work at the Embassy."

Pleased to meet someone from the Land of the Buddha, I could not resist telling this friendly chap, "I happen to be a great admirer of the philosophical traditions of your country."

"What do you mean?" he asked.

"I am a believer in the teachings of Gautama Buddha and I am also a great admirer of Boddhidarma [the patriarch who brought Buddhism from India to China and who came to be considered the founder of Zen]."

"Oh, well, then, you would certainly like the teachings of my Exalted Spiritual Master, His Most Holy Highness, Swami Hamarama Lamadingdong." (Or some name like that.) "He is one of the great spiritual masters of India today. He is a modern-day Buddha."

"Gee," I said, wondering if what he was saying was true. "I've never heard of him."

"Would you like to see his book?

"Well... sure."

It seemed apparent that karma had delivered me to this spot on Earth, at this time in my life, in this state of consciousness. Though spaced-out, paranoid and skeptical, I decided it would be irresponsible not to take what might be a first step on the much-sought-after, but ever-hard-to-find Path to True Understanding.

"Oh, that is good, but—I don't have the book with me. It is in my hotel room. Right there, across the street. Come on, I will show you. Are you interested?"

High as I was, I didn't want to go to anyone's hotel room. But, even more, I didn't want to insult this foreign gentleman's feelings or insult his guru or pass up this karmic opportunity, so I walked with him to his hotel and accompanied him up to his room. His name was Raj and he seemed very nervous. The hotel's interior was done in super-realism with moiré-patterned walls and easy-hallucinating carpets. The lobby, elevator and hallways might have been designed by Escher.

Raj's little cluttered room was stuffy and so was the book he handed me. No precious gems of wisdom jumped from the yellowed pages, just bad to worthless advice on what to eat, how to bathe, how to dress, how to crap, Holy Day rituals and the importance of avoiding contact with menstruating women.

While I leafed through this disappointing tome, my host poured me a hotel-bathroom glass full of Scotch, apologizing at length about not having any ice. Even Coca-Cola tastes like poison on acid; the last thing I wanted right then was a mouthful of warm Scotch, but Raj insisted I take it as he sat down next to me on the bed.

And that's when, suddenly, for the first time, tripping out on acid, holding a warm glass of Scotch in one hand and a bad swami book in the other, and having my knee rubbed by a nervous young man from India, did I realize I was being carefully, patiently, and methodically seduced like some bubblegum-chewing Bimbo from Palookaville. Amused and appalled, embarrassed and amazed, I informed Raj that it was time for me to leave.

"I can't... I'm not... I have to go."

On the one hand, as a practicing hippie, I was tolerant of other alternative lifestyles and I had no wish to hurt the poor chap's feelings, or worse, break his heart; on the other hand, I just wanted to get the fuck out of there! I bolted out the door, hurried down the corridor, descended in the elevator, raced through the lobby and dashed to my car, laughing all the way like a holy fool at my naivete, my pretentiousness and my power of self-delusion.

There are many other acid trips that stand out in my memory because they were magical and/or profound, acid trips that changed my perception and changed my life, acid trips that helped me recast habits of mind and habits of behavior, but these two—getting caught in a hailstorm in a paddle boat on acid and getting picked up by a gay guy from India on acid—stand out after all these years because they were so wonderfully, marvelously, incredibly and uniquely stupid.

Half Beard
Mike Serena

Once, while my wife, a friend of ours and I were tripping at our apartment, I got up to go to the bathroom. While I was in there, I looked into the mirror and decided that might be a good time to shave off my beard. I had some old shaving cream and razors, left-over from the last time that I had shaved... probably two to three years earlier. I started to shave, but soon realized that this might not be the best time to be playing with sharp objects.

I had removed a lot of hair from the right side of my face, but none yet from the left side. I then drew an imaginary line through the center of my face and carefully shaved off everything to the right of it, leaving the left side untouched. I then went back into the living room and sat down as if nothing had happened. My wife and our friend looked at me, and no matter what was going through their heads, they also acted as if nothing had happened. At the time I admired their ability to keep a straight face, or disdained their powers of observation; I wasn't sure which.

The next day, although I had come down a lot, I was still crazy enough that I decided to go walking around on the University of Cincinnati campus with half a beard. I got a lot of strange looks, and to those people who got close enough to almost ask (since nobody had the nerve to actually talk to a man crazy enough to have half a beard), I would say, "You think *this* is weird? You ought to see my *brother*," and leave them to try to imagine what my brother looked like.

My sister-in-law worked at that time in the Physics Department, so I decided to go see her. As I walked toward her office, I went past a door with that symbol used to denote radiation and a sign that read, WARNING! THIS DOOR MUST BE KEPT SHUT AT ALL TIMES! I went into the office that she worked in, but she wasn't there. When another woman approached, I looked her straight in the eye and said, "You know that door down the hall? Well, it's open," and pointed at my semi-beard. I thought that she was going to have a fit, but just then Joan came into the room, saw me, realized that I was up to some insane prank, and took over.

One of the reasons that I had gone to see her in the first place was that she had some Christmas presents for my brother that, even though it was now March, had not yet been delivered. After we talked for a few minutes, she gave me the presents to give to my brother and I departed.

There I was, in the middle of March, walking across the UC campus with half a beard and a stack of Christmas presents. This time, *nobody* got close enough for me to say anything. I felt like the poster boy for LSD, and at times wanted to laugh so hard that it hurt, but I felt that I was now involved in a live drama and that the theater involved in my walk required that I keep a straight face.

My Acid Trip with Groucho Marx
Paul Krassner

When I first told my mother about taking LSD, she became very worried.

"It could lead to marijuana," she warned me.

LSD was influencing music, painting, spirituality—and the stock market. Tim Leary once let me listen in on a call from a Wall Street broker thanking him for turning him on to acid because it gave him the courage to sell short.

Leary had a certain sense of pride about the famous folks he and his associates had introduced to the drug. He told me about prominent people whose lives had been changed by taking LSD—actor Cary Grant, director Otto Preminger, think-tanker Herman Kahn, Alcoholics Anonymous founder Bill Wilson, *Life* magazine publishers Henry Luce and Clare Boothe Luce.

"But," he told me, "I consider Otto Preminger one of our failures."

I met Preminger in 1960 while I was doing interviews on censorship for *Playboy*. He had defied Hollywood's official seal of approval by refusing to change the script of *The Moon Is Blue*. He wouldn't take out the word "virgin."

At the end of our interview, he asked, "Ven you tronscripe dis, vill you fix op my Henglish?"

"Oh, sure," I replied quickly. "Of course."

"Vy? Vot's drong viz my Henglish?"

I saw Preminger again in 1968. He was making a movie called *Skidoo*, starring Jackie Gleason as a retired criminal. Preminger told me he had originally intended the role for Frank Sinatra. Typecasting, I suppose.

I was hanging around with friends from the Hog Farm commune, who were extras in the movie. *Skidoo* was pro-acid propaganda thinly disguised as a comedy adventure.

However, LSD was not the reason why the FBI was annoyed with the film. Rather, according to Gleason's FBI files, the FBI objected to one scene in the script where a file cabinet is stolen from an FBI building. Gleason was later approved, though, as a special FBI contact in the entertainment business.

When *Skidoo* was released, Leary saw it, and he cheerfully admitted, "I was fooled by Otto Preminger. He's much hipper than me."

One of the characters in *Skidoo* was a Mafia chieftain named God. Screenwriter Bill Cannon had suggested Groucho Marx for the part. Preminger said it wasn't a good idea, but since they were already shooting, and that particular character was needed on the set in three days, Groucho would be playing God after all. I had met him—Groucho, not God—two years previously....

* * *

Lenny Bruce was staying in a second-floor room at the Swiss-American Hotel in the North Beach section of San Francisco.

Nearby, Hugh Romney (now Hog Farm leader and Ben & Jerry ice cream flavor Wavy Gravy) was working with a satirical troupe, The Committee, and distributing LSD in his spare time. He wandered around carrying a chromium lunch-box that had green velvet lining, a thermos bottle filled with hot soup, and his dope supply in the inner lining.

Lenny wasn't in his room, but guitarist Eric Miller was, so Hugh left a couple of hits of acid on top of the bureau. Lenny had never tried LSD before, and Hugh figured Lenny would just give it to someone else, not take it himself. Hugh also left another hallucinogen, DMT, with a note saying, "Please smoke this till the jewels fall out of your eyes."

Lenny returned, saw the package on his dresser, swallowed both hits of acid and smoked the DMT. He had never seen colors like this before. He was standing on the low window ledge, talking to Miller with great animation, when suddenly he lost his balance and fell backward, through the window.

It was an accident, but the instant he realized that he was *committed* to the fall, he called out in midair, "Man shall rise above the rule!" Then he hit the pavement below. Miller ran down to the sidewalk and tried to comfort him. Lenny's pelvis and both ankles had been broken, but he still managed to ask a nurse if she would please give him some head.

When Lenny got out of the hospital, he became the Hermit of

Hollywood Hills. Jerry Hopkins, a talent booker for the *Steve Allen Show*, had arranged for me to perform at the Steve Allen Playhouse in Los Angeles and, in one of his rare departures from the house, Lenny came to my show, both legs still in casts.

At one point during my monologue, I was talking about the importance of having empathy for other people's perversions. Later, during a question-and-answer session with the audience, Lenny stood up on his crutches and asked me to clarify what I meant by that.

"Well, I was in the subway once—it was rush hour and it was really crowded—and an elderly lady's buttocks kept rubbing against me, and I began to get aroused."

"You're *sick*," Lenny yelled.

The audience howled.

"Thank you, Mr. President," I said, ending the show.

Groucho Marx was in the audience, and Hopkins introduced him to Lenny and me.

"That was very smart, the way you finished," Groucho said, shaking my hand. "Besides, I was getting fidgety in my seat."

* * *

Now I was having dinner with Groucho. He was concerned about the script of *Skidoo* because it pretty much advocated LSD, which he had never tried, but he was curious. Moreover, he felt a certain responsibility to his young fans not to steer them wrong, so could I possibly get him some pure stuff—he had read about my first trip in *The Realist*—and would I care to accompany him on *his* first trip?

I did not play hard to get.

We arranged to ingest those little white 300-microgram tablets one afternoon at the home of an actress in Beverly Hills. Groucho was particularly interested in the countercultural aspects of LSD. I mentioned a couple of incidents which particularly tickled him, and his eyes sparkled with delight.

I told him how, on Haight Street, runaway youngsters—refugees from their own families—had stood outside a special tourist bus guided by a driver who had been "trained in sociological significance," and they held mirrors up to the cameras pointing at them from the windows, so that the tourists would get photos of *themselves* unsuccessfully trying to take photos. I also told him about that day when LSD became illegal and thousands of hippies gathered there to swallow tabs of acid as the police stood by helplessly.

"Internal possession wasn't against the law," I explained to Groucho.

"And," he added, "they trusted their friends more than they trusted the government. I like that."

We had a period of silence and a period of listening to music. I was accustomed to playing rock'n'roll while tripping, but the record collection at this house consisted entirely of classical music and Broadway show albums. First, we listened to the Bach Cantata No. 7.

"I'm supposed to be Jewish," Groucho said, "but I was seeing the most beautiful visions of Gothic cathedrals. Do you think Bach *knew* he was doing that?"

"I don't know. I was seeing beehives and honeycombs myself."

Later, we were listening to the score of a musical comedy, *Fanny*. There was one song, "Welcome Home," where the lyrics go something like, "Welcome home, says the clock," and the chair says, "Welcome home," and so do various other pieces of furniture. Groucho started acting out each line, as though he were *actually* being greeted by the clock, the chair, and the rest of the furniture. He was like a child, charmed by his own ability to respond to the music that way.

There was a bowl of fruit on the dining-room table. During a snack, Groucho said, "I never thought eating a nice juicy plum would be the biggest thrill of my life."

Then we talked about the sexual revolution.

Groucho asked, "Have you ever laid two ladies together?"

I told him about the time I was being interviewed by a couple of students from a Catholic girls' school. Suddenly, Sheila, *The Realist*'s Scapegoat, and Marcia, the Shit-On—she had given herself that title because, "What could be lower than a Scapegoat?"—walked out of their office totally nude.

"Sorry to interrupt, Paul," said Sheila, "but it's Wednesday— time for our weekly orgy."

The interviewers left in a hurry. Sheila and Marcia led me up the stairs to my loft bed, and we had a delicious threesome. It had never happened before and it would never happen again.

At one point in our conversation, Groucho somehow got into a negative space. He was equally cynical about institutions, such as marriage ("legal quicksand"), and individuals, such as Lyndon Johnson ("that potato-head").

Eventually I asked, "What gives you hope?"

Groucho thought for a moment. Then he said just one word: "People."

He told me about one of his favorite contestants on *You Bet Your Life*.

"He was an elderly gentleman with white hair, but quite a chipper fellow. I asked him what he did to retain his sunny disposition. 'Well, I'll tell you,' he said. 'Every morning I get up and I *make a choice* to be happy that day.'"

Groucho was holding on to his cigar for a long time, but he

never smoked it, he only sniffed it occasionally.

"Everybody has their own Laurel and Hardy," he mused. "A miniature Laurel and Hardy, one on each shoulder. Your little Oliver Hardy bawls you out—he says, 'Well, this is a *fine mess* you've gotten us into.' And your little Stan Laurel gets all weepy—'Oh, Ollie, I couldn't help it. I'm sorry, I did the best I *could*....'"

Later, when Groucho started chuckling to himself, I hesitated to interrupt his reverie, but I had to ask, "What struck you funny?"

"I was just thinking about this movie, *Skidoo*," he said. "I mean some of it is just plain ridiculous. This kid puts his stationery, which is soaked in LSD, into the water supply of the prison, and suddenly everybody gets completely reformed. There's a prisoner who says, 'Oh, gosh, now I don't have to be a rapist anymore!' But it's also sophisticated in its own way. I like how Jackie Gleason, the character he plays, *accepts* the fact that he's not the biological father of his daughter."

"Oh, yeah? That sounds like the ultimate ego loss."

"But I'm really getting a big kick out of playing somebody named God like a dirty old man. You wanna know why?"

"Typecasting?"

"No, no—it's because—do you realize that irreverence and reverence are the *same thing*?"

"Always?"

"If they're not, then it's a misuse of your power to make people laugh." His eyes began to tear. "That's funny," he said, "I'm not even sad."

Then he went to urinate. When he came back, he said, "You know, everybody is waiting for *miracles* to happen, but the whole *human body* is a goddam miracle."

He recalled Otto Preminger telling him about his own response to taking LSD and he mimicked Preminger's accent: "I saw *tings*, bot I did not zee myself." Groucho was looking in a mirror on the dining-room wall, and he said, "Well, I can see *my*self, but I still don't understand what the hell I'm *doing* here...."

A week later, he told me that the Hog Farm had turned him on with marijuana on the set of *Skidoo*.

"You know," I said, "my mother once warned me that LSD would lead to marijuana."

"Well," said Groucho, "your mother was right."

Originally published in HIGH TIMES.

Chapter 9

Disco Doses

Acid Confidential
Dave Marsh

There was the time I got busted on LSD, and the cops and EMTs (I had decided I could drive a car; I couldn't and put it into a semi-rural ditch) kept asking me how much I took, and I kept replying, "How much is there?"—under the illusion that all the world was just one big dose. I thought it was pretty damn funny at the time, you betcha. They didn't. They just kept asking me. They just made me think they were funnier.

Fantasy at *Fantasia*

It was the middle of winter when a bunch of friends and I went to see the re-release of *Fantasia* at the movie theater. It was the only time I ever took "windowpane" acid, and I kept having body rush after body rush.

It wasn't until we left and heard people on their way out asking for their money back that we found out the heating system was broken and all the "rushes" were just us shivering in the cold.

Little People

It was 2 a.m., and I'd already tried running in the moonlight with a stolen log, so I thought I'd see what it was like to watch TV on acid. I turned it on at random and got this Western. I watched, amazed at the bizarre distortion in my perceptions, and finally shook my head and went to bed. The next morning, I looked in *TV Guide* and found out that the movie I'd been watching was *The Terror of Tiny Town*, a musical with an all-midget cast.

Somersault
Rich Gore

It was 1975, in San Diego. I was riding my bicycle home from a local farmer's market, trying to balance a large paper bag of avocados on my handlebars and steer with one hand.

If I had been paying attention, I'd have noticed a guy wandering slowly down the sidewalk, and a pickup truck parked up the street with the gate down. But the paper bag was starting to tear, and I was concentrating on keeping it balanced and in one piece. So I didn't notice anything, not even that my bike was drifting toward the sidewalk.

Suddenly my front tire hit the back of the pickup truck, and in less than a second I flew up and over the bike, somersaulting and landing flat on my back on the pickup truck bed!

After I picked myself up out of the truck, checked out my bike, and started gathering up avocados, I noticed that the guy on the sidewalk had come over to stand by me. "Whoa, did you just *do* that?" he asked with eyes (and pupils) wide.

I admitted to him that I had, in fact, just done that.

"Wow," he replied. "I'm tripping on acid, and even *I* wouldn't have done *that*!"

Living Quarters
Pat Hartman

I think I was 20, wandering around my hometown alone and thoroughly psychedelicized in the middle of the night, when I realized I was out of smokes. There was a coffee shop ahead, but I didn't have any change either. I got through the ordeal of exchanging a dollar for quarters at the register and congratulated myself on passing for straight.

I put the quarters in the cigarette machine one by one, and that's when I noticed people looking at me. I realized too late that the front had been taken off the vending machine for re-stocking, and was leaning against a booth, and the quarters were on the floor.

Yo-Yo Glow

One night on acid, a friend of mine was twirling a glow-in-the-dark yo-yo. He had the end of the string and he was swinging it in big circles, and the tracers were kick-ass. Then, when we turned the light on to rejuvenate the glow of the yo-yo, we found that the string had slowly been ripping the skin off of his forefinger, and his bone was almost exposed. It was a trip.

Awakening
David Jay Brown

One spring afternoon, when I was 16, a friend of mine and I did some blotter acid. We were standing behind the back of his house, looking out toward the edge of his yard, where the lawn merged with a lush green forest. Through the slithering complex of shimmering plants and insects, I saw that everything was covered with eyes. All of the leaves on every tree and fern, every blade of grass, had eyes all over it.

As the acid was peaking, two Jehovah's Witnesses walked over across the lawn to us. I looked at them with my wide bulging eyes and was grinning widely. I couldn't stop smiling and laughing. One of the men asked me if I would like a copy of the magazine that he had in his hand. I looked down at the booklet and saw that it was called *Awake!* Then I looked up at the Jehovah's Witness, and looked back out at the forest.

I looked back at him again and giggled. All of the leaves still had blinking eyes covering them. Everywhere I looked, there were plants and insects covered with wide open, conscious eyes. I raised my trailing arm up, waved it across the landscape, and said, "*This*, my friend, is *Awake!* Everything around us is alive and conscious."

Then I just smiled, and kept smiling, as though I were revealing the secret mysteries of existence. The Jehovah's Witnesses both just looked at me, and didn't say anything. Then one of them just nodded his head and smiled, and they both walked away.

Peas With Eyes
G.A. Wood

I knew I shouldn't have done it. I was tripping in my room, but instead of pleading a strong lack of interest in eating, I thought I'd go to the family dinner table. I don't believe I said a word at the table. I just sat there taking it all in. The formality of it all struck me as funny, somehow.

I was afraid to open my mouth, however, because I feared my words would come out in some unknown language. Everything had an echo to it. I tried not to look at my parents' faces; I kept getting glimpses of horrible demons instead. Luckily, there were enough people at the table (a couple of brothers, a couple of sisters) that I wasn't entirely conspicuous.

I dutifully took each dish as it was passed around the table and took a small helping of each, delighting in the colorful textures. As the alien monsters made weird noises all around me, I pretended to be engrossed in my meal. Then I noticed the peas.

As I experimented with the difficult task of nudging some of them onto my spoon, I began to notice little facial features on them. A hundred green heads, all perfectly detailed. Two hundred eyes! I shot up from the table, muttering something to the effect that I wasn't really feeling all that well, and practically ran out of the room. Needless to say, I never tried that again.

Special Dinner
Charlie Peoples

Mike says, "I'm worried. It's my friend's first trip, and about an hour into it, he says he has to go home, something about his parents having a special dinner."

The phone rings, and after a brief conversation, I ask Mike how is his friend doing?

"Okay, I guess. He said he got through his parents' party, now his only problem was the rocking chairs and gorillas."

At that point, the call abruptly ended.

Horny
Hal Muskat

On my first acid trip, New Year's Eve '68, I was brought to an arty and dosed costume party in Paris where I was introduced to a young woman dressed as the Devil, horns and tail, all in red, and had my brains fucked out. Making love with the Devil on one's first acid trip may not be funny to you, but...

Organ Jokes
Robert Whitaker Sirignano

I had a friend who was tripping on LSD and stood up on a chair, saying, "My knees want to see that table!"

Deep into my own trip that lasted 24 hours, my body organs began to make jokes. My spleen, liver, pancreas and stomach began swapping jokes about the chromosomal makeup of various white blood cells originating in my left leg that were currently drifting around. The organs started laughing, quivering and making rude comments. I started to laugh, because I understood.

Now, even years later, I cannot recapture the reason why I found the incident funny. I can recollect the odd sequence of talking that the organs had with one another, but cannot recall the insight I perceived that made it so funny.

Dropping Acid
Dead Joe Jones

In an Albuquerque Sambo's parking lot, there were four of us dividing an equal number of blue microdots. All but myself had ingested theirs, and as I was grabbing mine it fell to the ground. It being nighttime, we had trouble finding it, so we went inside the restaurant and asked if they had a flashlight we might borrow. The manager said sure, but what are you looking for?

Deft thinkers that we were, we sez a contact lens. He sez okay and gives the loan of a light. We spent about 20 minutes looking for that little blue sucker, and couldn't find it. I think, why not go to ground level and try it that way. So I lay down on the ground and look across the parking lot.

There, about an inch and a half from my eyeball rests the little blue pill. Filled with jubilation, I snatched it up and shouted, "I found it." Just as the manager walks out of the restaurant and sez, "Let me see." I quickly pop it between my lips and feign dropping something.

"Oh, shit, I dropped it," I said.

So we spend another 10 minutes with the manager helping us look for a nonexistent contact lens. Then we blew off the hunt as hopeless, and, leaving the manager gaping after us, we giggly wandered off down the street.

Chapter 10

Two for the Road

Contact High
Mary Jane Oatman-Wak Wak*

It was the summer of '98 at the Lollapalooza tour at the Great Gorge Amphitheater in George, Washington, when I was approached by some buds of mine that wanted me to share my first 'A' experience with them. I have been a pot smoker since I was 15, tried the 'shrooms, but was a little scared to drop acid.

We arrived back at our camp after the concert and were laying out the goods. First Aaron stuck it in his mouth, then my sister Alicia and then our buddy Jamison. It was now my turn when a wind gust blew the foil package containing the white blotter sheet onto the ground.

By this time, it was one o'clock in the morning, and pitch black. I figured it was lost, but decided to give a look anyways. A group of about 10 people were walking by and asked if I needed help looking for my contact lens. I told them, "It's not my contact, it was a hit of acid." Then, all 10 of them, plus about 10 other people from surrounding camps, crawled onto their hands and knees to look for the single hit of acid. I told them that whoever found it got to keep it.

I turned to my buds and said, "I guess it just wasn't my time," but was now really bummed out because if 20-plus people were on the ground looking for one hit, it must be some good shit! But Aaron wouldn't let the night go down like that. We walked a whole three cars down to purchase a few more hits from "the man."

I laid the cute little sheet in my mouth, and waited, and waited. Just as I was about to let them know that I was not feeling a thing, I noticed the cornfields were dancing, the people were talking in another language, and I couldn't feel my feet. We walked around the campground of about 10,000 partiers, and I met the most amazing people ever. It's so great to be a stoner and still remember your first trips!

Mary Jane Oatman-Wak Wak (her birth name) is a member of the Nez Perce Tribe of Idaho. She is formerly from Kamiah, Idaho. Kamiah in the Nez Perce Indian Language translates to "Valley of Hemp."

A Kind of Tribute
Catherine Greenop ByWaters

Since your book on acid trips is already at the publisher and the chances of me getting a story included are slim, I have decided to send you just one. There are many I could send, but this one is special, because it is about my wonderful, handsome, creative, intelligent, witty, 26-year-old son, who is currently serving an 8-year prison sentence in Texas due to his use of, and involvement with selling, drugs. If it is at all possible to include this story, I know it would mean a lot to him, and I would consider it a kind of tribute to his refusal to cut a deal and receive a lighter sentence by ratting on others. Here goes...

There are two parts to this story but in the end both intertwine, as you will see. The first part is about me. I came of age in the glorious Sixties and, between the ages of 16 and 22, smoked a lot of pot and did my fair share of acid and mushrooms. Two things happened when I turned 22. I got married and quickly got pregnant, and I got saved. Being married and pregnant meant having to grow up and be responsible (that's how I saw things then) and being saved meant I would follow Jesus to the ends of the Earth and stay away from all tools of the Devil, which drugs most certainly were!

Lucky for me, I eventually got unsaved and started smoking pot again, but psychedelics were no longer a part of my life, mainly because I just didn't know how/where to get them. The years sped by and I found myself a mother of two teenagers. They loved hearing stories about my wild and crazy hippie days, the acid trips I took, the communes I spent time at, and the tree-house I lived in.

When my oldest son, Noah, was 16, he began acting like a typical adolescent: skipping school occasionally, didn't want to do his household chores, keep his room clean, stuff like that. I was a fairly permissive mom and, when dealing with these issues, tried to remember back to my own teenage years, but still we sometimes butted heads about these things, especially the skipping school.

We lived in a big city in Texas, and down the road from our house was a strip mall. It was all plate-glass storefronts, concrete, and a big paved parking lot. At the entrance to the parking lot there was a tiny little island of grass and flowers, meant to add a small measure of beauty to this asphalt jungle. Anyway, one day I got a call from a friend who said, "I don't mean to alarm you, but I saw Noah and a couple of his friends at the mall today when I was there doing my grocery shopping."

Damn! That meant he was cutting school again!

My friend continued on: "Noah was acting really strange. He was lying in that little grassy area by the mall entrance and it looked like he was talking to the flowers! He was there when I first got to the mall and was still there two hours later when I left, still talking to the flowers!"

Hmmmmm. What the heck? I got this call at 3 p.m., right about the time he was due home from school. So I waited for him to come home to get to the bottom of this strange situation. I waited and waited and waited. Finally at about 7 p.m., someone knocked on the door. It was one of Noah's friends.

"Catherine, Noah's out in my car, but he's afraid to come in. He knows he's in trouble for being late getting home from school. The thing is, he took LSD today for the first time and he's still flying high, and he wants to come home but he's afraid of what you're going to do."

Well, that explained the talking to flowers! "Tell him to come on in," said I, trying to hide my smile. And in he rushed, flying so high he could almost kiss the sky.

"Mom!" he exclaimed excitedly. "Mom! I learned so much today! I learned that everything you've been trying to tell me about life and stuff is right! I'm a butthead! I've been such a butthead! You're so smart, mom!"

Then he ran into the kitchen, grabbed the mop and filled a bucket with warm soapy water and started up the stairs to his bedroom.

"Noah! Where are you going with the mop and bucket?"

"I'm gonna go clean my bathroom, mom!"

A few minutes later he was back downstairs, again telling me how wise and smart I was. "Mom, you know what acid is? It's a progress-checker! You take it and everything becomes clear, all the bullshit falls away and you can see how far you've come or how far you've fallen behind! It's a progress-checker, that's what it is!"

Then he ran over to the bookcases (we read voraciously in our family), pointing to the books with a sweeping motion.

"Mom, look at all this knowledge! All this knowledge that you've absorbed! And you've done so much, and never sold out! Mom, you've made *so much* progress! You should be so proud of yourself! You've made so much progress, so much progress," he muttered as he ran back up the stairs to his room.

Progress-checker? The appropriateness of that term as it applied to psychedelics really struck a chord. Yes, it *was* a progress-checker, but had I really made so much progress as my son seemed to think? It had been 18 years since I tripped, but right then and there I decided it was time to check my progress!

After some asking around, I was able to get a couple of hits of good clean blotter from some Deadhead friends of mine, and a few weeks after Noah's first trip, I was flying high and checking my progress for myself. I've been checking myself on a regular basis ever since and ever since, in our family, acid has been affectionately referred to as Progress-Checker.